CLASSIC
Hand Tools

GARRETT HACK

Photographs by John S. Sheldon

The Taunton Press

Publisher
Jim Childs

Associate Publisher
Helen Albert

Associate Editor
Strother Purdy

Editor
Peter Chapman

Jacket and Interior Design
Carol Singer

Photographer (except where noted)
John S. Sheldon

Illustrator
Kathy Rushton

Indexer
Lynda S. Stannard

The Taunton Press
Inspiration for hands-on living™

Printed in the United States of America
10 9 8 7 6 5 4 3 2 1

Classic Hand Tools was originally published in hardcover
in 1999 by The Taunton Press, Inc.

The Taunton Press, Inc., 63 South Main Street,
PO Box 5506, Newtown, CT 06470-5506
e-mail: tp@taunton.com

Distributed by Publishers Group West

Library of Congress Cataloging-in-Publication

Hack, Garrett.
    Classic hand tools / Garrett Hack; photographs by
John S. Sheldon.
        p.   cm.
    Includes bibliographic references and index.
    ISBN 1-56158-273-5 (hardcover)
    ISBN 1-56158-507-6 (paperback)
    1. Tools — Collectors and collecting.   I. Title.
II. Title: Hand tools.
TJ1195.H12   1999
621.9'08'075— dc21   99-23719
                                              CIP

To Robert and Renée,
who taught me about the most important tools

Acknowledgments

Writing this book has been a constant adventure. Tool lovers, collectors, and users are a far-flung lot. As I traveled looking for tools, often with my good friend John Sheldon, we never knew quite what each day would bring. As you can see, we discovered lots of tools, from those in the hands of craftsmen whose work we interrupted to others in collections of rare Stanley and unusual American and British tools. We also found many friends along the way, who shared their tools, their stories, and often their homes. I am sincerely grateful to the following people who made this adventure both fun and successful:

Roy and Julanne Arnold, Clarence Blanchard, Bridge City Tool Co., Henry and Susanne Bucki, Bill and Sarah Carter, George and Jean Derbyshire, Footprint Tools, Jerry Glaser, Ted Ingraham, Craig Jensen, Paul Kebabian, Leonard Lee and Lee Valley Tools, Steve Lamont and Phil Brown (and all at the Barnsley Workshops), Vincent Laurence, Larry Meyers, Tony Murland, Max Ott, Ray Pilon, Mark and Jane Rees, Dave Sawyer, David and Ian Stanley, William and Caroline Wilkins, and Anne and Don Wing.

For his quick mastery of English roundabouts, for his good humor despite the hour or the challenge, and for his photographic savvy, I owe a hearty thanks to John Sheldon.

Ultimately, the success of this project depended upon the many talented folks at The Taunton Press. For their steady support, creativity, and friendship I am grateful to Helen Albert, Jon Binzen, Jim Childs, Zack Gaulkin, Carol Singer, and Matthew Teague. A special thanks to Peter Chapman, a friend and gifted editor, who has nurtured my confidence as a writer as I have taught him more than he needs to know about woodworking tools.

Contents

Introduction

Hand tools are invaluable to me. Over the years of collecting, tuning, sharpening, and working with them, my hand tools have become natural extensions of me, linked with what I make and how I make it.

As for machines, I have everything you'd expect in a modest and efficient shop set up to produce the high-quality furniture that has been my living for more than 20 years. Although it's nothing that I ever consciously set out to do, every year I use those machines less and hand tools more. While the brute force of a machine is useful (if you don't mind the dust, noise, and danger), it is nothing like the intimacy and pleasure of working by hand. As I work, hand tools allow me the flexibility that I rarely feel with machines. And it's the subtle marks they leave behind that I find most beautiful.

Not long ago, all woodworking was done with hand tools alone. It took two men to saw lumber from a log, and then a square, hatchet, planes, and handsaws to work each board to width, length, and thickness. With an even greater variety of hand tools, different trades turned the boards into chairs, chests of drawers, coffins, and coaches. Over hundreds and in some cases thousands of years, the craftsmen who depended on these tools constantly refined them to be more efficient and accurate.

It is from these craftsmen that we have inherited an incredible wealth of hand tools. Which of these tools do you need, and how do you tell a good tool from a poor one? How do you tune and sharpen them? How do you use each tool, and what is it capable of? These are some of the questions this book will answer.

I started this book by making a list of all the hand tools I use, as well as some peculiar and interesting ones worth knowing about. The tools are organized according to their basic tasks, such as boring, sawing, and planing. I explain the most important tools in the greatest detail, including some of the stories about how they evolved or about the trades that adopted them. My favorites, planes, deserve a book in themselves (which is why I wrote *The Handplane Book*; The Taunton Press, 1997). You'll also find information about making your own tools, buying used ones and restoring them, and vignettes about contemporary tool makers and the best tool auction in the world.

I have two biases when it comes to tools. One is that I favor Western tools, because this is the tradition I learned within (I have also included some Eastern hand tools, however). My other bias is for older tools, beautiful shopmade or classic woodworking hand tools manufactured up until about World War II. Some are still available, although far fewer than the seemingly endless variety that once appeared on the pages of Stanley, Sargent, Miller's Falls, and other tool catalogs. Old tools have stories; I feel connected with their history through the handles polished over years of use, the patina of wear, and an owner's or maker's name stamped onto the tool.

Learning to use hand tools takes time and patience, but the rewards are enduring. With this book as your guide, I hope that you too will relish the pleasures of working by hand, at a friendly pace, in harmony with your tools and the material beneath them.

What Are HAND TOOLS?

Learning about hand tools and how to use them is part of the joy and pleasure of working wood. Hand tools are part of our rich and inventive history, just as useful today as they were vital to an 18th-century furniture maker working wood without machines. If there was a need to cut wood in some way, you can bet that someone devised a hand tool to do it. Their beauty only adds to the enjoyment of using hand tools.

Working with hand tools, I understand wood on a most intimate level—in a way I might easily miss working with machines alone. Each of my tools leaves its own texture upon the surface as one more detail, one further subtlety of the wood. It's no wonder that stunning planes, beautiful handsaws, and delicate chisels have become symbols of fine craftsmanship. ❧

Marking gauges scribe fine lines parallel to an edge for laying out all kinds of joinery. The patented gauge on the right (1868) has two pivoting fingers for scribing around irregular curves; the one on the left (1864) has four stems for multiple settings.

Why Use Hand Tools?

With so many efficient woodworking machines available, why use hand tools? Quite simply, they are still the best tools for accomplishing many woodworking tasks. There are things that machines do well, such as surfacing and sizing rough boards to precise dimensions and cutting some joints, all with a lot less effort than would be required with a jack plane and other hand-powered tools. But it is the huge realm of working wood beyond machines—such as fitting common joints or cutting complex ones, planing surfaces to a polish, or splitting a log into parts for a chair and draw-knifing them to shape—where you can work more quickly, efficiently, and quietly with well-tuned tools powered by hand and body and guided by eye.

This might seem like a romantic vision of woodworking, and perhaps in a way it is, yet using hand tools is utterly practical. Generations of craftsmen have used and refined these tools, and I have no doubt that future generations will be using them as well. Learning what these tools are and where they came from is part of understanding hand tools. The rest is learning the skills and, by using them, gaining the confidence to pick up a dovetail saw and cut accurately to a line, to pare a tight-fitting joint with a chisel, or to plane a tabletop flat. Mastering one hand tool leads to success with others, and gradually to whole new ways of thinking and working.

Many hand tools will do multiple tasks, some better than others. I might pick up a shoulder plane to fit a joint, for example, while you might choose a paring chisel, and someone else a file. Each tool has advantages; no single tool is best. What tools you choose and how you use them is a matter of experience and personality. Few people use a tool in exactly the same way, or even agree on the basics of sharpening and tuning it. For me, this is what makes woodworking fun—to learn some new trick with a tool I thought I knew well, or to discover a clever tool I never even imagined.

Types of Tools

One of the advantages of hand tools is their versatility. Of course, some have very specific functions, but just as three woodworkers might pick up three different tools to fit a joint, most hand tools can do a range of different work. Still, they can be broadly grouped according to the work they perform: marking and measuring, striking, chiseling, planing, scraping, boring, and sawing. (This still leaves plenty of gray areas:

for example, dowel pointers and auger bits driven by a brace actually cut like little planes or chisels.)

MARKING AND MEASURING TOOLS

Marking and measuring tools—rules, squares, compasses, dividers, levels, marking gauges, bevel gauges, and chalklines—are the tools a woodworker uses to lay out cuts or joints. As construction proceeds, they are used for checking dimensions, aligning parts, or squaring up a frame or opening. Accuracy is important no matter what you are building, and marking and measuring tools are reliable guides.

STRIKING TOOLS

What could be simpler or more basic to woodworking than a hammer or an ax? But which hammer or ax is the right one to choose from the incredible variety? There are many such striking tools: wooden mauls for driving wooden nails into heavy frame construction; common claw hammers; axes and adzes for hewing and shaping; ball-peen hammers for metalsmithing, veneer hammers that aren't even used like hammers, and many others. Few of the specialized hammers and the trades that used them survive, but there are some new ones around, such as deadblow hammers and others with fiberglass heads and handles.

CHISELS

Chisels are all-purpose cutting tools. Chopping mortises and tenons, cutting recesses for hinges,

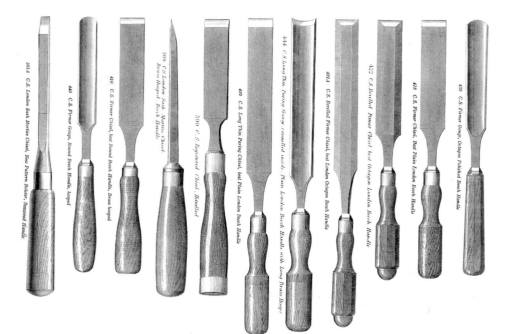

Chisels cut and fit joints and shape wood. The Sheffield Standard List of 1864 advertised a variety of first-class chisels with fancy handles, as well as carving gouges with curved cutting edges.

Planes are the most useful and beautiful of hand tools. These bench planes, which include a Norris #A6 smoother and Stanley Bedrocks #604, #605, and #607, can make delicate fitting cuts, shoot long straight edges, or flatten a surface to a polished sheen.

Norris bullnose, shoulder, and chariot planes for fine-tuning joinery are among the most beautiful planes ever made—and the most rare today.

and doing all sorts of paring and fitting involved in woodworking joinery are just a few of their many uses. Curve a chisel's cutting edge and you have a gouge. A gouge is primarily a carving tool, but it can also be used for making or refining moldings, for coping joints, or for creating small details, such as pulls. Lengthen the cutting edge of a chisel, add two handles at right angles, and you have a drawknife, a tool indispensable to chairmakers and anyone who works green wood.

PLANES

Planes are sophisticated chisels. Take a chisel-like iron and wedge it into a wood or metal body and you have a plane, capable of everything from cutting rough boards into dimensioned stock to smoothing any surface to a glasslike polish. Planes are used to cut and fit a variety of joints, as well as to create decorative moldings and to do much more. An 18th-century joiner would have used wooden planes; the planes we use today have long-wearing metal soles and easy-to-use adjusters. Planes are not easy tools to master, but they are arguably the most useful hand tools ever devised for working wood.

SCRAPERS, FILES, AND RASPS

Instead of a plane's chisel iron and knifelike approach to the wood, scrapers work at a much higher angle with a tiny, hooked cutting edge burnished—not honed—onto the steel. The most basic scraper is simply a piece of flat steel about as thick as a handsaw blade, with either a straight edge for smoothing level surfaces, or profiled for scraping curved shapes, such as moldings. A scraper blade can be secured in a wood or iron holder (much like a

From Stones to Stanleys

Handsaws haven't always cut accurately and effortlessly; it's taken thousands of years to refine the temper and composition of the blade and the shape of the teeth. Such has also been the case with augers, planes, braces, axes, and even with tools as simple as hammers. Some evolved in a spurt of ingenuity—an entirely new tool took shape—but mostly they improved slowly, one step at a time, and even a step backward now and again. It's harder to see, but the process is just as dynamic today as it ever was, for someone will always be looking for a way to pry just a little bit more efficiency from a tool.

All tools were hand tools until quite recently. The first were undoubtedly pounding tools—hard rocks with the right shape and heft to chip other rocks into axes and scraping tools. Lashing the ax heads to a piece of bone or wood, man extended the natural movements of his hand and arm for greater force, and so evolved the first woodworking tools.

From there, the evolution of tools followed in the wake of a growing knowledge of metallurgy—the ability to smelt first copper and then copper and tin into bronze cutting edges. Neither made particularly

Oversized hand tools were sometimes used as advertising props, but all of these tools are capable of extra large work, such as filing the huge bearings of a steam engine.

Sometimes the line between hand tool and machine is hazy. This interesting device probably was made by a cooper, who cleverly attached a round-soled plane to rails in order to make his efforts hollowing pail staves more efficient and uniform. In the background is a stoup plane for doing similar work freehand.

Joiners and cabinetmakers took pride in their tools. Many carved and dated them, although rarely to the degree of this Dutch plane dated 1752.

durable edges, but amazingly—and this was about 5,000 years ago—Bronze Age man fashioned workable saws, chisels, augers, and adzes. Once mastered, the ability to smelt iron ore, heat and hammer it into wrought (worked) iron, and then harden it in a delicate tempering process yielded tough tool steel. Ultimately, this led to modern hand tools as we know them.

Well into the 19th century, until the beginning of the Industrial Revolution, a carpenter's tool kit was basic: a few chisels and gouges, three or four planes, a few saws, a hammer, an ax and a hatchet, an adze, and some measuring tools. These would have been wooden tools with few metal parts. Ironically, just as hand tools were being replaced by machines—planers, molders, and saws driven by water or steam—the Golden Age of hand tools flourished. Creative minds modified old tools and invented new ones (and patented them) to suit the factory worker.

The second half of the 19th century saw the growth of factory production and industrial know-how, spurred in part by the Civil War. New manufacturing processes such as casting, milling, and making batches of identical parts changed the way tools were designed and made. It didn't take long for Stanley Rule and Level Company to put this technology to work making its famous line of cast-iron Bailey bench planes, and Stanley was not alone. The onset of the industrial age produced an offering of woodworking tools more varied than we will likely ever see again. Hundreds of patents were taken out for tool improvements—from better chuck designs to the auger bits they held—and for whole new tools born of the mere challenge of designing them.

Particularly amusing are the all-in-one tools that tried (but usually failed) to do it all—a combination tool that included a hammer, pliers, screwdriver, wire cutter, wrench, pry bar, and leather punch, for example, or a single compact tool handle that came with various

The quality craftsmanship of an 18th-century joiner is all the more impressive when you consider how few tools he had to work with and how crude and simple they seem.

The Civil War introduced factory production and the manufacturing of multiple parts (25 different ones in this Bedrock #604 alone). This technology made Bailey and Bedrock planes, manufactured by Stanley Rule and Level Company, not only possible, but economical.

Footprint Tools of Sheffield, England, still makes some hand tools the traditional way, by pounding red-hot steel beneath mammoth drop hammers.

A TOOL FOR ANY POCKETBOOK

THE GOLDEN AGE of hand tools—the decades between the Civil War and World War II—not only spawned a huge variety of tools but also produced different versions of the same tool in a range of qualities and materials to suit any taste or pocketbook. Take, for example, what could be a simple tool: a gauge for spacing clapboards. A carpenter could fashion a perfectly adequate one from wood. For the masses, Stanley manufactured a shiny nickel-plated, adjustable steel gauge with the nice feature of a handle that turns sideways to push out a small tooth to hold the gauge and clapboard in place. A gentleman could buy a fancier version still, such as Nester's patented model made of walnut and golden brass. It had a graduated rule for fine adjustment, a built-in spirit level, and a marker for cutting clapboards tight to trim. 🔩

Hand tools were once offered in a range of materials to suit different tastes and budgets. The three versions of the clapboard gauge shown here are shopmade (right), nickel-plated steel (center), and a gentleman's model made of walnut and brass with built-in level and rule.

screwdriver bits and other small tools as attachments. A factory worker need only carry one of these multipurpose gadgets instead of the many tools they were meant to replace. The ultimate combination tool was Stanley's famous #45 and later #55 planes with interchangeable cutters that did the work of dozens of individual planes. These tools were dubiously successful, but the understanding of metallurgy and factory precision that made them possible also transformed common tools. Metals replaced wood, allowing previously impossible innovations, such as ratcheting corner braces and adjustable iron spokeshaves.

Hand tools have steadily improved, with more precise and easier adjustments, longer-wearing parts, stronger steels, and even a successful new design now and again. Tool improvements are still going on, although I didn't feel this way 25 years ago when I started buying tools. Back then the only good tools were secondhand Stanleys, long out of production as machines further shriveled the hand-tool market. I knew of only one hand-tool catalog, and almost nothing of the few tool companies still hanging on here and in England. Now it seems every year I hear about some new company starting to make specialty tools—and thriving. I still love my classic Stanleys, but there are some mighty appealing tools in all those catalogs I get these days. Maybe the Golden Age isn't quite over.

Charpentier. *Gravure de G. Vogel. XVII° siècle.*

Seventeenth-century French carpenters used crosscut saws to cut logs to length, broad axes to shape the heavy timbers, and chisels to cut mortises. Other carpenter tools lying against the logs to the right include a hatchet, squares, a bowsaw, and a chalkline for marking the cuts.

How
HAND TOOLS
CUT

Woodworking is all about cutting wood. It's no mystery, then, that most hand tools are cutting tools. Saws, planes, chisels, drill bits, and rasps all cut wood in some way: by sizing, smoothing, joining, or shaping. Yet as different as the tools and the work may seem, they're really not that different at all. The cutting edge of a chisel is the same as that of a plane, a drawknife, a drill bit, or an ax. That edge either cuts the fibers of the wood or splits them apart.

Cutting the fibers is far superior to splitting, which is difficult to control. Whether along the fibers (long grain) or across them (end grain), a cutting action produces the smoothest surface. But while it might be the ideal, some splitting is inevitable. The challenge is to keep it to a minimum. ❧

Planes, especially tight-mouthed smoothers, favor controlled cutting of the wood fibers over splitting, producing an exceptionally smooth surface on the hardest of woods.

Cutting Dynamics

Many factors affect the results you will get with a tool. It might not be the right tool for the job. You might be using it ineffectively. The cutting bevel—the angle of the cutting edge—might be too fine or too large, or the cutting edges might not be sharp. A general understanding of how a tool cuts, with a beveled edge peeling off a shaving, will help you avoid some of these problems.

A sharp edge slices the fibers, whereas a dull one drives into them like a wedge. (Only in true splitting tools such as an ax or a froe is semi-sharpness a virtue.) A thin, knife-like cutting edge is ideal for slicing the fibers without wedging and splitting them apart. But a thin, sharp edge is also fragile and prone to chipping. Conversely, a large bevel is tougher, but it wedges and splits the fibers apart before the actual cutting edge does much cutting. A large bevel also takes considerably more force to drive into the wood. The compromise between these two extremes—the ideal bevel angle—depends on what kind of work you expect from the tool.

Take chisels, for example. A paring chisel has the finest of bevels (as small as 15°) because it is designed for light cuts and to be pushed gently and carefully by hand. A mortise chisel needs a greater bevel (about 30°) to cut tough end grain and withstand powerful mallet blows. Somewhere between the two are firmer chisels, which are pushed by hand and driven by mallet. In just about every wood-cutting tool, the

Aggressive chiseling with the grain is likely to split away some fibers rather than cut them, leaving a rough and uneven surface.

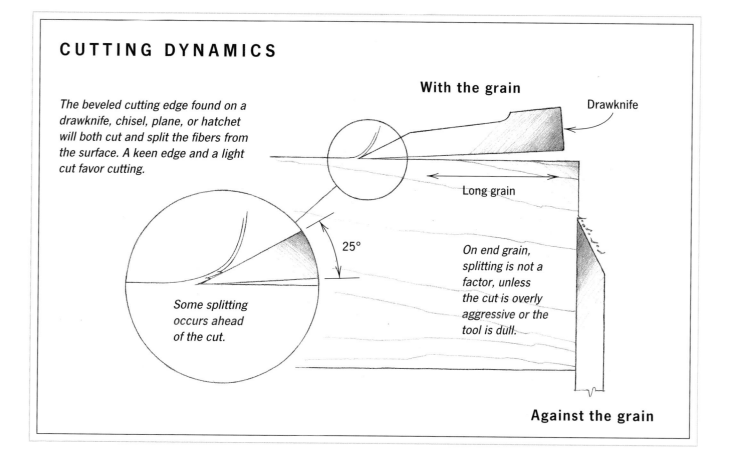

CUTTING DYNAMICS

The beveled cutting edge found on a drawknife, chisel, plane, or hatchet will both cut and split the fibers from the surface. A keen edge and a light cut favor cutting.

With the grain

Drawknife

Long grain

25°

Some splitting occurs ahead of the cut.

On end grain, splitting is not a factor, unless the cut is overly aggressive or the tool is dull.

Against the grain

ideal cutting bevel lies somewhere between the two extremes of 15° and 30°, for the simple reason that the physics of cutting wood remain constant (see the photo on p. 16).

Plane irons have similar bevel angles as chisels, but the way the wood experiences the bevel gives them a higher degree of cutting control. The difference is that the iron is wedged into place at an angle to the guiding sole: the bed angle. Some planes have a low angle, nearly equal to a chisel, and some have high angles, 60° or more (see the photo at left on p. 20). Common bench planes have a bed angle of 45°. The wood experiences this bed angle no differently than a cutting-edge bevel angle of 45°, with the

same resistance to the cut and potential for splitting. But what is not the same is that a plane has a throat, which effectively controls the cutting action.

As the shaving is cut, it's driven into the throat of the plane. The iron acts as a ramp for the shaving, levering it against the front of the throat. This levering action breaks the shaving repeatedly, which is what makes the shaving curl (see the photo at right on p. 20). Equally important, the sole of the plane ahead of the throat pushes down on the fibers, reducing the potential for splitting ahead of the cut. The actions of the sole and throat together favor cutting over splitting, explaining why planes can leave a smooth

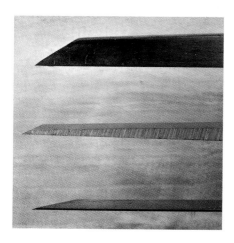

Chisel bevel angles range from a 15° bevel for a delicate paring chisel (bottom), to a tougher 30° bevel for a mortise chisel (top), used for chopping hard end grain. A firmer chisel (center) has a bevel angle somewhere between the two for varied bench work.

Plane bed angles vary, from an extremely low angle for slicing end grain (foreground) to a high angle for tough hardwoods (center), or somewhere in between the two for general-purpose bench work (rear).

As a shaving is cut and forced into the throat of a spokeshave, the cutter levers it against the front of the throat. The shaving breaks repeatedly (noticeable as tiny parallel ridges) and curls.

finish. In tough hardwoods, a high-angle plane is ideal—it curls and breaks the shaving more abruptly, with even less chance of splitting or tearing.

In theory, a low bed angle would seem to be an advantage, especially in softer woods. This is often the case, but what can also happen is that the iron drives into the fibers and some splitting goes on before the shaving can be levered and broken. As a result, low-angle planes are designed to cut end grain, where splitting is less of a problem and a low cutting approach is an advantage.

Many other tools have chisel-like cutting edges. The cutting lips of an auger bit are actually tiny chisels (you have to look closely to see them), and

a ripsaw has chisel teeth, too. With each saw stroke the chisel-like teeth scrape and pare tiny shavings from the bottom of the kerf. Those same teeth are less effective across the grain, because they cut and tear at the fibers in exactly the same way as a chisel cutting across the grain. This is why the teeth of a crosscut saw are not chisels, but rather beveled knives that score and slice the fibers. An auger bit, on the other hand, must cut across the grain half the time and with the grain half the time. The chisel-like lips would tear out badly cutting cross-grain if it

weren't for an added bit of sophistication: small knifelike spurs similar to crosscut saw teeth, that score the fibers ahead of the cut.

SKEWING THE CUTTING EDGE

There are no rules when it comes to choosing the best tool, although experience helps. Ultimately each piece of wood is different, and you won't know exactly how it will respond to a tool until you start working it. But whether you are cutting long grain or end grain, skewing the cutting edge introduces

Skewing the cutting tool (in this case, a drawknife) adds a slicing action for a better cut with less effort.

a slicing action that is almost always an advantage.

With tools such as an auger bit or an ax, you've got little control of the cutting edge once it's started into the cut. But with a chisel, plane, or drawknife, you can angle the cutting edge in relation to the force and direction of the cut. Simply skewing 10° requires noticeably less effort and produces less tearout.

A skew cut is not directly into the fibers (it's askew), adding the valuable element of slicing. It's no different than cutting a carrot with a

kitchen knife with a forward and downward slicing action, which is much smoother and easier than chopping straight down. A skewed chisel or plane iron isn't taking quite as wide a cut as it could, so there is less pressure against the cutting edge. Less force is needed to drive the tool. Plus, the wood "sees" a slightly lower bevel angle (because the cutting force is diagonally across the bevel and not directly into it). It's like angling your way across a steep slope rather than attacking it straight up.

Sharpening

Dull tools are nothing but constant frustration. They work poorly, tire you needlessly, and on top of that, they can be dangerous (because you will push too hard and possibly slip). It should go without saying, then, that the only way to gain confidence with hand tools is first to become confident at sharpening them. You will need a few good stones, a comfortable sharpening station, a basic knowledge of what you are after and how to get there, and a fair bit of patience. It helps

A sharpening station should be a place you don't mind getting a little messy. You should have everything you need close at hand: a grinder, stones, honing oil or water, rags, and good light.

This quiet honing station has excellent natural light and enough space for both waterstones (left) and oilstones (right). The large bottle contains soapy water to lubricate the waterstones.

more efficient and makes this task less of a chore.

You can learn a lot about sharpening by careful observation. Before you start grinding or honing, look at the bevel angle of the cutting edge. Try to think about how the tool is designed to cut. Recently I was sharpening an old reamer, and even though I knew that the beveled outside edge does the cutting, I didn't know the proper angle. Understanding the basics of how the tool works and following what was there, I sharpened the bevel to cut respectably. Sharpening this way sometimes can be a bit of trial and error, gradually tuning the tool until it works for a particular task. Luckily, the range of what works is quite wide.

Whether you are working with a new tool or a secondhand one, sharpening usually proceeds in stages: from grinding the bevel to lapping the back and finally honing the bevel and back to a polished, sharp edge. What follows is general enough to apply to many tools; more specific sharpening tips are included in each chapter.

If sharpening is comfortable and convenient, you'll be more likely to stop what you're doing and sharpen or just "touch up" your tools. Create a sharpening station close to your workbench with everything you need (see the photos at left). Ideally, you should have a separate area that can get a little messy (it will), excellent light, a mechanical grinder, and a few benchstones.

to relax, too. Your first attempts may not be perfect, but unless you are overzealous with a grinder, you're not going to ruin any tools by trying.

Some days I'll sharpen half a dozen times, spending only a few minutes each time to hone a few chisels or a couple of plane irons. I can't say it's my favorite part of woodworking, but I never fail to notice how much better a sharp tool feels, and how much easier it is to use. Sharpening often—and sharpening a few tools at once—is

GRINDING THE BEVEL

Like other machines in the shop, a mechanical grinder speeds sharpening by doing the heavy work that can be tedious by hand alone. You can get by without a grinder, doing the work on a coarse stone, a diamond lapping plate, or a fine file (for softer axes and adzes), but tool steel is tough. Save your time and energy for when it counts: honing the edge to sharpness on a benchstone.

There are plenty of commercial grinders on the market, ranging in quality and cost, and any one of them probably will work fine. I've used an oil-lubricated horizontal grinder, a benchtop version of an old sandstone clunker, and many common commercial grinders, all with good results. My current grinder is basic, even funky, but entirely functional. It's nothing more than an old ¼-hp motor from a washing machine that drives a simple arbor with a pair of coarse and fine stones. The tool rest is wood. It's just a little more advanced than the ancient, foot-cranked sandstone wheel lubricated by the steady drip from a tin can suspended above it, which I use for large tools such as my broad ax and drawknives.

A grinder is useful for bringing a dull tool (or one with a chipped edge) back to sharpness quickly. In addition to sharpening, a grinder can also shape a cutting edge (a cambered plane iron or scratch tool, for example) or restore the proper bevel angle. (A quick guide to a basic 25° bevel is a 2:1 ratio of bevel length to the thickness of the iron.) Besides sharpening, I use a grinder for tuning other metal parts on my hand tools and machines, and sometimes for making new ones.

Hollow grinding

A grinder speeds sharpening, particularly honing, by grinding a slight hollow across the edge bevel. Honing then becomes a task of removing metal from the cutting edge and the heel of the bevel, rather than across the entire bevel. The argu-

WHEN CHOOSING a grinder, look for a few basics: a slow speed (1,750 rpm, if possible) so there is less chance of overheating the tool from friction; a solid, adjustable rest; and coarse and fine stones at least 6 in. to 8 in. in diameter. Buy yourself a diamond or less expensive wheel-type dresser for keeping your stones true and sharp. If you have some money left, buy a couple of cool-grinding white aluminum-oxide wheels. ✺

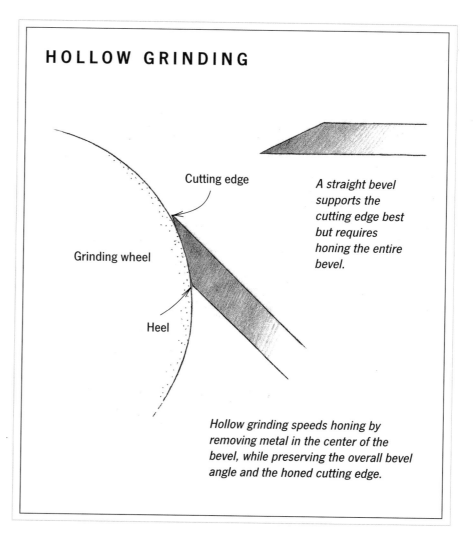

HOLLOW GRINDING

Cutting edge

Grinding wheel

Heel

A straight bevel supports the cutting edge best but requires honing the entire bevel.

Hollow grinding speeds honing by removing metal in the center of the bevel, while preserving the overall bevel angle and the honed cutting edge.

The chisel on the right is ready for a light grinding to renew the hollow across the bevel. The one on the left is just off the grinder. Grind as little as possible for the longest tool life.

ment against hollow grinding is that if the hollow is too deep, such as one cut by a small-diameter grindstone, the cutting edge will be thin and weak. This is especially true with Japanese laminated edge tools, where the very hard steel cutting edge needs the support of a wide, flat bevel.

With any tool, my approach is to grind close to the cutting edge but leave some of the polished edge remaining. This preserves the shape of the edge, if there is any (such as a gently cambered smoothing plane iron), and it minimizes the amount of steel removed so the tool lasts longer. It also leaves a bevel wide enough to support the cutting edge.

LAPPING THE BACK

Every cutting edge has two faces: a beveled side and a back. The beveled edge gets all the attention, even though the back makes up half the cutting edge. Therefore, the back should be every bit as polished as the bevel (see the photo below), and in most tools it should be flat. There are exceptions, of course, such as axes sharpened with two bevels and drawknives that some craftsmen prefer to round slightly on the back for better control. Even with curved cutting edges, such as a gouge, the back is still flat, even if it might be curved along the length of the tool.

ONE WORD OF CAUTION about grinding: It's easy to ruin a cutting edge quickly. If you heat the edge enough to discolor the steel, you will alter the temper. The edge might sharpen, but it won't last. Grind only until the tool begins to warm (the fine edge heats most quickly) and then let it cool in the air. No part should be uncomfortable to the touch. Avoid the need to quench in water; this causes microscopic cracks in the cutting edge.

For a truly sharp edge, the back or nonbeveled side of a cutting edge should be just as polished as the beveled side.

A flat back serves at least two purposes. In a chisel, the flat back guides the tool in a straight line. If the back was even slightly bowed from handle to cutting edge, the chisel would tend to cut in a curve and would be difficult to control. A flat back also makes sharpening chisels, plane irons, and other cutting edges easier. There is no guesswork to laying the back flat on a stone and honing away.

To maintain a flat back on your cutting tools, you will need a lapping table. Think of a lapping table as a large, coarse bench stone. It can be used not only for flattening the backs of cutters but also for maintaining the soles of planes and benchstones. Lapping tables can be as simple as a sheet of 120-grit aluminum-oxide paper (or finer) stuck with spray adhesive to a piece of ¼-in. (or thicker) plate glass. An alternative is to sprinkle silicon-carbide grit on the glass and lubricate with water or kerosene. Plate glass should be dead flat, but use your lapping table on the bed of a table saw or jointer for extra support.

Start lapping your plane iron or chisel with 120-grit aluminum-oxide paper. Move through successive grits so that at each stage the back has a uniform polish at least ½ in. wide behind the cutting edge. Use light pressure to avoid deforming your cutter (which is possible), and keep the back flat on the lapping table (avoid the temptation to tip the tool to polish closer to the cutting edge). Bring the back to a higher polish on your sharpening stones in the same way.

ALL CUTTING EDGES have two faces, and most of the time only one face is beveled. The other is honed flat to optimize its ability to cut and, in the case of a chisel, to guide the tool in a straight line. But there are some tools that cut with two bevels, such as axes, froes, and knives. Two edge bevels are quicker and easier to sharpen, because you don't have to worry about honing the back flat.

So why not do the same on a plane iron or drawknife? You can hone a back bevel by lifting the cutter slightly, rather than keeping it flat on the stone. A tiny back bevel (in a tool such as a bench plane, which cuts with the bevel down) can even be an advantage in cutting figured woods, because it steepens the angle of the cutting edge in relation to the work. The problem is that it is easy to get lazy and hone the back bevel a little higher each time, gradually changing the cutting dynamics for the worse. ❊

HONING THE BEVEL AND BACK

Honing the bevel and back on benchstones is the final stage in sharpening a cutting edge. An edge off the grinder, coarse stone, lapping table, or fine file can feel sharp, but magnified it looks serrated and rough. Using progressively finer stones, any grinding marks and microscopic grooves left by the previous stone are honed away, creating a smooth, sharp and long-lasting edge.

Not long ago all stones were natural, quarried from the earth for their particular ability to cut tool steel. Natural stones have uniform and tough grit particles weakly bonded together so that new abrasive particles are constantly exposed (but not so soft that the stone will erode easily with wear). Buy new

A lapping table made with silicon-carbide powder or a sheet of abrasive paper on plate glass is ideal for flattening chisel backs, plane soles, and sharpening stones.

NATURAL STONES, man-made oil or waterstones, ceramic stones, diamond stones, and diamond paste on a cast-iron plate—there is certainly a bewildering variety of sharpening possibilities. Are they all that different? Not really. Some cut faster, some wear quickly and require frequent maintenance, some are messy, but the truth is they all share the ability to sharpen and polish cutting edges. Try different ones. Learn to use what you choose—how to get a good edge on them and how to maintain them. Most important, use them often.

Natural stones are found all over the world, with exotic names to match: Washita, Turkey, Charnley Forest, Tam O'Shanter. Even the little New England town where I live has an outcropping of novaculite slate (similar to better-known Arkansas stones). Natural stones have a consistent, silky feel and work wonderfully. Their only disadvantage is that they can be quite expensive. (Keep your eyes out at a flea market for an old one that just needs a good cleaning and flattening.)

Some of the many stones the author uses: black Arkansas, Belgian, and other natural stones, along with man-made India and diamond-impregnated stones. Some work with light oil, others with water.

Less costly and nearly as impressive are man-made stones manufactured from synthetic or natural grits. Man-made stones designed to work with oil as a lubricant tend to wear more slowly and need less maintenance than fast-cutting and quick-wearing waterstones. You can buy special honing oils, use kerosene as I prefer, or even try olive oil or light machine oil.

Diamond stones have a layer of microscopic diamonds bonded to a steel plate or other backing. They come in a range of mostly coarse and medium grits well-suited for lapping the backs of cutters, flattening other stones which have worn hollow, and restoring nicked edges. Diamond stones stay flat and last a long time (monocrystaline diamonds longer than polycrystaline), but they don't last forever. Lately I have been making my own diamond stones from 10-micron and 4-micron diamond paste spread on a cast-iron plate.

Ceramic stones are relatively new. They have the look and feel of porcelain, are quite fine, and are best suited for the final honing and polishing of an edge. These stones need no lubricant and maintenance other than an occasional flattening and rinsing with water. 🞖

stones today and you're more likely to get man-made stones that mimic natural stones, or diamond-impregnated "stones" (they're not really stones at all). Whether a stone is natural or man-made, it usually requires some sort of lubrication, generally water or oil, to flush the surface of spent grit and steel particles (*swarf* as it's known). Both water- and oilstones, whether natural or man-made, have their advantages and disadvantages (see the sidebar above). Whatever you choose, you will need a coarse, medium, and fine grit and individual lidded boxes to keep them clean and protected.

Natural or man-made slipstones hone curved or small edges such as gouges and molding-plane irons. Many useful shapes are available, but if need be, you can shape your own against a diamond stone.

Honing is the hardest part of sharpening to master. The challenge is to hold the cutting bevel at a consistent angle to the stone while moving it back and forth. Some rocking around is unavoidable, but this slows sharpening because sometimes you're honing on the back of the bevel, sometimes on the cutting edge. With large tools such as a drawknife, it's easier to hone by bringing the stone to the tool. And for honing curved cutting edges, such as gouges and molding plane

irons, you'll need a few shapes of slipstones. (You can make your own by wrapping a dowel or other shape with a strip of fine abrasive paper.)

I've seen some wild honing techniques, from long back-and-forth strokes to jitterbugging all over the stone. Whatever technique you use, it's important to relax. I start by rocking the tool on the stone to feel the bevel, then I loosely lock my arms and wrists when I feel I am right on it. I then start stroking in loose figure eights up and down the stone, using nearly all of the stone to wear it evenly. A natural tendency is to work in the same pattern which, over time, puts a slightly skewed edge on the tool rather than a square one. This isn't necessarily bad, but in some planes, any skew makes the cutter harder to set parallel with the sole. Simply working in a reverse figure eight half the time keeps the cutting edges square.

Some craftsmen hone on a small "microbevel" (about 5°) on the cutting bevel by lifting the cutter slightly and honing the very tip of the edge more heavily. It's a natural thing to do anyway, and speeds sharpening somewhat. The advantage of a microbevel is that the cutting edge is tougher, albeit steeper, but the overall bevel has not changed.

With the bevel honed, hone the back of the cutter by keeping it dead flat on the stone. Resist the temptation to lift the rear of the cutter and hone just the cutting edge. I've seen this done with plane irons—essentially honing on a back

bevel—but if you do this with a chisel, it will not cut true. Once the back is evenly polished on your finest stone, there should be no reason to go back to a coarser stone.

As you might expect, there are all kinds of jigs and fixtures available to take the guesswork out of honing, but I don't think you need any of them. Honing will feel awkward at first, but down the road relying on your hand and eye to guide you will be every bit as accurate, and much faster.

A piece of leather charged with rouge, an extremely fine abrasive, makes a good strop for the final honing of curved or straight cutting edges.

WORKSHOPS,
Benches, and Clamps

For most craftsmen, there's no place they'd rather be than in their workshop. It's a place to be creative, to make piles of shavings and scraps, or to seek quiet refuge from the demands of daily life. You too will need a shop space, for no matter how wonderful your collection of hand tools, they're not worth a lot unless you have a place to use them. A shop for using hand tools doesn't have to be big, as long as you have good lighting, a sturdy workbench, and a convenient way to store your tools.

A bench is the heart of any shop, the most useful of all tools. A few planks or a sheet of plywood on sawhorses can suffice for a simple bench—at least until you get around to building a proper one. For that, you'll want to install a vise or two and learn a few tricks with clamps and specialty vises for holding unusual projects. 🪡

Light from skylights reflects off the white walls to illuminate the bench and sharpening station (at left). Tools are stored on shelves, in an old chest, and hung from nails and racks.

Workshops

Workshops are as different as the craftsmen that use them and the work they do there. I've been in tiny shops so organized and efficient that every cubic inch was used. Others I've seen have been as vast as small factories. Two advantages of working with hand tools are that they take up less space than machines, and they are so quiet that even a spare bedroom could be made into a workshop. But no matter how much space you have to work with, you'll need some basic organization of your space, your tools, and your materials.

The most important element of any workshop is your bench and the area immediately around it. While a bench secured to a wall is sturdy, a freestanding bench allows you to work around all four sides, which comes in handy for large projects. Give yourself enough space to joint long boards without running into anything. A large area nearby is ideal for a couple of sawhorses to set work upon, or to spread out parts in various stages of construction. This leaves your bench uncluttered. Make your tools accessible: Put them in hanging cabinets nearby, in drawers built into the base of your bench (which adds to its stability), on shelves, or in banks of drawers along a wall.

My shop is divided in half, with a bench and extra space for ongoing projects at one end. At the other end are my machines, wood storage, clamps on wall racks, drawers of hardware and more tools, and all of the things I need less often. My bench is in a corner about 4 ft. from each wall, lit from two sides by four large windows. The organization and layout of my workspace took many years to refine and it's still evolving. Some days I think about how nice it would be to have a bench area completely separate from all the dusty machines.

Whatever your circumstances, take the time to create a good working environment for yourself; it is the key to working productively with hand tools or machines. Whether you are there to make a living or just for the pure pleasure of being creative, make your shop a place you want to spend time.

LIGHTING

Lighting in a workshop is often an afterthought, but it shouldn't be. Good lighting is vital to working with any tools, but especially hand tools. Choose a spot for your bench that has the best natural light. Long before my shop was finished, I knew exactly where I wanted to put my bench—in the southeast corner that has consistent light all day long.

Natural light is preferable for a number of reasons. It is the most even light, especially when you have more than one window. Even lighting creates few shadows and best illuminates your tool and your work, allowing you to do things by day that are far more difficult with artificial light at night. Natural light also is more restful, even though at times it can be glaring and hard to

ONCE YOU HAVE a workbench and you start to use hand tools—even if you use machines primarily—you'll need to store all the tools you accumulate. It's best if they are near your bench; after all, that's where you'll use most of them. And while there are lots of creative storage solutions—whole books on the subject, in fact—they basically can be broken down into drawers, shelves, and hanging racks.

The traditional solution is a tool chest with many fitted compartments and drawers for specific tools. It's a great idea, but not always easy to use. I prefer drawers—lots of drawers of various depths to suit tools of different sizes and heights. Tools stored one deep are easy to find quickly and can be protected from one another by simple dividers (strips of wood glued to the drawer bottom, for instance). Tools in drawers stay clean and are somewhat protected from moisture and swings in temperature that will cause metal parts to sweat and rust.

Shelves are like open drawers and are just as useful, except that

Drawers, shelves, and racks make every cubic inch of this tool chest accessible and organized. Cabinet doors seal out dust.

your tools will get dusty. Shelves are a great way to store planes, when all you need to see is the end view to choose the right one. As with drawers, make shelves of different heights and not more than one or two tools deep. A couple of tips from experience: It's easier to find a tool on a shelf when it is well below eye level, and shelves made from closely spaced dowels stay cleaner because they allow shavings and dust to pass through.

Hanging tools from racks or nails driven into the walls near your bench works fine, too. Racks with holes are better for small tools, such as chisels and auger bits, and you can see at a glance when tools are missing. Peg racks are an easy way to store saws, drawknives, spokeshaves, and anything else with a hole in the handle. At one end of my shop I have a huge rack specifically for all the different clamps I use. ▩

control. Make natural adjustments to your habits. After spending some time at your bench, for example, you will discover when the lighting is best for cutting dovetails. Every shop should have some natural

light, even if it is nothing more than a couple of high narrow windows throwing light into a basement shop. On a purely emotional level, even one window gives you a view

to rest your eyes and sense the day outside.

Even if you have fantastic natural light pouring into every corner of your shop, you'll still need some artificial light. Overhead light is a

and down the entire length there are holes for bench pins or dogs. Made of beech, the top is almost 3 in. thick, heavy, and solid. I bought the hardware for the end vise, which took me as long to build and fit as the entire bench took to make. The legs have strong mortise-and-tenon joinery and they are well braced. The only maintenance it needs is an occasional flattening with a jointer plane, and a coat of linseed oil every year.

A bench's height—typically between 34 in. and 36 in.—is more important than its other dimensions. A bench that's too high will be uncomfortable for hand-planing for any length of time. It will also be more tiring, because less of your upper body will be providing power. On the other hand, bench height for chiseling and sawing is less im-

good start. Fluorescent lights are the least expensive and produce an even light, but I prefer incandescents, which mimic sunlight more closely. At times you'll also need a raking light to see surface details—when planing across a tabletop, for example. For sawing dovetails, I prefer light from behind. A light on a movable arm right over the bench works well, as does a clamp-on light. It's best to have a few options for the most flexibility.

Workbenches

Everyone has an opinion about what makes the ideal workbench. Some woodworkers are content working on a large flat table and using clamps instead of a vise. Others prefer a long bench with multiple vises. Nevertheless, there are a few bench basics most would agree on: a flat top of modest width but long, rock-solid construction, and at least one but preferably two vises. Many modern benches are based on a versatile traditional European woodworking bench, which has a large side vise, an end vise with dogs for clamping work flat upon the benchtop, and a narrow tool till or recess running the length of the bench.

I built my own bench based on the one I learned upon, because at the time I knew no better design. It's 7 ft. 8 in. long, 29 in. wide (including a narrow tool till running the entire length), and 35 in. high. On the front, at one end, I have an old cast-iron side vise. At the other end, there is a heavy end or tail vise,

The large end or tail vise on the author's bench clamps work securely between wooden dogs, leaving him with both hands free to control the tool.

portant. There are certain rules of thumb about the proper height of a bench—one is that the bench should be as high as your wrists when you're standing with your arms hanging—but it really comes down to personal preference. Try out a temporary bench with saw-horses and boards, or work at differ-ent table heights to see what feels comfortable. A bench too low is better than one that's too high—and it's easy to remedy by jacking it up with a board or two under the legs.

A bench doesn't have to be fancy to work well, so don't think you have to spend a small fortune to buy the best. I know cabinetmakers who work on the most basic of benches half the size of mine. You can make a perfectly acceptable bench by laminating plywood or planks to-gether to build up a couple of inches (or more) of thickness. Set this on some legs that are mortised, bolted, or securely nailed and braced to-gether, and you've got a strong and stable work surface. You can buy a ready-made benchtop, too. Just be careful that you don't make the bench too long without bracing the top (or making it thicker), because it could sag and cause you endless problems. I highly recommend building your own bench—it's a wonderful project.

BENCH VISES

The purpose of a vise is to secure your work in the right position so that you have two free hands to power and control the tool. A vise can also serve as a clamp for gluing or assembly. The simplest vise is a

Don't do heavy pounding or mortising in a vise—you risk damaging it. Instead, put the work on top of the bench, a much more stable surface. In this case, two clamps—a handscrew and a holdfast—secure the work.

side vise, a two-jawed affair that bolts onto the side or end of a bench and clamps shut with either a quick-action screw or a traditional screw. The advantage of the quick-action screw is that, with a half-turn of the handle or lever, you can slide the movable jaw in or out, and then crank it up tight. There are lots of other versions of this vise, with wooden screws instead of metal, double screws, or one or more bars to guide the vise parallel with the fixed jaw.

You don't need a massive side vise, nor one that opens more than

8 in. to 10 in. Do buy the best vise you can afford, however, not one of the small homeowner types you're likely to find in a local hardware store. Add wooden jaws, not only to avoid marring your work but also to save a tool edge if you slip. My side vise gets a lot of use holding boards on edge so I can joint edges, mor-tise in hinges, or pare a joint—all relatively light cutting with general-ly parallel-sided stock. A side vise is also ideal for holding boards with curved or uneven edges that would not lie flat on a bench. Heavy pounding on a vise can ruin it, so

Pairs of half bench hooks are a stable way to hold boards just above the benchtop for sawing tenons or planing tenon shoulders. You also can butt work against wooden dogs that fit into the holdfast holes.

Protect your benchtop from sharp tools by using a board or bench hook for chiseling small pieces (such as this inlay). The raised back makes a nice stop for planing, sawing, or chiseling small work.

If you are holding work in one side of a vise, place a scrap block on the opposite side for even clamping pressure and to avoid racking the screw. To help support large panels, add a bar clamp across the benchtop.

for work such as chopping joints, use the top of your bench; it is more stable, anyway (see the photo on p. 33). And for tapered work or awkward shapes that require creative shimming to secure in a side vise, clamp them to your benchtop with bar clamps or a holdfast.

I do a lot of light sawing in my side vise, such as cutting dovetails with the work clamped upright. A common problem with this setup is that most of the time the board has to be clamped to one side of the vise screw. As soon as you snug up the jaws, they rack out of parallel, stressing the screw. The jaws don't hold anything very securely this way, either. One solution is to clamp a block, about the same thickness as your work, in the other side of the jaw, as shown in the bottom photo at left. (Drive a brad into the block to keep it from falling out every time you loosen the vise.) I keep different sizes of blocks on hand in my bench till (this is one good reason to have a till). If you do a lot of this type of work, you might consider buying or making a two-screwed side vise large enough to clamp wide boards between the screws.

Whatever side vise you choose, make sure to mount it with the fixed jaw flush with the front vertical edge of your benchtop. That way you can clamp a long board into your side vise (for jointing, for instance; see pp. 115-118) and the front edge of the bench will give the board extra stability. This also allows you to clamp the far end of the board against the front edge of the bench with a bar clamp.

Besides a side vise of some kind, benches in the European tradition have an additional end or tail vise. After working with one for as long as I can remember, I cannot imagine an easier and more stable way to clamp work upon a benchtop. The clamping action is between two bench dogs or pins, one in the end vise and the other somewhere along the bench surface. (This is why a long bench is helpful.) The sliding end vise also forms a small but powerful clamping vise within the benchtop (see the photo on p. 32).

You can make or buy end vises with double screws and double pins or buy just the hardware and make your own. Either way, you'll need to mortise or drill holes for bench dogs about 6 in. apart. The dogs can be as simple as a length of 1-in. dowel, or rectangular dogs with a built-in spring to hold them at any height. Stick with wooden dogs over metal ones; they are easily shaped to fit odd work, quickly replaced, and a lot gentler on tools.

No matter how well made or well fitted an end vise, the wooden jaws will eventually sag slightly below the surface of the benchtop. You can level everything with a jointer plane, although a little sag isn't a big problem, as long as any work clamped to the benchtop is supported on the bench and not on the movable jaw of the vise. It is more stable this way, too. Sometimes this setup requires taking up slack with a scrap block between the movable jaw and the work (see the photo on p. 32). When using any vise (especially an end vise), just

A VERSATILE VISE

THE EMMERT VISE is an unusual side vise that's a useful addition to any shop, especially if you work with a lot of oddly shaped pieces, as patternmakers do. (The wooden patterns they make for casting metals can be almost any shape imaginable.)

The jaws of this vise clamp out of parallel, and they have double bench pins for clamping large pieces flat on the benchtop; the entire vise rotates 360°, tilts, and locks in any position. Versatile, you might say. ❧

The Emmert patternmaker's vise swivels, tilts, locks in any position, and clamps odd shapes with pivoting jaws.

snug the vise enough to hold the piece; too much pressure can easily deform your work.

Holdfasts and bench stops are alternatives to an end vise. A holdfast is a quick-clamping arm mortised into holes along the benchtop to secure work on the top of the bench (see the top photo on p. 36). A stop is simply a fixed bench dog that

A holdfast is a quick and secure way to hold work upon the benchtop. Traditional holdfasts slide into a hole and hammer tight; this one works quietly with a screw.

A small carver's vise such as this benchtop model has a table with a screw for attaching the carving. The table turns and tilts, locking at any angle you need. The ebony block ready to be carved will be a decorative finial.

works as a single point to butt work against when planing or chiseling. You can use it alone or in combination with a holdfast for added stability. There are steel stops, sometimes with little teeth to help grip the work, that are mortised into the benchtop (usually on the left end) and flip down when not in use. The simplest is a tight-fitting wooden dog that can be tapped up or down. Bench stops take some getting used to, but they are a wonderfully quick and simple way to hold work.

SPECIALTY VISES

If you plan on doing some carving or making a Windsor chair, it's worth knowing about carver's vises and shaving horses. Three-dimensional carvings (as opposed to flat carvings, such as signs) are often too awkwardly shaped to clamp easily onto a bench. The simplest solution is to use a carver's screw that fastens into the bottom of the carving through the bench or a board (one is shown in the engraving on the facing page). A more versatile solution is a carver's vise that swivels, rotates, and locks in any position. (The work is mounted onto the vise with a screw, as shown in the bottom photo at left.)

A shaving horse is a vise and a bench in one. You sit on the shaving horse and push against a foot pedal to clamp your work between the wooden head and an angled shelf. The harder you push, the more clamping pressure you apply. To reposition the work, simply let up on your foot. It's the ideal place for

Chairmaker Dave Sawyer uses a shaving horse for drawknifing and spokeshaving the fine tapered spindles that form the back of his Windsor chairs.

KEEP ALL CLAMPS clean and free of dried glue and rust, wax the bar, and occasionally oil the screw. It's easy to distort a clamp by applying more pressure than it was designed to handle, so either use more clamps—which is better for even pressure anyway—or find a bigger, stronger clamp. Keep the length of the screw that extends from the head to a minimum by taking up slack with scrap blocks or by snugging up the movable head before applying pressure. Use nonmarring pads or pieces of leather on the clamping heads to protect finished work.

using a drawknife, or for shaping anything from chair spindles to shingles. You can customize the clamping head with leather (as shown in the photo above) to protect delicate work, or cut a small groove in the head to grip chair spindles.

Clamps

You can never have too many clamps. I've done complex laminations when I've used just about every clamp in the shop—and believe me, I have a few—and I still could have used more. Glue-ups are just one of the many uses for clamps. Think of them as an extra pair of hands (or several extra pairs) to hold work while you drill, chisel, saw, or plane.

Traditional clamps come in a few basic types: bar clamps, handscrews,

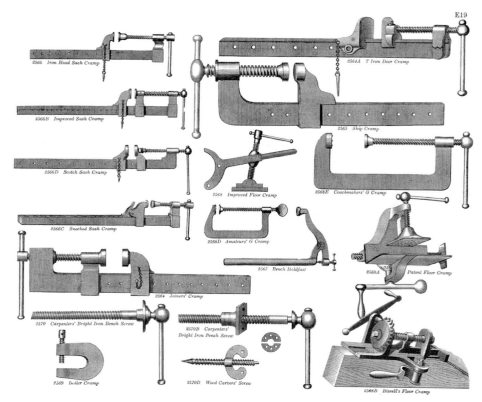

You can buy an interesting assortment of clamps today, but certainly nothing like the variety once offered in the Sheffield Standard List, which contained everything from floor clamps to coachmaker's clamps.

C-clamps and spring clamps are ideal for securing small work or for use in tight places, although they can be quite large and powerful, too.

C-clamps, and spring clamps. Few woodworking tools are as simple as a clamp with a screw or spring to deliver pressure, and a frame to hold the work and direct the pressure. Most clamps are made of malleable (slightly flexible) iron or steel, although handscrews and shopmade bar clamps are often wood. Clamps differ in their construction, their rigidity (which affects how much pressure they can apply), their size, and the depth of their jaws.

Bar clamps have a modest reach, they adjust quickly, and they have

Wooden handscrews have three useful features: they can clamp securely with the jaws out of parallel, the wooden jaws don't damage work, and they have a deep reach.

the advantage of a rigid, straight bar to keep large panels and carcases flat and true during glue-ups. The clamps I usually reach for in my shop are light-duty bar clamps, 6 in. and 12 in. long, which I use for small glue-ups and for holding jigs or work to my bench. I also have heavier ones—36 in. long and even longer—with larger screws and deeper jaws, and I use these nearly as much. You can buy clamping heads and make your own wood or pipe clamps any length you need. Pipe clamps can be threaded together to make extra-long clamps.

Taper the legs of a staple into opposing wedges and you have a pinch dog, a simple and useful clamp for aligning parts or clamping joints.

Part clamp, part shooting board, a miter jack was once a common shop tool that helps to plane an exact 45° miter—or 90° using the rear face. The planes are unusual Spiers miter planes.

C-clamps are best for small work and modest clamping pressure. I have some with 1-in. openings and larger ones with deep jaws. C-clamps adjust slowly, however. To speed up adjustment, I either slip in a scrap block to shorten the distance I have to adjust the screw, or I grab the end of the screw and spin the clamp. Spring clamps, which are really just oversized clothespins, come in a range of sizes and clamping pressures for all kinds of light clamping work. They work quickly, but not very positively. For very delicate work, clothespins work just fine, too.

Wooden handscrews have largely been replaced by other clamps, which is a shame considering how useful they are for clamping odd shapes and for holding work in their large jaws with even pressure. Handscrews have two screws: Use the screw that goes through the middle of the jaws to snug the clamp in position and the end screw to apply the pressure. To open or close the jaws quickly with the clamp off the work, hold the two handles and pedal it like a bicycle.

Clamping odd shapes, such as coopered cabinet doors, is an interesting challenge. If the curve is shallow, some creative jigging along with a bar clamp might work. Much simpler is a pinch dog tapped into the end grain, straddling the joint. Pinch dogs are like heavy-duty staples, with wedges for legs, that draw the joint tighter the farther they are driven into the work. They are a wonderful example of a simple solution to a difficult problem.

Marking and
MEASURING
TOOLS

If you remember anything from your high school shop class, it's probably the old adage "measure twice and cut once." Not only is this good advice to help avoid errors, but it also speaks to how basic measuring and marking out is to every aspect of woodworking. From the initial drawing to the completed project, marking and measuring tools make the work easier and more accurate.

A rule and square are the most important measuring tools. After you master them, add others, such as dividers, mortise gauges, bevel gauges, and angle dividers. While there is a certain degree of precision inherent in each of these tools, bear in mind the degree of accuracy required. A ¼ in. one way or another might suit a barn frame, but the slightest gap looks sloppy in a fine piece of furniture. 🔧

Marking knives and awls are superior to pencils for marking out joinery because they cut a fine, distinct line, sever the fibers (preventing chipout), and provide a groove for seating a chisel edge or saw.

Rules

Rules are as old as antiquity. As early as c. 2500 B.C., Egyptians had developed standardized measurements (based on the length of a human foot or an outstretched hand or arm), which they used in the first rules, made of stone or wood. The Romans had bronze folding rules, but they were rare and the average craftsman had a knife-marked lath—a straight wooden rule he probably made himself. Not until the 17th century were rules graduated into inches and then quarters, and it was a full century later before eighths and sixteenths came into common practice.

As the scales became more sophisticated, rules in common use also started to fold. Beginning in the 17th century, and roughly every century since, rules folded first twice, then four times, then as many as 15 times with long Stanley Zig-Zag Rules. Now we have the

Tools for Marking Out

There are all sorts of options for marking out your work: Some craftsmen like to use a micro-point mechanical pencil, others a ball-point pen or a sharply pointed awl. Pencils are fine for much marking out work. A pencil line is easy to see and erases easily, but even the thinnest line is not as distinct and fine as a knife or awl mark.

I prefer a marking knife for two reasons: First, it cuts a tiny groove that is perfect for holding the edge of a chisel (or some other cutting tool) dead on the line. Second, it

scores the fibers to reduce chipping. A marking knife should be sharpened to a point, with a fine bevel. For extremely thin knives, a double-bevel works well, but for the greatest accuracy a single bevel is better (use the flat of the blade against a rule or square). I own a few different knives, one of which is narrow and long for marking in tight spaces.

For marking the face of a board or its position in a glued-up panel, where I want bold marks to avoid making a careless mistake, I use a red or blue lumber crayon, available at any hardware store. Lumber crayons are also useful for marking out cuts and potential matches (faces and edges), and for marking grain direction during the milling process.

FOR ABOUT 500 YEARS, since it was decreed by King Edward I of England, an inch was three dry barley corns (grains) laid side by side. In the 19th century, rules were standardized for inches and feet, but still every major trading center in Europe had a slightly different foot. Not so long ago manufacturers made rules with a Paris foot on one side and an Amsterdam or a London foot on the other. This shouldn't seem odd: today we still can't agree if we will measure in millimeters or inches. 🎲

ultimate folding rule—a tape measure. But some carpenters will tell you that folding rules are still the best—easier to use than a tape in awkward places, such as measuring the inside of a wide door opening. Some rules have another nice feature: extension or caliper ends for accurate inside dimensions and depth measurements.

Fine rules traditionally were made of boxwood with brass joints. One notch higher were ivory rules with German silver fittings. Boxwood may not be as fancy, but it is a logical material for making a rule. It is extremely fine-grained and stable, and its light color displays the rule markings well. Ivory is a questionable choice for rules. Although it shows off the markings clearly, it is a decidedly unstable material that swells and shrinks quite readily with changes in humidity. At a cost six times that of boxwood, many ivory rules must have been gentlemen's tools, more for status than use. Occasionally you may run across an ebony rule.

In keeping with the ingenuity of toolmakers, there are lots of rules that not only measure length but also do some of the thinking for you. Take, for example, a "shrinkage rule" used by patternmakers (one of these rules can be seen on the far left

of the photo on p. 40). The wooden patterns they make are for casting metals that shrink about 1% of their total volume as they cool after being poured into the mold. For example, a 2-ft.-long shrinkage rule for cast iron, which shrinks ⅛ in. per foot, actually measures 24¼ in. Likewise, sawyers have lumber rules that, when laid across the diameter of a log, calculate the number of board feet of lumber that the log will yield. "Wantage rules" measure liq-

uids in barrels and tell you how many gallons are "wanted" to fill it. There are many other clever rules.

It's useful to have a few straight rules of various lengths. Steel rules can take rough use, and the markings are easy to read (especially on bright steel). They can be used as straightedges, flexed to lay out shallow curves, or you can clamp two together for accurate inside measurements. A 36-in. steel rule is useful for making drawings and layouts,

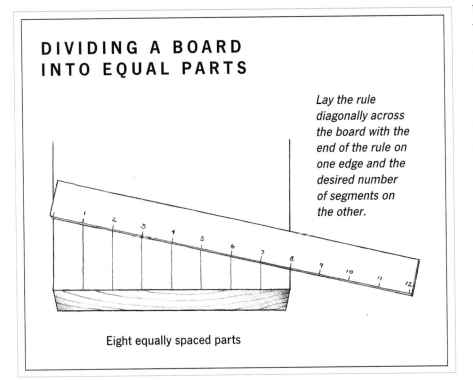

DIVIDING A BOARD INTO EQUAL PARTS

Lay the rule diagonally across the board with the end of the rule on one edge and the desired number of segments on the other.

Eight equally spaced parts

but perhaps too long for daily bench work; 12-in. and 24-in. rules are about the right length, and a 6-in. rule is handy for measuring in tight places.

For the greatest accuracy, be sure to read a rule with its edge—not its face—against the work. Straight rules can do things other than simple measuring, too. One useful trick you can do with a straight rule is to divide a board into equal segments across its width (for laying out dovetails, for example). To divide a 6-in. board into eight equal parts, I place the rule diagonally across the board, with the "0" on one edge and the "8" on the other, and mark off a

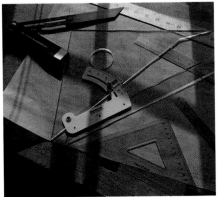

Stiff steel rules and plastic triangles aid in drafting accurate patterns and drawings, and for transferring measurements. Use a bevel gauge (top left) to transfer angles from a drawing to the work.

Patterns and story sticks are simple devices for transferring dimensions and helping you avoid errors commonly made when repeatedly measuring with a tape or rule. They also store those dimensions for later use.

segment at each inch marking (see the drawing on the facing page). This method works for any number of equal parts, depending on the scale you choose.

Patterns and story sticks are extremely useful measuring tools that can save a lot of time in the layout phase. A good pattern can be used again and again to lay out cuts, a more accurate method than measuring repeatedly, which can introduce small errors into your measurements. A pattern can be as simple as the first piece you cut, a cardboard template, or a story stick. A story stick is a thin strip of wood, as long as you need, with pencil marks at important reference points. They tell a story: for example, every element of a cabinet, from rail widths at top and bottom, to panel height, overall height, toe space, and so on.

Squares

It's ironic that so many woodworking cuts are at 90°, or square, considering there is nothing square about the trees we get our lumber from. Nevertheless, we live in a rectangular world. When building almost anything, you will have to make sure some part lies square to

These squares speed the layout of large work. The house framing square (top) has engraved rafter tables and a pair of adjustable gauges for laying out stair stringers; the unusual bridge builder's square is used to lay out large mortises and tenons. The square below it is hand-graduated and stamped 1804. A 12-in. square (bottom) is a useful size for a shop.

TRUING a framing square is a surprisingly easy thing to do. Whether the square is new or you've dropped it a time or two, check to see if it is square. Line up the tongue (the shorter of the two legs) against the straight edge of a piece of plywood and make a fine pencil line along the long leg. Flip the square over so that it is on the opposite side of the line and draw a second line parallel to the first. If the two lines are exactly parallel, your square is dead on. If they are wider apart at the bottom, your square is more than 90°; if it is narrower at the bottom, it is less than 90°.

The trick to correcting an out-of-square square is to move some of the metal along the imaginary miter between the blade and the tongue. Rap a center punch smartly on the inner corner to spread the square apart slightly, or on the outer corner to bring the legs of the square together. Punch a few times if necessary, but check your square after each punch so you don't push it too far the other way.

This framing square is not accurate, as shown by the two test lines. You can spread the legs of the square by tapping a center punch on the inside corner. To bring the legs closer together, place the punch on the outside corner.

some other part, and most likely you will be doing a lot of this. As a result, you'll need the following: an accurate try square or combination square for bench work (preferably both a 6-in. and a 12-in. size), and a framing square for larger work, such as laying out cuts on plywood sheet goods.

You can establish the squareness of a rectangle (such as a carcase or large panel) by measuring the diagonals; if the diagonals are equal, the rectangle must have square corners. You also can check squareness with a framing square (for large work) or a smaller try or combination square (for work at the bench). A framing square has one blade or "body" 24 in. long and 2 in. wide (useful for laying out mortise-and-tenon joinery in timber-framing) and a narrower "tongue" 16 in. long and 1½ in. wide (also for timber-framing). I have one with a 12-in. blade, a very useful size. The name "framing square" comes from its common use framing houses, as evidenced by the complex table of rafter lengths stamped onto the face of some squares. In theory, one could lay out all of the dimensions of a complex roof with a square alone. You can make a square of any size if you remember Pythagoras' rule that the three sides of a right triangle are in the ratio of 3:4:5.

Bench squares can be metal combination squares—meaning they have a 45° face for checking miters—or they can be wood and metal "try squares" (so-named because they "try" the squareness). The

For bench work, a small square is useful: either an elegant wood and metal try square (top), a metal square with movable rule (center), or a fixed engineer's square (bottom left).

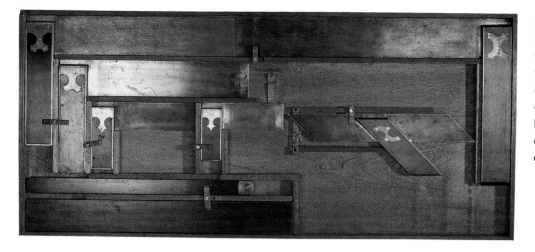

A beautiful collection of squares, miter squares, and winding sticks (bottom left) is fitted into the till of a 19th-century joiner's tool chest. The care with which they are fitted both protects them and speaks of their value to an unknown craftsman.

wide blade of a try square is fixed at right angles to the body, whereas combination squares have a movable blade graduated as a rule. (In a pinch, a combination square works as a marking gauge, as shown in the photo at right.) Both squares can be accurate, but older try squares are the more beautiful of the two, often made with rosewood bodies, steel blades, shapely brass rivet plates, and edges trimmed in brass.

To mark a square cut with these tools, hold the body of the square tightly against the work and use a pencil or knife to mark along the blade. To check the squareness of the end of a board or joint, hold the square the same way and sight under the blade; the amount of light you see clearly shows the degree to which the edge is out of square (provided your square is accurate). Squares are delicate instruments and can easily lose their accuracy, so be careful not to drop them or otherwise manhandle them. If they're not true, they're not worth much.

A combination square and pencil make a quick marking gauge, but it's almost as accurate and faster to wrap a couple of fingers over the corner of the board for gauging a pencil line.

For transferring one or two angles, the St. Johnsbury Tool Co.'s cabinet-maker's bevel gauge (bottom right) has two blades locked in position by a thumbscrew. The A-shaped L. C. Stephen's patent folding inclinometer rules with spirit levels (top and bottom) are for measuring angles such as roof pitches.

Fancy combination gauges for the well-heeled craftsman are bevel gauges, levels, squares, and inclinometers all in one.

A miter square is fixed at 45° for consistent and accurate miters. The modern steel Japanese miter square in the foreground is used no differently than the traditional English one at top.

Bevel Gauges

If you work with anything other than square edges, you'll need a bevel gauge. A miter square is one kind of bevel gauge, fixed at exactly 45° for miter cuts. A sliding bevel gauge, on the other hand, is adjustable. As with squares, there are many variations of bevel gauges: some are wood, some metal, and some are beautiful combinations of the two. All have an adjustable straight blade and stock. By tightening a nut at one end, the blade can be locked in any position; when loosened it folds into the stock. One variation has a small steel square for a blade that makes the tool even more flexible in transferring angles.

Most bevel gauges will do a serviceable job, but there are some things to look for when you're buying one. Avoid gauges with a nut or tightener proud of the stock where the stock and blade join—this gets in the way and makes them awkward to use. Better are bevel gauges with a wing nut on the end of the stock. They feel more positive, the nut is not in the way, and you can tighten the bevel no matter what side is up (not so with the first type).

A bevel gauge works like an adjustable square. You can set it with a protractor, from a drawing, or from the work itself. Tighten the nut just slightly before setting the blade so it will hold its position, and then cinch it down when you have it set where you want it. (Make sure the blade is flush or proud of the stock above the joint to get an accurate

Set a bevel gauge from the work, from a drawing, or from a protractor. The Italian brass protractor is marked 1701 and has scales for laying out polygons of up to 12 sides. A combination protractor and bevel gauge (top) is an extremely useful tool for all layout work.

A quality metal rule is an accurate straightedge for checking the sole of a plane or the flatness of a jointer bed.

MARKING and measuring tools generally don't need a lot of tune-up—either they are accurate or they are not. You can adjust a framing square, but not other squares, at least not very easily. Start with quality tools and try not to bend them or drop them, especially on concrete floors. The most maintenance you should have to do is to keep your marking knife, and the pins of your marking gauge, compass, and dividers, honed sharp. 🌑

measurement.) When I have to keep track of multiple bevels, I use two bevel gauges. (Shipbuilders, who work with bevels constantly, use bevel gauges with two blades.) Once set, treat the tool gently, so you don't run the risk of changing the setting. It's also a good idea to

transfer important angles to a board for later reference, or to keep track of many bevels. One of the nice features of a bevel gauge is that it gives you an angle and its complement, which can be helpful when setting a table saw for a bevel cut.

Similar to a bevel gauge are angle dividers, which look and work like bevel gauges with two blades, but the blades are connected to the stock so that they open and close in unison. Just as the name implies, the tool bisects any angle and yields the appropriate miter angle. Angle dividers are not that common anymore, but they come in handy for coopered work or for fitting woodwork in old houses with out-of-square corners.

Straightedges

Shop straightedges come in two types: precisely machined metal straightedges for checking the flatness of a plane's sole or a machine setup, and wooden straightedges used as fences to guide tools or to test the flatness of large work, such as doors, where precision is less critical. A good metal rule 24 in. or 36 in. long is accurate enough for much of the work in the first category. To see if a straightedge is straight, hold the edge against a known flat surface, such as a jointer bed or saw table, and then rotate the straightedge end for end to see if they agree. The faintest sliver of

A chalkline need be no more complicated than a spool of line and a hunk of chalk. Chalklines are used to mark out a long straight line, such as the one along the wany edge of this board. Also shown are traditional wooden line reels, and a modern one that also functions as a plumb bob (on the board).

pear twice as big. I hang the wooden straightedges when not in use to keep them from warping.

Chalklines

A chalkline marks a straight line much as a straightedge does, but the advantage is that it allows you to mark any length you need. It is simply a reel of cord that you charge with chalk, stretch between two points, and snap sharply to leave a line. Some versions use ink instead of chalk for a sharp, distinct line. Most chalklines store the cord and powdered chalk inside a case; you merely pull out the chalked cord as you need it. The simplicity of the system is that as long as the cord is stretched tight, the line will be straight. If I'm snapping onto an uneven surface or if the line is long, I'll hold it tight against the work at the midpoint and snap each half separately.

A lot of the lumber I work with has what is known as "wany edge," which means that the bark was left on one or both edges. It takes more work to mill wany-edged lumber to size, but the advantage is that you can get wider boards (and less wood goes into the scrap pile). To create a straight edge on wany-edged lumber, I use a chalkline; although the line is nowhere as fine as one made with a straightedge and pencil, it's entirely adequate to follow with a bandsaw. For the most part, however, a chalkline is a carpentry tool for marking lines to install shingles or to lay out lines for nailing.

light is about 0.001 in. wide, but if you want to be precise, you can measure any gap with a feeler gauge.

You can buy hardened metal straightedges (of any length) machined to whatever tolerances your budget will allow. A hardened edge is nice if you are going to use the straightedge for cutting veneer, because the edge will hold up to a stray knife cut. Another option is to make a straightedge. Buy a piece of cold rolled steel roughly ¼ in. by 1¼ in. (from any steel supplier), belt-sand the faces clean, and take it to a machine shop to mill one edge straight.

Simpler yet are shopmade wooden straightedges. For short work I use my metal straightedges, but for longer work I use 54-in. or 96-in. wooden ones. The 54-in. straightedge is an old quartersawn oak board with one good edge trued with a jointer plane; the 96-in. one is a plywood offcut. Both are accurate enough to get a fair idea of the flatness of a large cabinet or tabletop. I occasionally check them against each other, or alone by tracing the profile of one edge on a piece of paper or plywood, then flipping the straightedge end-for-end to see how the edge aligns with the pencil line. Any errors will ap-

Levels and Plumb Bobs

To determine whether a surface is level (horizontal) or plumb (vertical) you can use a level. To test or establish long verticals, the better tool is a weight on a string, or a plumb bob. At one time they were made of lead (hence *plumb*), but more modern plumb bobs are usually brass or iron with steel tips. (Some are quite ornate and beautiful, further examples of the tool maker's art.) Ancient Egyptians combined the ideas of plumb and level in an A-shaped wooden tool, where the chord between the two legs of the A was level when a plumb bob suspended from the top of the A hung exactly in the center of the chord. Another version has a plumb bob hanging along one leg of a square. When the bob is centered on the leg, the square is both

Hang a plumb bob on a line and gravity does the rest. A smooth profile and dense weight are important so the bob does not flutter in the wind.

Levels are among the most beautifully made tools. The inclinometer level at center was made by L. L. Davis Level and Tool Co., and the brass-bound and rosewood levels are by Stratton Bros. of Greenfield, Mass.

Levels come in many styles, from the fanciful cast-iron Davis level (second from top) to the practical modern level with digital readout (center). At the top is a brass-bound rosewood level (with level sights for use as a transit); in the foreground are various small levels (including one that clamps onto a square) and a circular level for measuring an incline.

plumb and level—a simple use of gravity.

Spirit levels, the common levels of today, use another aspect of gravity: the fact that liquids will form a level surface. The variations in such levels are endless, from tiny pocket levels to carpenter's levels 6 ft. long. The most beautiful are made with exotic woods and bound in brass to preserve their square and straight edges. Their precision is due to the slightly curved glass vials nearly filled with alcohol (hence "spirit") or antifreeze, which are set in plaster parallel to the length of the level or perpendicular to it. When the bubble inside the vial floats to the center (encouraged by the vial's curve), the level is exactly horizontal or vertical. This simplicity makes it easy to imagine small levels that

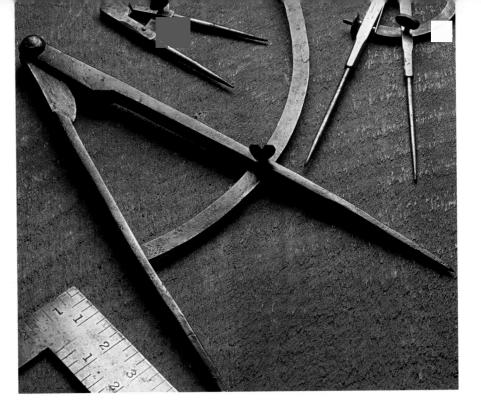

Dividers have two stiff legs with a thumb screw for locking them in place, and sometimes the handy feature of an additional screw for fine adjustment of the setting. Use them to transfer dimensions or "step off" equally spaced increments.

Trammel points, which can be fitted to a wooden beam of any length, can scribe large circles or arcs, or transfer long dimensions. For fine-tuning the distance between the points, the standing pair has a screw adjustment. Trammels were commonly shopmade or school projects, and few are identical.

clamp onto squares, levels that measure a fixed angle, or "variable-pitch adjusters" that clamp onto one end of a level for laying deck joists or plumbing at set angles.

Compasses, Dividers, Calipers, and Trammel Points

For drawing a circle, transferring dimensions, or measuring dimensions on a turned piece, compasses, dividers, and calipers are essential. Each of these tools has two adjustable legs and some method to

hold them at this setting—either a stiff hinge, a spring with threaded rod and nut, or an arm between the legs that can be locked in position with a thumb screw. These interesting tools range in size from the tiny to the huge, and in material from shopmade wood to precisely machined steel.

On a compass, one leg usually has a sharp steel point and the other a pencil point to draw circles or arcs of circles, or to scribe lines parallel to an edge. Whenever you have to fit a piece of wood to an uneven wall, you can scribe it with a compass. Hold or clamp the wood tightly in position against the wall, open the compass as wide as the biggest

Hand-forged or manufactured from cast steel and decoratively filed, calipers measure inside and outside dimensions. Some hold their setting through friction of the hinge alone; others have a spring joint between the legs with a screw adjuster to hold them in position.

IT IS EXTREMELY difficult to accomplish most woodworking tasks without a good rule, a square, and a few other basic layout tools, but several of these tools you can fashion yourself. You can make a workable compass, dividers, or trammel set from a scrap of wood and a couple of nails or pencils. Likewise, a simple wooden or plywood pattern can substitute for a bevel gauge.

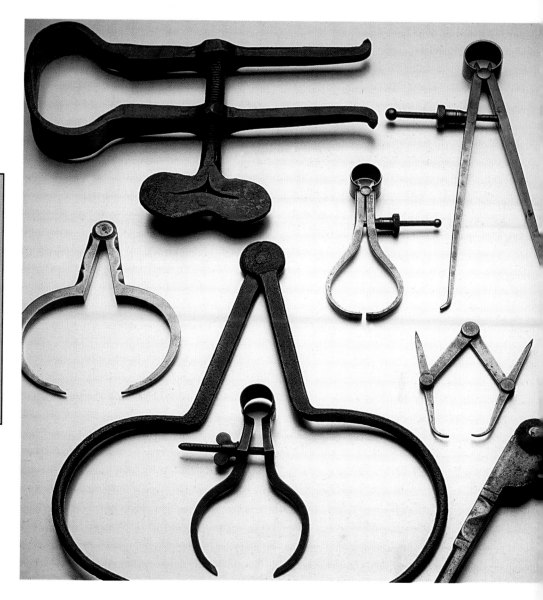

gap and—keeping the compass in the same orientation—guide the point along the wall. The pencil point will draw a line on the piece, perhaps a cabinet or a molding, that parallels every irregularity. Log home builders and timber-framers use this technique to fit parts and to lay out joints.

Unlike a compass, dividers have two sharp points (no pencil). They can do the same work as a compass, but what they do best is transfer dimensions accurately, when laying out dovetails, for example, or when marking a board for equally spaced holes. Prick the dividers into the wood and walk one leg after the other down the length along a straight line. You can see right away if the spacing works, readjusting the

dividers if it doesn't. Dividers are also an accurate way to transfer a dimension from one place to another, such as from a full-scale drawing to the workpiece. I hone divider points on a fine stone to keep them needle sharp.

Proportional dividers have two legs that form two pairs of dividers joined end-for-end with a common movable hinge point, similar to a pair of scissors. By changing the hinge point (making one set of

dividers half the length of the other) you can transfer dimensions and, at the same time, double or halve them.

Trammel points are half a set of dividers, you might say. They come in pairs and generally are used on a strip of wood (any reasonably rigid scrap will do). Some trammel sets have two steel points and are used as dividers for transferring large dimensions; others can be outfitted with a pencil for drawing large circles or arcs of circles (and many come with both options). Some are unique, with beautiful brass details and fine adjusters to move the points. I don't own any trammel points, mainly because an alternative is so easy to make: To scribe a large circle or arc, I drive a nail into one end of a stick and drill a hole for a pencil the right distance out (the radius). A notch in the side of the stick for the pencil point also works, with the advantage that I can fine-tune its position by cutting to one side or the other and move the apex of the notch just a little.

A set of dividers and a compass have straight legs; calipers usually have curved ones. They work the same way your fingers do when pinching something and are used for measuring the diameter of a turned table leg or the thickness of a bowl. Reverse the pinching action, and that's how some calipers measure inside dimensions accurately, especially in places you can't reach (and certainly a lot more easily than with a small rule). Perhaps to prove that tool makers have a sense of humor, they've made dancing calipers, with shapely female legs or a dancing couple; the toes measure inside and the arms outside. Because calipers often were customized by blacksmiths for some particular purpose, there are many variations for specific trades, with double openings for two separate dimensions or with rules that convert a caliper's opening to a measurement, or vice versa.

With a single setting a vernier caliper measures the thickness of a tenon and the width of its mortise, or a tenon length and mortise depth. A depth gauge (center) that is also a small bevel gauge is another useful measuring tool.

Why make a plain tool when you can have some fun with the design? Calipers with fanciful and shapely legs have toes for inside measurements and arms for outside dimensions. The leg on the marking awl is a pocket clip.

Patternmakers rely on inside and outside calipers for transferring dimensions from drawings to accurately size the round section of wooden patterns for casting anything from gears to shafts and wheels.

Designed with multiple functions, the A. Williams patented marking gauge (bottom right) combines a single-pin marking gauge with a double-pin mortise gauge, and a knife-pointed slitting gauge. The G. Kenny gauge behind it does all this and is a trammel set, too.

The caliper I use most often is a vernier caliper (see the photo at right on p. 54). It's really more of a machinist's tool, able to measure 0.001 in., which is impressive but not the main reason I like it. Rather, it is because the jaws open 6 in. and give three measurements simultaneously: inside dimension, outside, and depth. This allows me to measure a tenon thickness with the outside jaws, and without changing anything, I can test the mortise width with the inside jaws. I can also check a tenon length and mortise depth without actually measuring either, reducing the possibility for error. I have a little depth gauge that also does this job (shown in the same photo), but a vernier caliper is more versatile. Because its jaws are deep and parallel, I can use it to check whether the two cheeks of a tenon are parallel, or to see if a long mortise is the same width at both ends.

Marking Gauges

Marking gauges include a variety of tools, all with a similar function: to scribe or cut one or more lines parallel to an edge. There's one type of marking gauge, called a mortise gauge, that works on a similar principle to my vernier caliper: With one setting I can lay out both the

A large panel gauge marks out the width of a board parallel to an edge in preparation for ripping.

tenon thickness and mortise width. It consists of a sliding beam with a fixed and movable pin, and a head that clamps on the beam with a thumb screw. It scribes two lines parallel to a face or edge, much more accurately than a pencil.

Other gauges do similar layout work, such as a marking gauge with a single fixed pin for dovetailing, a much larger panel gauge for marking the width of a board parallel to one edge (used when boards were ripped by hand), and a cutting gauge with a knife in place of the pin. There are plenty of other unusual gauges made by Stanley and other manufacturers—butt gauges with multiple pins for marking out mortises for butt hinges, and metal gauges with thin wheels in place of pins, to name two. At a minimum you will want a mortise gauge, one of the most common and versatile.

When woodworking was done by hand, every shop had a number of gauges, purchased from catalogs or made in the shop from ebony, rosewood, or beech, sometimes with brass inlay at points of wear. Because they were such important tools, someone always was tinkering with the design to produce a tool that combined multiple tasks or worked more accurately and easily. Some designs were patented, but most were as individual as the craftsmen who used them.

The shape of the pin or knife further distinguishes the different gauge designs. Naturally, you would expect a cutting gauge to have a knife. If you are going to use one for cutting veneer strips for inlays as

PROBLEM: how do you mark the centerline of a tapered workpiece? A similar problem: How do you mark the four equal bevels on a square and tapering piece (such as a pencil post) to shape it into an octagon in section? Careful measuring is one tedious but workable solution, but there is an easier way.

Take a scrap of wood and drill a hole in the middle for a pencil. Then hammer a 16d nail an equal distance to either side of the pencil so they project at least 1 in.

Straddle the gauge over the stock so the two nails ride along the edges as the pencil marks the center.

For dividing square or tapered stock into an eight-sided piece (for the posts on a pencil-post bed, for example) use two pencils spaced from the pins in the ratio of 5:7:5. The divider will mark the location of the bevels for shaping the octagon. With a little bit of creativity, you can use this idea to make similar gauges for many marking tasks. 🪚

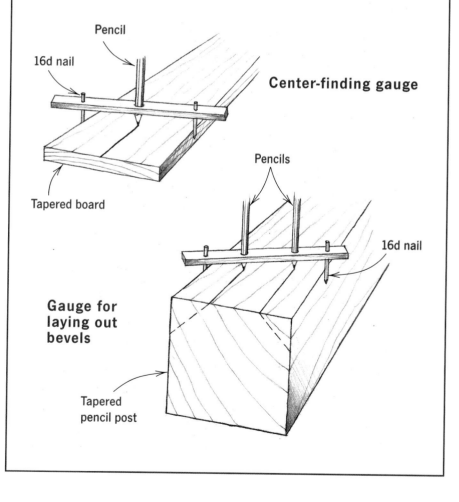

Pencil

16d nail

Center-finding gauge

Tapered board

Pencils

16d nail

Gauge for laying out bevels

Tapered pencil post

A gauge with a pin works well for cutting with the grain, but across the grain a knife scores the fibers more cleanly.

(A shallow mark is easier to plane away if you don't want it to show.) Be aware that the knife will tend to follow the grain. To avoid or at least lessen this tendency, sharpen the point so it angles away from the fence. If you do this, the knife point will pull away from the edge, drawing the gauge tightly to the work. This works just as well if you decide to push your gauge.

A marking gauge is used whenever you need a line parallel to an edge. It can be used for inlay work, for dimensioning a board to a consistent thickness by hand, or for cutting dovetails. For marking out mortises and tenons, set the two pins of your marking gauge as wide as the chisel you will use to chop the mortise. Don't rely on the rule on the beam of some gauges, but rather set the gauge by measuring the distance between the pin and head. Or better still, set it directly from the work.

I do, a rounded knife cuts more gently than a finely pointed one. For marking across the grain, a knife (think marking knife) is superior to a pin (think awl) for cutting the fibers. With the grain, a pin works well. Rather than having a number of gauges, I sharpen my mortise gauge with slipstones until I get a knife edge that works well in most circumstances.

A marking gauge is designed to be pushed away from you, but I've always found pulling less awkward. The point need only project $\frac{1}{16}$ in. or so from the surface of the gauge. To scribe a line, rest the beam on the work, hold the fence tightly to the edge, and drag the point along. You can control the depth and size of the line by rotating the beam, from the point fully buried in the wood to just the faintest scribe line.

The fine steel fingers of a profile gauge conform to any contour, producing both a positive and negative profile.

Profile Gauges

Working with moldings—or with any shapes for that matter—there are many times when you need to transfer complicated contours or profiles. Wooden patterns are one solution, but they take time to make. A good alternative is a profile gauge, a stack of thin metal (or plastic) fingers bound together yet able to slide past one another and conform to almost any shape. One side is the negative of the profile, the other the positive (see the bottom photo on the facing page). The more fingers per inch, the more detail it captures.

The whole idea behind a profile gauge or any gauge, or for that matter any of the marking and measuring tools discussed in this chapter, is to improve your accuracy and efficiency. Making gauges is something I do quite often when building a piece of furniture: a dovetail gauge of a certain pin angle made from a beveled scrap of wood and fence glued together, or a small story stick for setting my router to cut evenly spaced grooves. They aren't fancy and they usually don't take a lot of time to make. Most of the time I use them once, so I don't want to spend a lot of time making them.

The beauty of knowing how to use hand tools—and being able to improvise new ones when you need them—is that it allows you to work to whatever degree of precision you desire. Many times $\frac{1}{16}$ in. is accurate enough (that's all some rules can measure anyway). At other times, the precision of an engineer is called for. Don't forget that you're working with wood, a material with a personality of its own, and one that will change dimension no matter what you do.

A jack-of-all-trades, a Stanley Odd Job will do the work of many tools, including a level, plumb, square, miter square, marking gauge, depth gauge, and compass.

STRIKING TOOLS

Axes built America. Facing a seemingly endless forest, settlers used axes to clear land and hew trees into fences, stockades, homes, barns, and ships. To make all the wooden necessities of daily life, from barrels to water pails, wagon wheels to ox yokes, an ax or adze did much of the work, hewing parts out of a log and shaping them to size.

While a hatchet is still an ideal tool for shaping wood quickly, machines have largely replaced the work of axes and adzes. Similarly, air nailers and screw guns have diminished a carpenter's reliance on his most basic striking tools: the hammer and mallet. But no machine can replace the sensitivity and the pleasure of swinging a hammer—setting a nail or nudging a part into place—or the feel of a well-balanced mallet driving the wooden handle of a chisel. 🪲

Bronze Age tools, such as these axes and knife from Luristan, Persia, show the sophistication of tools made nearly 3,000 years ago. The cast ax at the top, with reinforced edges on the tapered blade and a cross-hatch decoration, would have needed constant whetting to maintain a sharp edge on the soft metal.

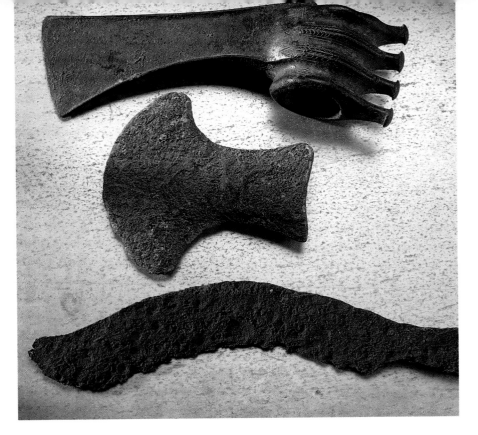

Axes vary in weight and width for many tasks: felling trees, shaping them into timbers, and cutting joints. British designs that arrived with the colonists, such as those illustrated in the Sheffield List (below), gradually evolved into a new American style with a heavier poll for better balance and more power.

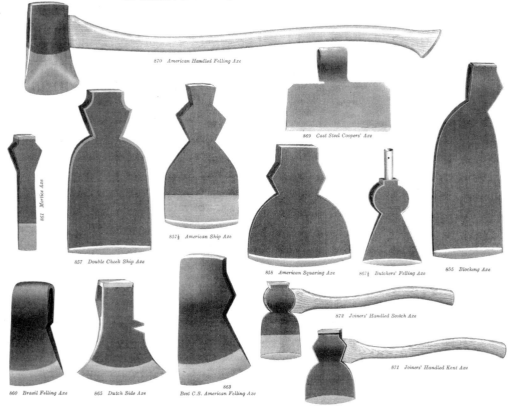

870 *American Handled Felling Axe*

869 *Cast Steel Coopers' Axe*

861 *Mortice Axe*

857½ *American Ship Axe*

857 *Double Cheek Ship Axe*

858 *American Squaring Axe*

867½ *Butchers' Felling Axe*

855 *Blocking Axe*

872 *Joiners' Handled Scotch Axe*

871 *Joiners' Handled Kent Axe*

860 *Brazil Felling Axe*

865 *Dutch Side Axe*

863 *Best C.S. American Felling Axe*

Axes

The first tools were surely stone hammers of some kind. By chipping a flint cutting edge with a hammer and lashing it onto a split wooden or antler handle, man made an ax. To work well, the ax head had to have enough weight, which stressed the connection with the handle. During the Bronze Age, in one of the more curious detours in the development of modern tools, ax heads were cast with an open end perpendicular to the cutting edge, not parallel with it as is typical today. This design strengthened the connection between the ax head and handle, but it meant that the handle had to be L-shaped to orient the ax head properly. Naturally, the durability of the tool now depended on the strength of the handle.

It was not until the Iron Age that the prototype of the modern ax emerged, a design made possible by bending a rectangular strap of wrought iron in half, forming a handle hole parallel with the cutting edge. Steel was so valuable it was reserved for only the cutting edge welded between the sides. When it wore down, which it did, a blacksmith "rebit" it at the forge with a new steel edge.

Little has changed since then, although the size of the tool and the profile of the cutting edge have certainly evolved. Axes for felling trees need weight for powerful blows, a slim profile to cut deeply with each stroke, and a relatively narrow cutting edge with two equal bevels. Splitting axes work best with a more pronounced wedge shape and a stout bevel. On the other hand, axes for hewing and squaring timbers to size—called broad or side axes—are more efficient when they have a long cutting edge. Beveled on one side only, and with a handle slightly bent to give your hands clearance when working close to a surface, a broad ax is capable of paring wood nearly as flat as a plane.

An ax is the most basic woodworking tool. In skilled hands it is capable of a range of work, from splitting parts from a log to sizing and some joinery. A 17th-century settler could build a house with an ax alone and—I am exaggerating only a little—much of the furniture,

Early continental broad axes had long blades, as shown in this 1493 illustration of the building of Noah's Ark. The axes were probably harder to control than later, more symmetrical designs.

too. If you look closely at barn or house beams, or the back of an 18th-century cupboard, you will see the distinctive marks left by an ax or its cousin, the adze. By the late 19th century, when machines began to replace hand tools, catalogs still offered an impressive range of axes, each having a slightly different weight or edge to suit the various trades: wheelwright, shipwright, cooper, carpenter, and woodsman. Each was named for the localities or trades that favored that style: Kent, Kentucky, Canadian, Norfolk, and Newcastle.

HATCHETS

Unless you are going to do a lot of green woodworking or hew a house frame out of logs, an ax is not going to be a tool you'll use that much. A hatchet is another story. Hatchets are light axes, less than 3 lb., with similar variations in shape and function. The one I use most often is an old multipurpose shingling hatchet. It has a blade for splitting shingles to size, a hammer head, and a small notch for pulling nails. It's similar to a lather's hatchet, which is used for nailing plaster lath and making the

WOOD IS THE IDEAL material for handles. It's easy to shape and has just the right amount of springiness to absorb vibration. But wooden handles can split or snap, leaving a broken stub in the head. To work the stub out, drill a number of closely spaced holes into the wood with a metalworking twist bit (which won't be damaged by running into the metal wedge likely to be there) and punch out the stub bit by bit.

Use hickory or ash for the new handle. The white sapwood makes better handles than the darker heart, as do handles split rather than sawn. Bandsaw and

Using a favorite handle as a pattern, split out the stock for a new handle and shape it to fit your grip perfectly with a drawknife and spokeshaves.

drawknife the handle to shape using the broken handle or another favorite as a pattern. Fine-tune with a rasp or spokeshave.

Fit the handle by trial-fitting it in the head repeatedly and shaving down the high spots (they'll show as dirty areas from rubbing inside the head). Check that the head and handle are in the same plane by sighting down the handle. When the handle fits the head snugly and is about ½ in. from going fully home, saw a kerf for a wedge across the long axis and nearly as deep as the head.

Drive the handle into the head by rapping hard on the opposite end while holding the handle vertically. Hammer in a hardwood wedge and saw off any excess. Start a slot with a chisel at right angles to the wooden one and drive in a metal wedge. Finish the handle with a scraper and sandpaper and wipe on a coat of boiled linseed oil and varnish. ❧

lath by splitting a wide board from each side and opening it up like an accordion (a lather's hatchet is shown in the engraving on p. 71).

For rough sizing work, rounding a piece of wood to spin fairly true on a lathe, or wasting the bulk of a bevel cut along the underside of a curved tabletop, a hatchet is a remarkably quick and accurate tool. Mastering this tool is much easier than gaining the confidence to take a whack at your work with a tool you know can also do a lot of damage. As with any tool, accuracy comes with practice. Swing a hatchet with your arm and not your wrist. A hatchet sharpened with two equal bevels, like a felling ax, works well for most work. Sharpened with a single bevel and a flat back, a hatchet is more accurate for paring to a line or cutting a flat surface, such as a large tenon on a timber or that beveled table edge. In this case, a hint of a back bevel is recommended. In either case, the overall bevel can be as small as 20°.

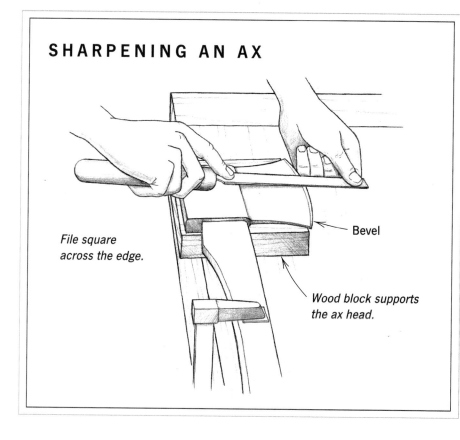

SHARPENING AN AX

File square across the edge.

Bevel

Wood block supports the ax head.

Hatchets are useful tools for rough shaping and quick removal of excess wood. Here, a chairmaker is rounding a leg billet with a hatchet before turning it on his lathe. The chopping stump has two levels, so that he can work at a comfortable height whether shaping long or short pieces.

SHARPENING AXES AND HATCHETS

Axes and hatchets are sharpened the same way. Often, the steel is soft enough to be cut with a file (a softer edge will hold up to the shock of chopping, especially into a hard knot). A file is the best tool to establish the overall shape and bevel. You can also use a grinder, but be sure to use a grinder with a large-diameter wheel; a small bench grinder leaves a hollow ground and a somewhat fragile edge. (If this is all you have, use the side of the wheel.)

File square across the edge, either away from it or into it, if you feel brave. Sight down the cutting edge to see that you are keeping the bevels equal. Finally, hone the edge by bringing the stone to the tool. Sharpen a broad ax or side hatchet the same way, only keep the back flat and polished. Hone just the slightest back bevel onto the edge to encourage the tool to angle out of the cut with every stroke. This will give you a bit more control over the tool.

Adzes

Turn the cutting action of an ax 90° and you have an adze. A short-handled adze is swung like a hammer for close-in shaping work. Adzes with longer handles are used the same way you might chop with a pickax. In sure hands, an adze is

TWYBILL, TWO-BILL, and mortising ax all describe variations on an ancient tool—a cross between an ax and a chisel. Some twybills are swung like a small double-bitted ax with the cutting edges at right angles to one another. They are used for chopping and picking out the waste from large mortises (probably drilled out beforehand). Other twybills are like huge chisels, or single-bitted axes, with long chisel-like cutting edges. Continental woodworkers used them—and still do—but for some reason they were never popular with English and American craftsmen.

One twybill I've seen was an iron bar over 4 ft. long, flattened at one end into a 1½-in.-wide paring chisel. The other end was a stout mortise chisel, and in the middle was a short hollow socket just the right size for a wooden handle—or at least you might think so. But if a hapless apprentice had been sent in search of such a handle (along with a left-handed hammer, to the amusement of his coworkers), the search would have ended in vain because such a twybill never had a handle. A handle would have made the tool ungainly and impossible to swing. Instead, a workman would rest the bar against his shoulder, grasp the short socket and, using the weight of the tool, chop out a mortise with one end and then pare it to size with the other. 🏵

A sculptor's adze has two blades of different curvature for roughing out a chair seat and then shaping it to a smooth, finished surface. The oval handle ensures a secure grip; choking up on it provides a measure of added control.

capable of accurate shaping and flattening, but it also is a far more dangerous tool. Swung like a hoe, the blade of a foot adze finishes cutting near or under your toe.

It's easy to see how a moment of inattention could have disastrous consequences. No wonder it is said that the adze is the only tool the Devil is afraid to use.

Until recently, I thought foot adzes were obsolete. So I was surprised to find a shipwright at Mystic Seaport, Connecticut, straddling a 60-ft.-long log of purpleheart, hewing it to a taper to form the keel of a reproduction of the schooner *Amistad*. Nearby was another shipwright shaping a massive rear stem with a broad ax. A century ago this would have been a common sight in any shipyard.

Hand adzes, although no longer common, are useful and still available both new and used. Many trades still use them, such as chairmakers to hollow seats, coopers to cut a consistent bevel on the inside of the barrel staves, and wheelwrights to shape the curved parts for wheels and wagons. The "poll"

Adzes combine the heft of an ax and the curved cutting edge of a gouge to quickly hollow everything from bowls to barrel staves or to flatten a surface as smooth as if cut by a plane. The narrow adze to the right is called a "joug adze" and is used for shaping wooden bucket yokes.

or hammer face of the adze is used in place of a hammer to knock parts into alignment or to drive nails. The long, round poll of a shipwright's adze is used to drive spikes or nails deep below the surface, well out of reach of the cutting edge. Some of these adzes have a straight cutting edge for leveling wide surfaces. Others have turned up ends, or a pronounced curve to the cutting edge like a gouge, for severing and paring the fibers when the tool is worked across the grain.

SHARPENING ADZES
Sharpen an adze similarly to an ax. On a foot adze, the handle gets in the way of sharpening, so quite cleverly the handle is wider toward the end that fits in the "eye" of the adze head and can be driven out and removed. The eye is quite deep, for a strong connection between tool and handle, especially important since the handle isn't permanently wedged into place. You can then grind, file, and hone the edge. An overall edge bevel of 25° is a good place to start. Because the back of the tool forms part of the cutting edge and guides the paring cut, it should be flat and polished, with only a slight back bevel. As

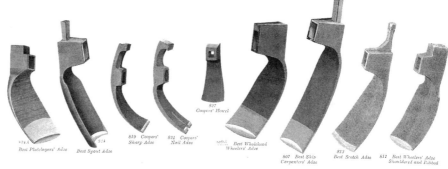

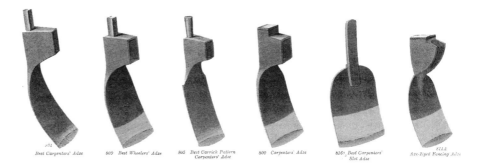

Adzes are used by every trade: shipwrights, coopers, wheelwrights, gutter makers ("spout adzes"), and carpenters. The hammer-like polls on some are useful for banging parts into alignment or for sinking a nail below the surface and out of range of the cutting edge.

Struck with a mallet, a froe splits a log into chair parts or tool handles with minimum waste and, most important, along the grain for maximum strength.

Using the froe as a lever or wedge helps open the split. Because the split wants to run out to the weaker side, pressuring against the heavier side of the bolt keeps the split running true.

with a side ax, the back bevel provides added control as it guides the edge out of each chopping cut. The curve of the blade also helps.

Froes

Imagine a long steel blade with an eye forged into one end for a perpendicular wooden handle, and you have a froe. It could be mistaken for an ax, and is used along with one, but it isn't a true striking tool. Rather, it is struck with a wooden club that drives it into the end grain of a block for splitting out anything from chair parts to shingles. Because it splits rather than cuts the fibers, semi-sharpness is all that is required.

Splitting parts from a log has a few advantages. For one, it's quicker than sawing for producing straight parts such as chair rungs and legs (provided the stock has straight grain). Using a froe and club only, chairmaker Brian Boggs can split the 15 parts he needs to build a chair in about 20 minutes. Another advantage is that the parts will be stronger than if they had been sawn, because the splits follow the grain. In a quality log, hardly any of the wood is wasted (there is no saw kerf), and when it comes to shaping with a drawknife, split parts work far more easily. A cooper's curved froe has one further advantage: The curved blade splits out staves partially shaped to the curve of the barrel or pail.

A froe might be a simple tool, but using one takes skill and strength. The split is started by hitting the top

Wooden mallets are gentle on wooden chisel handles. These simple, shopmade ash mallets have tapered handles that slip into a mortise in the head, wedging the handle in place. The striking faces are angled about 10°, in line with the arc of a natural swing, and they are large so there is less chance of missing the target.

of the blade with the club, driving the froe into the end grain. In a good log, it is then just a question of using the froe to lever open the split, tapping when necessary, and working the split to the end.

It gets tricky when the pieces get smaller—the thinner of the two parts bends, and the split drifts toward the bent side, cutting the piece progressively thinner. One solution is to split a large "bolt" or blank in half (or quarters, if necessary), so the pieces are close to equal in size and will tend to split evenly. You still may need to resort to another solution: pressuring against the thicker side, so that it bends slightly and the split works toward that side. To do

this, lay a bolt heavy side down and push down as you lever, using gravity as much as you can (see the bottom photo on the facing page). Or you can hold the work as it is traditionally done: in a tight fork of a tree known as a riving break.

Mallets

The wooden club used to drive a froe is a type of mallet, similar to one a carver might use for driving chisels. The simplest mallets are nothing more than a limb of hardwood, gnarly burl, or root, with one end shaped into a comfortable handle. Large wooden "beetles" or

"commanders" are for driving together house and ship frames, where a lot of heft is necessary. A length of tree trunk with a few feet of a limb attached for a handle works quite nicely. The beauty of these simple mallets is that they are easy to make and, for the effort, they last a long time.

The most common mallets are wooden hammers, 1 lb. or so in weight, with large striking faces more gentle on wooden handles, treenails, and furniture parts than the face of a metal hammer. Take a hammer to a chisel handle (other than a steel or plastic one), and you will probably split and ruin it. The larger head of a mallet also gives you a good chance of delivering a stout blow while watching the work (and not the mallet or chisel handle). In the case of driving a mortise and tenon together, a mallet, unlike a hammer, won't mar the wood.

There are two common types of traditional carpenter's mallets: They can be rectangular with slanting faces, similar to a chunk of beam, or cylindrical with a wedged handle at

PART OF THE RICH heritage of woodworking hand tools is the wonderful names that some of these tools carry. Among striking tools alone, there are names such as the curious "beetle," the imperious "commander," and the persuasive "go-devil." Some tools aren't content to have a single name—a "twybill," for example, also goes by the name of two-bill, mortising ax, and grubbing ax.

right angles to it. Both use tough end grain for the striking face. The handle in a rectangular-headed mallet fits in from the end and tapers wider, so it wedges into the head and stays tight. It also has the ergonomic advantage of slanting faces perpendicular to the arc of a natural swing. This delivers a solid, square blow with maximum force. One of the more interesting of the cylindrical-type mallets is a caulker's mallet—a very long, narrow, and iron-bound mallet for driving oakum caulking into the seams between a ship's wooden planking.

Modern mallets usually have rubber or rawhide heads, if they are not made entirely out of plastic. Their

A turned carver's mallet is the ideal tool for all sorts of chiseling and carving work.

main purpose is for assembling woodwork, although a hammer and block of wood work just as well. For all-around chisel work, I still prefer a round carver's mallet made from a dense wood such as lignum vitae. Because it is round, any way you hold it works. Choking up on the handle close to the head gives me maximum control when chiseling or carving, while still producing quite a bit of force. Gripping the mallet farther down on the handle, I have the power for heavier work, such as driving a mortise chisel into oak.

Once you get practiced at it, tapping with a mallet rather than working freehand will increase your control. Push a chisel by hand, and there is always a chance of slipping and making large mistakes.

Never hit metal with a mallet or you risk damaging the head. Reflatten a worn head with a block plane and chamfer the edges well. The steady pounding on the longgrain fibers of a carver's mallet eventually separates them (in much the same way that a basketmaker pounds along an ash log to detach long, thin strips for weaving). Turn a new mallet out of any dense wood and, if you want, bore a hole in the end of the head for lead shot or pennies to add to its mass.

For assembling furniture parts, or disassembling trial fits, mallets with rubber, rawhide, or plastic heads deliver hefty blows without marring wooden surfaces.

Hammers

There will never come a day when
hammers are obsolete in the carpentry trade, because there is no
more versatile tool than a claw
hammer for driving nails, pulling
bent ones, knocking things into
position, or prying them apart.
Hammer designs may have changed
in subtle ways since antiquity, with
fiberglass or tubular steel handles
replacing wood and bone, but they
are still the most basic of tools that
combine the very different functions of pounding and levering.

During the 19th century, hammers blossomed into a multitude of
different forms and functions and,
like axes, they were named after
specific trades or functions, or for
the towns that originated the particular pattern. Naturally each trade
favored a certain type of hammer—
its weight, or some variation in its

THOMAS TURNER & CO., SUFFOLK WORKS. SHEFFIELD.

860. Ladies' Claw Hammer
861. London Upholsterer's Hammer
862. Best Carpet Hammer
863. Benwell Upholsterer's Hammer
864. Gents' Claw Hammer
865. Cabriolet Hammer
866. Common Upholsterer's Hammer
867. Farrier's Claw Hammer
868. Geologist's Hammer, with Pick
869. Geologist's Hammer, with Pean
880. Bright Kent Hammer
883. Tack Hammer
884. Slater's Pick Hammer
870. Bright Lath Hammer
871. Bricklayer's Hammer
872. Improved Shoe Hammer
873. Common Shoe Hammer
874. Best Coal Hammer, with Pick
875. Cast Coal Hammer
876. American Adze Eyed Claw Hammer
881. Grocer's Hammer
877. Special Exeter Hammer
878. Special Warrington Hammer
879. Canterbury Hammer

Every trade had its own special hammers, used for everything from driving wooden
shoe pegs to punching holes in roofing slates. Few of the dozens illustrated in this early-
20th-century catalog—or the trades that used them—survive today.

shape or size. Some had claws, others
two faces of different shape, for
driving nails and light riveting, for
example. Handles were wood, light
and delicately shaped for gentlemen
and ladies, sometimes 4 ft. or longer
for reaching way up on walls for a
bill hanger's hammer, or stout for
heavy sledges.

No hammer is more basic than
a claw hammer, so-called because
opposite the head is a curved or
straight claw—ingeniously designed
for pulling the nail you just bent
over. The opening in the claw tapers
toward the head and its inner edges
are modestly sharp to get a good
grip on a wide range of nail shanks.

A curved claw has better leverage for pulling nails, due to the way it rolls on the claw as you apply pressure to the handle. Straight claws have their advantages too, mostly to carpenters for all kinds of prying—much like a wrecking bar.

The connection between hammer head and wooden handle must be strong and rigid to hold up to constant pounding and levering. The eyes of early hammer heads were round, which were easy to make but not as strong as an oval or rectangular eye common today. And while tapered wooden handles have wonderful flexibility and can absorb vibration, they leave less wood for the handle-to-head connection. Moisture changes also take their toll—as the wooden handle shrinks and swells against the confining eye of the hammer head, the fibers eventually compress and the handle becomes loose.

A solution that originated in the Middle Ages was to forge two long straps to the head and rivet these to the handle, or to clinch straps through the eye after the head was forged. For rugged small hammers—such as a grocer would use as much for hammering as for prying open cases—another solution that led to modern Stanley and Estwing hammers was to make the head and handle in one forging. In 1840, David Maydole, a blacksmith in Norwich, New York, took yet another approach. By forging a much deeper eye like that of an adze, he created a so-called adze-eye hammer, which became the design for nearly all claw hammers since.

For general-purpose shop work, a curved claw hammer from 12 oz. to 16 oz. is ideal. It's a compromise, but this size can drive a brad and also deliver a good whack to seat a tenon in its mortise. (Having both a light and a heavy hammer is a better solution.) Round faces are the most common, although an octagonal face is an advantage when working in a corner.

One of the few specialty hammers still available and favored by

Making a strong connection between a handle and hammer head has always been a challenge, but especially so on early hammers with narrow heads and shallow eyes. One solution was to rivet a pair of straps to the handle and then clinch them over the head. A more secure method was to forge straps as part of the head (second from left).

These unusual hammer heads might seem like playful mistakes, but the designs are surprisingly useful. Double claws make practical sense—the extra claws give you a choice if you need more leverage. The head with two claws (and no apparent striking face) is possibly a shingler's hammer. Notice the head with the corrugated face (far left) for a good grip on the nail.

From massive sledges to a delicate coach-trimmer's hammer with a tiny side claw, hammers are as varied as the tasks for which they were designed. Contrast this array of hammer heads from the mid-19th century with the varieties sold in hardware stores today.

Octagon Coach Trimmers Hammer Head. 1125

1125G Clinch Cutter

1125A Manchester Spike Hammer

Round Coach Trimmers Hammer Head. 1124

1125D Plumbers' Hammer Head

Warrington Hammer Head. 1119

1117 Exeter Hammer Head

1118A Warrington Hammer Head

1118 Exeter Claw

1123A Cloggers' Hammer Head

1125B Farriers' Shoeing Hammer

1125K Best Flooring Hammer Head

1125F Farriers' Shoe Turning Hammer

1125C MINERALOGISTS' HAMMERS

1122 London Veneering Hammer Head

1125L Framing Hammer Head

1116 Rivetting Hammer Head

1125E Farriers' Sledge Hammer

1121 Best Clench Hammer Head

1125J Saw Setting Hammer Head

Veneer hammers are not designed to be swung but rather pressed across a veneered surface to squeeze out trapped air and excess glue. The hammer at left is shop-made with a brass edge; the cast hammer at right has a poll for setting pins that hold the veneer in position.

Designed in the same vein as handles with interchangeable tools popularized in the Victorian era, this modern hammer patented by George Derbyshire has interchangeable heads stored in the handle: a stainless-steel head for nails, lead and plastic heads for dead-blows, a copper head gentle on metal, and a ball-peen head for riveting and light forging.

some cabinetmakers is a Warrington pattern hammer (one is shown in the engraving on p. 73). Instead of a claw, it has a wedge-shaped cross peen an inch or so wide, with a slightly rounded face. You'll appreciate this narrow head the first time you try to start a tiny brad; you may even find it easier to use than a claw hammer with a larger face. A Warrington hammer is also a good riveting hammer and ideal for tightening the knuckle of a knife hinge or tapping in a steel bolt when doing machine maintenance. A ball-peen hammer is another useful machinist's hammer for riveting and metalwork.

As the old joke goes, when things are really going together hard, you just need a bigger persuader. For driving big spikes, a 20-oz. (or larger) framing hammer with a long handle for maximum leverage is one solution. Another is to have a sledge or two. A 3-lb. sledge with a short handle is perfect for giving something a good whack and still maintaining control. For splitting logs (for chair parts or tool handles), a heavier sledge, along with a few wedges, is the best tool.

TUNING A HAMMER
If there was ever a tool that needed little or no tuning, a hammer is it. That isn't to say there is nothing you can do to make your bench hammer a bit more useful. On cheap hammers and well-worn ones, the claws are no longer sharp

One common use for a sledge is to drive a wedge for splitting a log. A wedge or froe allows you to direct the split more easily than with an ax, especially if the split is defined with a saw kerf first.

Glazier's hammers are used to set small "points" to secure a pane of glass in a window. The large flats of the head ride along the pane of glass. Two styles are shown here, one with a fixed head and the other with a rotating head. The other glazier's tools include a square, pliers for breaking glass, a glass cutter, and modern pliers for setting points.

enough to grip the shank of a nail (only the head). Sometimes filing along the back curve of the claws will sharpen them, or you could try a small file between them. Then file the end of one of the claws into a chisel-like edge, so you can reach into tight cracks and pry things apart.

TOOLS USED WITH HAMMERS

In my shop in a typical week, I could be working on a piece of furniture one day and tuning a machine or making a piece of hardware the next. Besides different hammers, the variety of the work requires an assortment of punches, nail sets, and

cold chisels. Look for them at tool sales or buy them as the need arises.

It's impossible to do blind nailing without a nail set. This is the tool for setting the tiny head of a finish nail below the surface of the wood (see the photo on p. 77), or for driving one in an awkward place. Rather than risk marring the wood,

For many woodworking and metalworking tasks, especially for making and repairing tools, you'll need some small cold chisels of different sizes (at right) as well as (from left) a center punch for marking drill holes, nail sets, punches, and a ball-peen hammer.

I often use one for driving a nail the last ¼ in. You'll need at least two: a nail set with a very small tip for fine nails and brads, and a slightly larger one for common finish nails. New nail sets have a concave tip, supposedly to grip the nail head better. A flat point works okay, but better yet is to grind the end to a blunt point and it will prick into the nail head like a center punch and stay put.

A center punch is another essential tool used with a hammer. It pricks the location of a hole before drilling, to prevent the bit from wandering by giving it a place to start. Center punches are usually metalworking tools, but they work just as well with wood, especially for such work as marking pilot holes for hinge screws. A similar punch with a flat end and a long, tapered shank is sometimes called a drift pin. It is ideal for driving out stuck bolts, hinge pins, or a broken-off handle in a hammer head. Another useful tool you should always have on hand is a cold chisel, which can be used for cutting metal, too (such

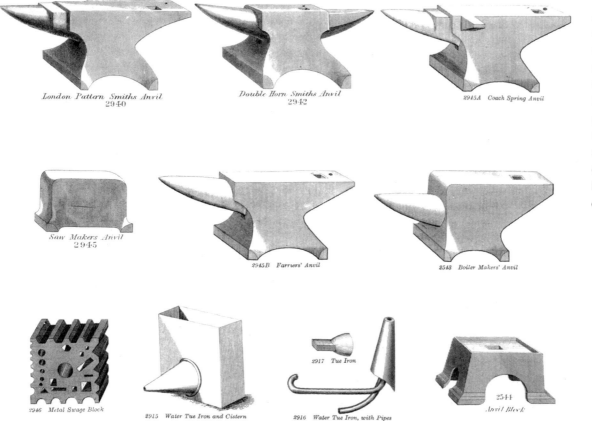

London Pattern Smiths Anvil
2940

Double Horn Smiths Anvil
2942

2945A Coach Spring Anvil

Saw Makers Anvil
2945

2945B Farriers' Anvil

2543 Boiler Makers' Anvil

2946 Metal Swage Block

2915 Water Tue Iron and Cistern

2917 Tue Iron

2916 Water Tue Iron, with Pipes

2544
Anvil Block

Anvils used to be available for every conceivable trade. A large floor anvil or even a smaller bench model is good for forging, riveting, flattening a bent hinge leaf, or driving a new handle into an ax or hammer head.

as a nail in an awkward spot or to enlarge the slot in a damaged screw). You should have a few sizes, and keep them sharpened.

Somewhere along your wood-working road you'll probably need an anvil—the equivalent of a work-bench for metalworking. A good machinist's vise often has a flat area behind the jaws that works well as a small anvil. (A machinist's vice is useful to have for any number of holding and sharpening tasks away from your woodworking bench, where you can afford to be a little messy.) Better yet is a bench anvil, a small, portable anvil that can take heavier pounding. Meanwhile, keep your eyes out for a 125-lb.

IF YOU EVER WANT to upset an overconfident carpenter, wax the face of his hammer. The hammer will slide off the nail head every time, no matter how good his aim. For the opposite effect, sanding the face of a hammer gives it a bit more grip. For this reason, a shingler's hammer is almost always checkered, and Stanley once offered hammers with corrugated faces.

(or heavier) floor anvil. With a round, tapered horn and a large flat surface, this is the right tool for hot or cold forging, or for lighter work such as flattening a bent hinge leaf or peening over a rivet.

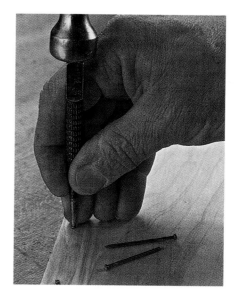

Use a nail set to sink the small head of a finish nail below the surface. A slightly pointed tip (similar to a center punch) pricks the nail head and stays put. A finger or two against the wood surface helps steady the nail set.

CHISELS,
Gouges, and Drawknives

A chisel is a simple tool.

It's a blade with a beveled cutting edge and a handle to hold, guide, and drive the tool. Essential to hand woodworking for paring a joint to fit, chopping joinery of all kinds, or shaping wood, a chisel is simple in design but not necessarily simple to use. All of the control comes from the skill and coordination of the user, not from the design of the tool.

Gouges and drawknives are simple tools as well, with the same chisel-like edges, except that they are curved, or in the case of a drawknife, elongated and powered by two handles rather than one. As with chisels, you can vary your technique within a single stroke to go from cutting a coarse shaving to making a fine, paring cut. 🪲

A typical set of bench chisels, ranging in size from ⅛ in. to 1¼ in., for chopping mortises, cutting tenons, or paring joints. This set was made by Buck Brothers, of Millbury, Mass., one of largest and best-known makers of chisels and gouges.

Chisels

Chisels and chisel edges show up everywhere in hand tools. A plane is a sophisticated chisel, a saw or file a series of chisel teeth, an auger a chisel turning around a center point, and an ax or adze a chisel swung from a long handle. In its most basic form, a chisel is a rectangular steel blade sharpened to a beveled edge and connected to a handle. As with all the basic woodworking hand tools, there are endless variations for specific purposes.

Making sense of the various types of chisels can be bewildering, especially when it comes to choosing a set of chisels for everyday bench work. Which of the various types do you need? Is one style or length more useful than another? The questions can go on and on, because even with fewer choices than there once were, there are still many types of chisels available. In Sheffield, England, the historic center of edge-tool manufacturing, makers such as Robert Sorby, William Marples, and Ward and Payne offered an array of chisels. American makers such as Buck Brothers of Millbury, Massachusetts and Peck, Stow & Wilcox of Southington, Connecticut, among many others, at one time offered dozens of various types and sizes of chisels. Naturally, the many woodworking trades favored particular styles of chisels, each with a slightly different shape, length, weight, or handle.

Chisels can be divided into three types: firmer, mortise, and paring. Each type comes in a range of sizes from about ¹⁄₁₆ in. wide to 2 in. wide or even wider (except for mortise chisels, which are usually under 1 in. wide). Firmer chisels are the ones that spring to mind when you think of "bench chisels," and for good reason—they are generally the most useful. They have modestly long blades, a beveled or flat top face, and a cross section with enough steel to hold up to mallet blows. Mortise chisels are stout, deeper in section than their width to withstand the heavy work of cutting mortises. The longest and lightest in section are paring chisels. They are pushed by hand alone and are far less common than they once were.

All chisels have either flat faces or, on better chisels, bevels parallel with the long edges. Beveling the face was once a laborious process of hand grinding on huge water-powered grindstones, which added to the cost but makes for a more beautiful tool. Bevels also lighten a chisel without sacrificing strength and reduce its profile so that it can work in tight places, such as inside a dovetail, where the thicker edge of a flat-faced chisel may not fit. Cabinetmaker James Krenov grinds the faces of his bench chisels into two wide bevels, giving them a triangular profile. Even some mortise chisels have a slight bevel along the sides to give the blade a bit of relief when working in a tight mortise.

Vital to the strength of a chisel, especially one worked hard with a mallet, is a strong connection between the blade and handle. The simplest, yet by no means the easiest to make, is a blade forged into a tapering tang and driven into a wooden handle. (Skill is involved forging the tang strong enough to take the stress, yet not so hard that it becomes brittle, or so soft that it bends.) A brass or steel ferrule around the handle resists any splitting action caused by the tang. An improvement on this system was to forge a "bolster"—a widened area at the base of the tang for the handle to butt against and help absorb the force from handle to blade. Mortise chisels have large bolsters, paring chisels much smaller ones. On good chisels, a leather washer between bolster and handle further absorbs some of the shock of a mallet blow.

The most costly chisels have a superior method of joining the handle and blade: with a forged, tapered socket instead of a tang. The end of the handle has a mating taper, so that the harder the chisel is driven the tighter the connection. No fer-

Chisels vary in size, handle style and material, and blade shape (either beveled or tapered in thickness). This array of common chisels includes (from left) a timber-framing chisel, a small mortising chisel, a paring chisel, a Japanese firmer chisel, and two beveled firmer chisels.

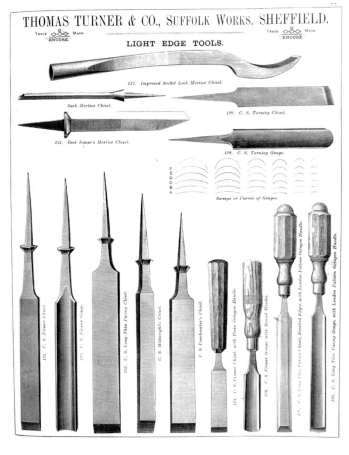

THOMAS TURNER & CO., SUFFOLK WORKS, SHEFFIELD.

LIGHT EDGE TOOLS.

Quality chisels and gouges such as the ones advertised here have tang construction, which would have been fitted into handles either bought separately or made in the shop.

Chisel blades are designed for specific types of work: the short, tapered, and beveled blade of a bench or firmer chisel (top) provides careful control; the long and thin blade of a paring chisel, sometimes beveled, guides fine cuts (middle); and the thick, tapered, and square-edged blade of a mortise chisel is for hard chopping (bottom).

rule is required, since the end of the handle is captured in the socket. On heavy-duty chisels such as framing chisels, the top of the handle is sometimes "hooped" with a steel ring that keeps it from mushrooming over, or it is fitted with a leather washer to cushion mallet blows. Unfortunately, it is common to find used socket chisels with the handles long gone and the socket deformed by years of abuse with a hammer. If the socket isn't split or excessively deformed, it can probably be restored.

There are no simple generalizations about handle styles: it's a personal choice. Most are round, some are oval, often they taper for a more comfortable grip or have flat facets for the same reason (and so the chisel doesn't roll off the bench). Because handles were sold out of the same catalogs that sold chisels (and in just as much variety), a cabinetmaker could fit a favorite handle style to all his chisels. The most prized (and the ones usually fitted to the finest chisels) are those made of boxwood, sometimes delicately turned and detailed with incised rings. Ash and beech handles are more common.

Secondhand or new, there are many different chisels to choose from. One approach is to buy a set of new firmer chisels (or used firmer chisels in a range of sizes) and add a few mortise chisels or paring chisels as you find them or need them. Everyone has their own opinions about which chisels are best, but as with many tools, learning to tune and use what you have is more important that owning a wide variety of tools.

In the old days, you could buy tool handles from a catalog if you needed a replacement and you chose not to make your own. Such handles came in all sorts of styles, from octagonal beech to fancy boxwood handles, for socketed chisels or those with tanged blades.

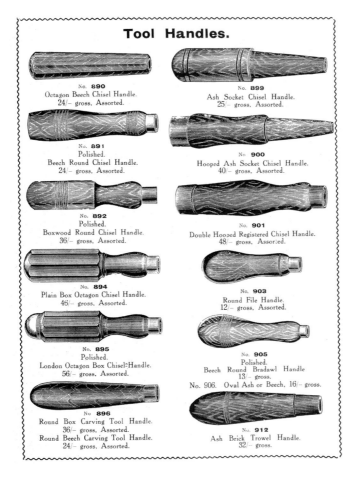

Tool Handles.

No. **890**
Octagon Beech Chisel Handle.
24/- gross, Assorted.

No. **899**
Ash Socket Chisel Handle.
25/- gross, Assorted.

No. **891**
Polished.
Beech Round Chisel Handle.
24/- gross, Assorted.

No **900**
Hooped Ash Socket Chisel Handle.
40/- gross, Assorted.

No. **892**
Polished.
Boxwood Round Chisel Handle.
36/- gross, Assorted.

No. **901**
Double Hooped Registered Chisel Handle.
48/- gross, Assorted.

No. **894**
Plain Box Octagon Chisel Handle.
46/- gross, Assorted.

No. **903**
Round File Handle.
12/- gross, Assorted.

No. **895**
Polished.
London Octagon Box Chisel Handle.
56/- gross, Assorted.

No. **905**
Polished.
Beech Round Bradawl Handle
13/- gross.
No. 906. Oval Ash or Beech, 16/- gross.

No **896**
Round Box Carving Tool Handle.
36/- gross, Assorted.
Round Beech Carving Tool Handle.
24/- gross, Assorted.

No. **912**
Ash Brick Trowel Handle.
32/- gross.

FIRMER CHISELS

Firmer chisels are general-purpose bench chisels. Speculation as to where the name came from—perhaps a corruption of "former" or "forming"—suggests the importance of firmer chisels for the preliminary shaping and cutting of joints. In fact, they are well suited to contemporary woodworking, where most work is done first by machine and then at the bench with chisels or other tools. As something of a compromise between the stoutness of a mortise chisel and the fineness of a paring chisel, they will do either task adequately.

There is such a range of firmer chisels that it is hard to get too specific about what they look like (it is easier to say that they do not look like mortise or paring chisels). The blade can be as long as 8 in., which isn't much shorter than some paring chisels. The body of the blade is modestly thick, enough to hold up to being driven with a mallet, but not so thick that the chisel feels heavy. Yet on framing chisels, a type of firmer chisel, the blade is quite thick for cutting joints in large timbers.

MORTISE CHISELS

Mortise chisels have a distinct shape that sets them apart from firmer and paring chisels: a thick cross section, often quite a bit deeper than they are wide. They need to be massive to take the constant beating of a mallet. They also need to be thick to give the cutting edge plenty of support. Lighter versions of this design, for more delicate mortising, are called sash mortise chisels. Before there were routers and mortising machines—the tools most likely to cut mortises in a shop today—a mortise chisel was the tool for the job. To cut a ½-in.-wide mortise, all you needed was a ½-in. mortise chisel and a mallet.

In softwood, a skilled cabinet-maker can cut all four mortises for a small cabinet door, by hand, in 10 minutes or less. I've seen it done. To work this fast with a simple tool takes skill and flawless technique. But there are subtleties of the design of a mortise chisel that help. Generations of joiners have refined these tools to make them easier to use, with more predictable results.

"EVERLASTING" CHISELS

SHORT FIRMER CHISELS are known as butt firmer chisels. These are the style of the Everlasting line of chisels that Stanley produced early in this century, with blades as short as 3 in. and heavy steel-buttressed handles (to take the shock of a hammer, rather than a mallet, used by a careless carpenter). They were advertised as ideal for cutting butt and other hinge mortises, but in fact they have another advantage. The short blade means your hand stays close to the edge, giving you a lot more control than chisels with longer blades. The disadvantage is that butt chisels are useless for any sort of deep mortising or paring, because the blades just aren't long enough.

Stanley "Everlasting" beveled firmer chisels are easy to control, and the design of the tang makes for a very rugged chisel that can withstand hammer blows.

Mortise chisels have thick tapered blades, large bolsters with leather washers to cushion mallet blows, and oval handles for a comfortable grip for twisting the blade into alignment with the mortise. They sometimes are sharpened with a rounded bevel, making it easier to lever out the chips.

The long blade of a paring chisel, sometimes so thin it's slightly flexible, guides the cut as if it were a plane's sole. Fancy London pattern handles are typical on such fine cabinetmaker's tools.

When chopping a mortise, one cut follows another along the length, going deeper each time and levering out the waste. Understanding this helps to see another virtue of the deep profile of the blade: A thick blade helps guide the chisel in a straight line, cutting a mortise of consistent width. Some mortise chisels have a slight bevel from back to face, giving the blade clearance and allowing for some twisting of the blade to keep it on course. And because a large part of the work with a mortise chisel is levering out the waste, rounding the bevel is a small refinement that works like a rounded hammer claw, for when you're levering with the bevel down.

PARING CHISELS

Paring chisels are the most refined. They are lighter, with wide face bevels, and often ornate boxwood handles. Used mainly by joiners, cabinetmakers, and patternmakers, paring chisels have long, thin blades—some even flex slightly—for delicate paring and fitting, and for getting into tight places unreachable with a shorter chisel. One variation on a typical paring chisel has a handle offset from the blade, known as "cranked" or trowel-handled, for such work as paring the bottom of a long groove. Paring chisels should never be struck with a mallet, but driven by hand alone.

One of the more unusual paring chisels is called a slick. Slicks are heavy and huge, as big as 4 in. across, with long handles bulging into a knob for placing a shoulder or palm against. A canoe builder I know uses a slick for every sort of cutting task imaginable—in fact, it's one of the few tools he uses—from paring joints between planking to fitting ribs and decks. Traditionally, slicks were used by house joiners and shipwrights for the same sort of careful fitting of large parts. A slick's weight and balance turn what might seem like an ungainly tool into one capable of precise paring or aggressive shaping. A slick is sharpened no differently than a paring chisel, except that the cutting edge is shaped into a slight curve for maximum control.

With blades as wide as 4 in. and handles 12 in. or more in length, slicks are the largest chisels, but they are capable of finer work than their size suggests. They were traditionally a shipbuilding tool, used to pare, level, and fit decking and frames.

Japanese bench chisels typically have short blades for precision work and backs ground hollow to make the chore of flattening them easier.

EASTERN CHISELS

In terms of function, Japanese chisels are not much different from their Western counterparts. But it doesn't take a very close look to see that Japanese chisels are, for the most part, much shorter and stockier. The handles are connected differently, the blades are laminated, and the backs of the chisels are flat only around the edges (they are ground hollow in the middle). I have a few Japanese chisels mixed in with the rest of my hand tools, and I use

As much for decoration as function, high-quality Japanese bench chisels sometimes have multiple hollows ground into the back. For a strong connection with the handle, they have another characteristic feature: a combination socket and tanged blade. A Japanese paring chisel (second from right) looks short compared to its western counterpart (right).

them regularly. As Japanese tools have become more available in the past 20 years, many craftsmen have adopted them, and while some are more qualified to explain the subtleties of these tools, I offer these observations.

For one accustomed to Western chisels, the most noticeable difference in Japanese chisels is their shorter, stockier blades, more like short butt chisels than typical long-bladed firmer chisels. The advantage of this design is that your hand is closer to the work, giving you more control and reducing the amount of blade through which you must transfer the force. The handles are rigidly connected by a combination of tang and socket. A heavy tang unites the blade and handle, with a long socket-shaped ferrule fitting between them. Below the ferrule the tang widens into the same tapering shape and functions as a bolster.

A profound difference between Eastern and Western chisels is in the forging of the blades. Rather than being cut from one piece of high-carbon steel, Japanese blades have a hard steel cutting edge forge-welded to a softer, wrought-iron back (the soft steel sometimes is made from old anchors or anchor chains). The softer back absorbs most of the cutting stress, enabling the cutting edge to be quite a bit harder than Western chisels. Such edges stay sharp longer, but they are more brittle and require a stouter bevel angle.

Because you can't use more than one chisel at a time, tool designer George Derbyshire made a single handle with interchangeable blades (right). On the left is a prototype for an ergonomic handle that encourages a firm grip for both paring and chopping.

The key to sharpening a chisel is flattening the back, either on a lapping table or working from coarse to fine stones. The hollowed Japanese chisel (right) illustrates that the entire back need not be flat, only the area near the cutting edge.

SHARPENING AND TUNING CHISELS

To work properly, the back of a chisel must be dead flat and polished. A flat back mainly serves to guide the cut, but it is also half of the cutting edge. For shorter chisels, the last inch or so should be flat; on longer paring chisels, at least a few inches. For either, the area close to the cutting edge must be flat. While this sounds easy to do in theory, getting the back of a chisel flat—even a brand new one right out of the box—takes patience. Take heart in knowing you'll only flatten the back once.

To flatten the back, you'll need a lapping table (see p. 25). The most difficult chisels to lap flat are those that have a back that is slightly con-

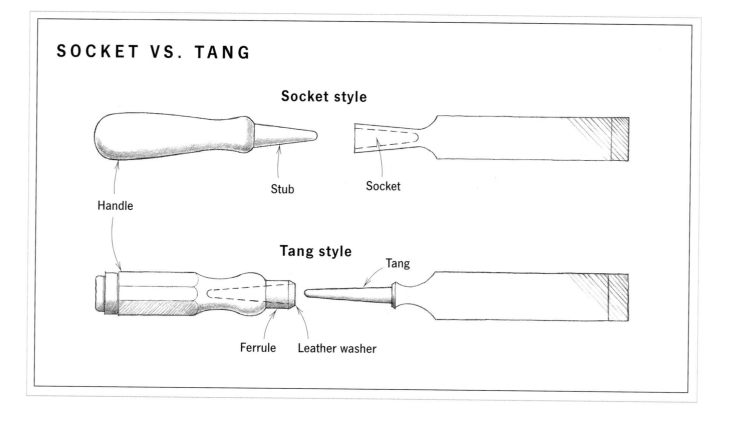

SOCKET VS. TANG

Socket style

Handle

Stub

Socket

Tang style

Tang

Ferrule

Leather washer

---

vex along its length (chisels with a concave back are considerably easier to flatten). On these chisels, you must remove most of the high area toward the middle first, in order to flatten up to the cutting edge (and the chisel will rock around while you do this). Japanese chisels have hollow backs to make flattening easier, but for Western chisels, it's a matter of persistence, moving from a coarse to a finer grit, and finally honing the back on ever-finer sharpening stones. If there is any pitting near the cutting edge, you'll need to lap it out. Finally, with your finest stone, dull the corners of the blade along the sides. They can be extremely sharp, and you will come into contact with them regularly.

Sharpen the bevel as you would any other—straight across, except in the case of a slick, when a bit of camber helps. Bevel angles vary from as low as 15° for paring chisels, 20° to 25° for firmer chisels and everyday bench work, and 30° for mortise chisels. As with tuning

HOW DO YOU TELL if a chisel is really sharp? There's the old fingernail trick for testing a sharp edge—seeing if it grabs rather than slides along a fingernail—or you might try shaving some arm hair. But the best test is to use the chisel on wood: Only a truly sharp edge will easily pare pine end grain and leave a glass smooth surface. A less than perfect edge will tear out fibers and leave noticeable streaks where areas of the edge are the slightest bit dull. ✄

any edge, these bevel angles are guides—good places to start. Don't be afraid to fine-tune your chisels to the specific work you do, if you are so inclined. Use a lower overall bevel and hone on a 5° microbevel if you want easier sharpening and better performance. Just be careful with mortise chisels for use with hardwoods. This is heavy work that demands a stout edge. Don't hollow-grind mortise chisels, but rather hone the edge with a modest microbevel, or convex, to give the cutting edge extra support.

Replacing a chisel handle

Chisel handles usually don't need much tuning, but the handles on your workhorse chisels may need replacing from time to time. Socket chisels are the easiest to replace, es-

Bevel up or bevel down? Keep the bevel up to the waste side for paring or, as shown here, chopping the waste from a mortise. Turn the bevel down to use the chisel in the same orientation as a plane iron, or for levering out the waste.

The most accurate way to cut to a line is to use the widest chisel that will fit and creep up on the line slowly. Waste as much as possible this way so that the final cut just pares to the line. A knife line, seen here on this tenon shoulder, also helps by creating a tiny groove to hold the chisel's edge.

pecially if you have access to a lathe. Remove the broken stub by drilling it out. The only tricky part is sizing the tenon to the socket. I measure the diameter of the socket at the top, its depth, and guess the diameter at the bottom. I then turn the tenon to these dimensions, scraping and fitting by hand from there.

Every trial fit leaves marks on the handle where the high points rub. You want the two parts to mate closely to keep the handle firmly connected. But be sure to leave a small gap between the top of the socket and the corresponding shoulder on the handle, and cut the handle shy of the bottom so that, over time, the handle can seat more fully into the socket.

To replace a tang-type chisel handle, shape it to suit your hand and turn one end to the inside diameter of your ferrule. I cut my ferrules from brass pipe, thin-walled for light chisels and thicker for heavier chisels. You can cut the ferrule with a hacksaw or pipe cutter and file the inside smooth.

The hardest part of fitting the handle is drilling a hole along the centerline to receive the tang. If you are adept at turning, you can do a lot of this drilling on the lathe after turning the handle; otherwise, set the handle upright in a vise. I drill a hole with three diameters: one the full depth of the tang and equal to its smallest dimension; the second about half as deep and equal to the dimension of the middle of the tang; and the third hole ½-in. deep, and just a bit smaller than the largest part of the tang. The wood will compress to accommodate the tang, but you don't want to split the handle either. Cut a leather washer for the tang and drive the handle on.

USING CHISELS

Much of woodworking involves the use of chisels. Some chisel work is careful fitting, some is aggressive chopping; no single technique works for it all. Even a simple task such as chopping a mortise has endless variations depending upon how you learned and what you are after, so I am going to leave descriptions of cutting dovetails and joinery to books better suited to that subject. Instead, I'll describe some techniques that will improve any work you do with chisels.

The first question that typically comes up is whether to use a chisel bevel up or bevel down. The simple answer is bevel up, or to the waste side, but it really depends upon the work you are doing. When paring or chopping accurately to a line, the flat back of the chisel against the line guides the cut. If the back has any sort of back bevel or a back that's not truly flat, you won't have this reference surface to help guide you.

However, if you are paring the bottom of a groove, or cutting with the chisel angled off the surface, the flat back is no longer a useful guide. Besides, it's hard to use a chisel that way—the angle of approach is too high and all the chisel wants to do is dig in—so turn it around with the bevel down. Use the bevel to guide the cut, and adjust the cutting

Simple jigs can make laying out and cutting complex joints quicker and more accurate. This pair helps cut matching haunched mortises and tenons.

BUYING USED CHISELS

THERE'S NO EASY way to tell a good chisel—or any edge tool for that matter—from a mediocre one. The quality of the steel used in the chisel is paramount, but you can't just look at the steel and tell much about it. The composition of the steel certainly affects how a chisel will sharpen and hold its edge, but far more important is how the steel was forged and heat-treated. Short of sharpening and using the chisel, though, you won't know if it was tempered too hard (meaning it will be brittle), or if it is too soft and will dull quickly.

But buying a used chisel isn't entirely a shot in the dark. You can tell a lot just by looking at the chisel. Does it appear as though it was carefully forged and finished? Are the bevels consistent? Is the socket (if the chisel has

one) robust and in line with the blade? Is the back of the chisel flat? If necessary, check it with a straightedge.

Craftsmen usually made their own handles, so the quality of the handle isn't always a reliable guide. However, if a chisel has a shapely handle that looks like it has seen much use, you can bet that someone valued it. The best guide to quality is to look for particular manufacturers with stellar reputations: Reliable names include T. H. Witherby; James Swan (number one in my mind); Peck, Stow, and Wilcox (marked as P, S & W); L. and I. J. White; Underhill Edge Tool; and Charles Buck (Buck Brothers is better known but has an uneven reputation for quality). ⊗

For cutting angled mortises accurately, a wooden block with a fence makes a good guide for your chisel. Use a chisel with a long blade, as wide as possible, and take paring cuts.

A chisel functions as a flat-backed knife for light paring cuts, such as trimming the end of a delicate table leg. Use your thumb for leverage and a slicing or skew cut. Chamfer the edges first to prevent breaking out the fibers.

depth by raising or lowering the chisel handle and levering against the bevel.

The first impulse when cutting to a line (when chopping a mortise, for example) is to put the edge of the chisel right on the line and start chopping. Resist this temptation—it's impossible to work accurately this way. Because of the shape of the cutting edge, pressure against the beveled face drives the back of the chisel hard against the work. Chop deep enough and the pressure will be so great the chisel will compress the fibers and drift beyond the line. The only way to overcome this is to creep up on your lines, wasting what you can before getting close, and finishing with as light a paring cut as possible.

I prefer to mark out with a knife or mortising gauge because it gives me a very fine groove to locate the cutting edge for this final cut. For a straight, true cut (on a tenon shoulder, for instance), work with the widest chisel that will fit. You also can hit a wide chisel more aggressively than a narrow one. Be careful of one last thing: When cutting all the way through a piece, cut from both sides rather than just one—you'll be less apt to split out the fibers.

Chiseling with a mallet is usually more controllable than working by hand alone. The exception is paring. When paring a surface, use both hands—one hand pushing and the other guiding the blade, especially when working close to an edge, where the back of the chisel has little support. When you have no choice but to work against the grain, pare with a light cut for the smoothest surface. Another way I like to pare is to use a curving and slicing action, with the chisel flat on the work, using my thumb for leverage. The trick is to take a light cut, using a corner of the cutting edge and skewing it across the work.

SOME UNUSUAL CHISELS

While firmer, mortise, and paring chisels will perform the bulk of your chiseling needs in the workshop, there are a few unusual chisels that can come in handy. These include skew chisels, scraper chisels, drawer-lock chisels, and lock-mortise chisels.

A bench chisel ground to a skew, anywhere from 10° to 20°, makes an incredibly useful chisel for paring the waste out of dovetails or other fine joinery where space is tight. Grind a right and a left skew for the most versatility.

A chisel ground with a very steep bevel (70° to 90°) might seem too blunt to be useful, but such a chisel works like a high-angle scraper, for controlled paring such as truing the bed of a wooden plane. The flat back helps guide the cut.

Skew chisels

Skew chisels are similar to paring chisels, except that they have a skewed cutting edge rather than a square one. It always strikes me as curious that I've never seen a used skew chisel—and I've only recently seen them in catalogs—because this is a very useful tool. Woodturners use skews, but evidently not many joiners. I made one many years ago from a broken chisel I found in a discount bin at a woodworking supply store. By chance, the blade was snapped off at about a 20° skew, so I sharpened it that way to see how

it would work. For paring end grain in tight places, no other chisel is quite as handy. While you can now buy a pair with opposing skews, you can also grind any chisel with a skewed edge.

Scraping chisels

A scraping chisel is another simple idea. The tool couldn't be easier to make and is capable of the most controlled scraping and cutting. In-

stead of a 25° bevel, a scraping chisel is ground and honed closer to 90° (as low as 70° also works). Such an edge is anything but blunt if sharpened well. For trimming a haunch in a mortise, or for its traditional use—cleaning up the bed of a wooden plane—a scraping chisel produces fine, consistent shavings without digging into the wood. The flat back provides excellent control.

TOOL MANUFACTURERS love to make tools and sell them with the promise that they are just what we need to increase our speed, improve our accuracy, or both. Take corner chisels, for example. Made to chop the corners of mortises perfectly square in one pass, they're really no faster than a firmer chisel and far more difficult to sharpen. Trying to get a single bevel sharp is one thing, but honing two bevels—side by side with no room between them—can drive you crazy. No matter how you do it, one edge will be either slightly longer than the other, out of square, or you will leave a little hook in the corner. Corner chisels might be useful for chopping large mortises (although I doubt it), but they are certainly superfluous in furniture making. Stick with your simple and versatile bench chisels. ✖

Corner chisels are designed to create perfectly square corners by cutting adjacent sides of a mortise simultaneously. Although great in theory, in reality they are difficult to sharpen and align in the mortise, making them no more efficient than a firmer chisel.

In this cutaway view of a mortise, a lock-mortise or swan's-neck chisel levers against the side to pare the bottom—a task difficult to do with a bench chisel. Originally these chisels were designed to cut a deep lock mortise through a door stile and into the tough end grain of the rail, but they are just as useful in any deep mortise.

Drawer-lock and lock-mortise chisels

Very different, but just as useful for those unusual chiseling jobs, are drawer-lock and lock-mortise chisels. They are related only in that both have uses chiseling mortises for locks. A lock-mortise chisel (or swan's neck chisel, as it is also called, because of the gentle curve of the blade) can cut with the same sort of scraping action as a scraping chisel. Imagine a deep mortise for a lock–

set, so deep you have to cut into the end grain of the lock rail. A lock-mortise chisel is designed to lever from the sides of the mortise and neatly pare the end grain away. Sharpen the blunt edge as you would for scraping, or with a fine bevel for paring long grain in the bottom of deep mortises.

What do you do when you want to fit a lock to a small drawer after the fact, or chisel in an area too small even for a butt chisel? A drawer lock chisel is the answer. Z-shaped and struck with a hammer, it has two chisel ends at right angles to one another, so it is able to cut at right angles or parallel to an edge. I've never seen a new one offered anywhere, but it would be simple enough to forge one yourself.

A drawer-lock chisel works in the tightest spots, as when retrofitting a lock to a small drawer. Both ends of the Z-shaped tool have flat chisel blades at 90° to one another. The chisel is hit at the bend with a hammer or mallet.

Gouges and Carving Tools

Carving is a skill with its own special techniques and tools, and entire books have been written about the carving cousins of chisels—gouges and other carving hand tools. As a generalist when it comes to furniture making, I carve as little as I need to get by. Nevertheless, I use a number of carving tools, especially gouges. Think of them as curved chisels, useful for shaping curved joints, fairing the transition between moldings, and adding small decorative touches.

Gouges come in two basic types: in-cannel or paring gouges sharpened with the bevel on the inside,

A typical set of gouges has blades of different curvatures, with bevels on the inside for curved paring cuts (or copes, as seen in background), or on the outside for carving. The two cranked patternmaker's gouges (right) will smooth the bottoms of long troughlike shapes.

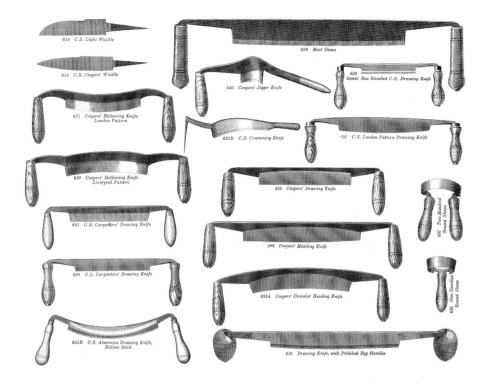

614 *C.S. Light Whittle*

615 *C.S. Coopers' Whittle*

638 *Mast Shave*

640 *Coopers' Jigger Knife*

639 *Gents' Box Handled C.S. Drawing Knife*

625 *Coopers' Hollowing Knife, London Pattern*

625B *C.S. Crumming Knife*

631 *C.S. London Pattern Drawing Knife*

630 *Coopers' Hollowing Knife Liverpool Pattern*

622 *Coopers' Drawing Knife*

621 *C.S. Carpenters' Drawing Knife*

623 *Coopers' Heading Knife*

637 *Two-Handled Round Shave*

620 *G.S. Carpenters' Drawing Knife*

623A *Coopers' Circular Heading Knife*

636 *One-Handled Round Shave*

621B *C.S. American Drawing Knife, Hollow Back*

619 *Drawing Knife, with Polished Egg Handles*

Coopers used many drawknives: one for beveling the head and bottom of the barrel, another for shaping the staves inside and out, another for leveling an area for the head (a cooper's jigger), and yet another for smoothing the inside of the barrel.

There's no better place to use a drawknife than at a shaving bench or horse with a large jaw to hold the work securely.

Drawknives

When I started this chapter extolling the virtues of simple tools, I had drawknives in mind. Here is a tool that in the right hands can hog great jagged shavings, and on the next stroke pare so fine that the shaving almost floats off the edge. There is no magic to this tool—it has the same edge as a chisel. The advantage of a drawknife is that it is used two-handed, with handles at right angles to the edge for maximum power and leverage.

Coopers, spar makers, chairmakers, wheelwrights, shingle makers, and many other trades adopted drawknives and altered them to suit their particular work. Some have long, wide blades, others are shorter and narrower, or have blades curved to work in unusual places, such as inside a barrel. Carpenters created an ingenious variation with handles that fold over the blade, protecting both the tool and its owner when he reaches in his toolbox.

I have three common drawknives, all of which have a role in my furniture making. One is for the roughest of work, like taking the bark off the wany edge of a board. I use a smaller knife with a 6-in. blade for wasting large chamfers, such as on the facets of a pencil-post bed or the bevel along a curved tabletop. I also have a very small gentleman's knife with a blade only 4 in. long, which I use for the most delicate chamfers and shaping. All three knives cut more quickly than a plane and, with care, produce just as beautiful a surface.

TUNING AND USING DRAWKNIVES

Whether to use a drawknife bevel up or bevel down is a matter of some debate. I use them bevel up for most work and bevel down only when I am cutting within a concave area, when it seems to work better that way. Sharpening has something to do with my choice. Basically, a drawknife is sharpened like a chisel with about a 20° bevel, except I hone on a very small back bevel that gives me extra maneuverability working bevel up. No longer does the cut have to follow the flat of the back: I control the cutting depth by lowering or raising the handles.

To hone the bevel (and the back bevel), it is easier to bring the sharpening stones to the tool. There isn't much else to tune on a drawknife, except to replace a broken handle (as you would a tanged chisel). To tighten a loose handle, try peening the end of the tang coming through the handle. If this fails, try squirting some Super Glue adhesive into the tool end of the handle.

Chairmaking is one of the few trades left that depend upon the versatility of drawknives, from working up rough legs and other parts, to their final shaping and fitting. While you can work at a vise or bench with a drawknife, a shaving horse is designed just for this kind of work. You can sit, shave, quickly reposition the work or clamp in a new piece, all at a comfortable height to deliver the most power and control to the tool.

SCORPS

Some chairmakers use an unusual form of drawknife called a scorp or inshave for hollowing and shaping a plank seat. Essentially a curved drawknife, a scorp works like a two-handled gouge. Coopers used them

to smooth the insides of barrels, as did wooden shovel and scoop makers. True to the ingenuity of craftsmen who relied on hand tools, I've seen an interesting variation— a one-handed scorp. The interior between the curved edge was filled in with wood like the sole of a wooden spokeshave, giving much more control by transforming a simple cutting tool into a more complex plane.

Sharpen a drawknife as you would a chisel, with about a 20° bevel and slight back bevel. It's easiest to hold the tool steady on a surface and bring the stone to the blade.

Hand-forged scorps or inshaves are used one- or two-handed for hollowing plank seats, scoops, or for smoothing the insides of barrels.

7 PLANES

Imagine a time when nearly everything was made by hand. Not just furniture and houses, but every necessity of daily life, from kitchen utensils to farm wagons. The labor and sweat to make even the simplest piece of furniture was enormous; every board had to be flattened to a uniform thickness, then sized by hand with a jack plane. Planes were easily the most important hand tools in any shop, and they still are. It's no wonder they have become symbols of fine woodworking and meticulous craftsmanship.

Integrating planes into your routine will get you thinking in new ways about how you make things. And you will enjoy the process far more, because there are few pleasures as wonderful as curling up translucent shavings, smelling their aroma as they float to the floor, and feeling a surface so polished it shines. 🪵

This iron miter plane from the late 17th century is not much different from a Roman plane of 2,000 years ago or a modern low-angle bench plane. Even the construction is ancient: The sole is connected to the body with two large tenons that are peened and clinched.

A Legacy of Planes

Woodworking made a great leap forward when planes appeared. You would think that a tool as vital as a plane might have been around forever, as far back as the dawn of woodworking, when man started chipping stone scrapers and chisels. The Egyptians left no evidence of having used planes, though it is amazing that they made such intricate and sophisticated furniture without them. They used adzes instead, and it's not too hard to imagine some craftsman who eventually started pushing his adze instead of pulling it, and then lengthened the body into the sole of a crude plane. By mid-morning, historically speaking, the first planes appeared. Some were found in the ashes of Pompeii (A.D. 79), quite rusty and missing wooden parts, but still with all of the important elements of the design.

Through the Middle Ages and up to the 18th century, planes were quite basic. A joiner's or carpenter's kit contained a number of wooden planes: a smoothing and longer jointer or jack plane for general work, a few molding planes, and some joinery planes such as a plow

Until the Civil War, a joiner or carpenter relied on wooden planes for preparing and sizing stock, smoothing surfaces, and jointing long edges. Fashioning his own planes from wood, he could make any length needed.

Patternmakers adapted (and in some cases made themselves) an unusual molding plane with interchangeable soles and irons. Compact and efficient, such a tool was used to cut hollows or coves in wooden patterns for casting metals.

and rabbet plane. Either because of the conservative nature of craftsmen or because such planes served their purposes, changes during this time were slight and usually just affected the shape of the handle or body of the tool rather than the way it functioned.

All this started to change in the 18th century. Rising wealth and a growing middle class with a taste for fine furniture, elaborate houses, carriages, and other consumer goods created a demand for skilled craftsmen. This, in turn, created a demand for the tools—especially planes—to make such craftsmanship possible. Joiners and cabinetmakers needed

fancy molding planes for house trim and casework, a greater variety of bench planes for sizing and shaping, heavier smoothing planes for working the difficult timbers suddenly in vogue, and more accurate planes of all types for cutting joinery, raising panels, and plowing grooves. For

every trade, planemakers supplied the planes needed, and although new in some ways, they were still only variations on the same basic wooden tools of centuries before.

Things likely would have continued this way except for the scientific and mechanical curiosity spurred

LEONARD BAILEY left his mark—sometimes quite literally—on nearly every cast-iron bench plane ever made. Many of the features that make modern planes so easy to use, features we almost take for granted, were his invention: an adjustable frog, a knuckled lever cap that holds the iron in place, a vertical adjuster for the iron, and rosewood for handles and knobs. When he started tinkering, cast-iron planes were a novelty—wooden planes ruled. He knew cast iron would make a superior and economical plane, as long as he could devise a simple way to clamp the iron in place and adjust it.

In 1855, at age 30, Bailey took out his first patent for a rocking adjuster later used in Stanley's cabinet scrapers and scraper planes. Thirteen years later he had a line of a dozen cast-iron planes in production (plus another dozen spokeshaves and combination cast-iron/wood planes) with most of the features we have come to know. When he joined forces with Stanley a year later, his reliable designs—coupled with Stanley's marketing savvy—hastened the acceptance of Bailey bench planes as the preferred plane throughout the world. 🪰

Advances in technology spurred by armament manufacturing during the Civil War helped companies such as Stanley Rule and Level produce cast-iron planes with long-wearing soles and simple adjusters for the iron (top and bottom). Meanwhile, British makers such as Thomas Norris refined smoothing plane designs (center).

by the Industrial Revolution, and later the Civil War. While water- and steam-powered factories turned out millions of wooden planes, inventors and small-town mechanics tinkered with ways to make planes easier to use. They created new adjusters and better mechanisms for holding the iron in place, and they began to use cast iron for longer-wearing soles.

Leonard Bailey and Stanley Rule and Level are the two names we most associate with these changes, transforming the humble plane into a tool for every man. Ironically, while Stanley engineers devised more and more sophisticated planes for every conceivable need, they couldn't overcome a market that was steadily shrinking as thickness planers and other woodworking machines replaced hand craftsmanship. What remains of this Golden Age is our rich legacy of classic planes.

Types of Planes

Leaf through any tool catalog and you're apt to see a couple dozen or more planes offered. Any good used-tool shop might have a hundred or more classic Stanleys and others for sale. I've seen collections of nearly a thousand planes. How are all these planes different from one another, and what are they used for? And what exactly distinguishes them as planes?

Planes are complex tools. Think of them as sophisticated chisels, where the design of the tool controls the size and quality of the shaving.

THOMAS TURNER & CO., SUFFOLK WORKS, SHEFFIELD.

TRADE MARK. "ENCORE."   TRADE MARK. "ENCORE."

415 Moving Fillister

422

489

503

Sash Fillister   Plough Plane   Rabbet Plane

Smooths   350   355   Trying Plane   452   Pair Ovolo Sash Planes

405   532   534   535   536

Chamfer Plane   Iron Bull-nose Plane   Bull nose Beech Plane   Boxwood Chariot Plane   Iron Chariot Plane

537   Jack Plane Handle.   434   Dado Grooving or Trenching Plane   352 Jack Plane

391   Sash Gouges   Side Templet   Saddle Templet

456   457   474   465   462
Ovolo   Ogee   Ogee

468   458   450   459   386   447   436   452
Ouurk Ogee & Ouurk Bead   467   Ovolo   Ouurk Ovolo & Astragal

This page from an 1890 catalog offers a typical array of workaday wooden planes for every shop task from sizing and smoothing stock to cutting joinery, moldings, and window sash.

Specialized planes designed for a single purpose can be hard to categorize, such as this witchet and rounding tool, which cut round tenons.

The important elements are a sole that guides the cut and regulates its depth; a slender mouth that accepts the shaving, which is then curled against the cutting iron; and the pitch or angle of the iron to the work, which determines how fast the shaving is bent and curled. There is a little more to it, but essentially it all adds up to a self-regulating tool that's relatively easy to use.

As for what a plane can do, so far plane designers have had no trouble thinking up new and interesting ways to make planes that can cut everything from dovetails to ornate cornice moldings. This variety can be distilled into four basic tasks: sizing and preparing stock, cutting joinery, flattening surfaces to a smooth polish, and shaping curves and decoration. There are also specialized planes, usually associated with a specific trade and designed for a single purpose, such as cutting round tenons or half-round core-boxes. And while it would be interesting to organize planes into one of these groups, many are capable of multiple tasks.

PLANES FOR SIZING AND PREPARING STOCK

When you picture a plane, it's probably a bench plane, for the simple reason that they are the hardest working and most common of all planes. Named for their work at the

These late 19th-century bench planes by Mathieson of Glasgow, Scotland, do not have cast bodies but are made of steel plates dovetailed together. Combined with an overstuffed wood infill (like over-risen bread), they are massive enough to work figured or ornery timbers more easily than comparable Bailey planes.

bench (where most planes are used), bench planes range from the tiny Stanley #1 to the #8 jointer, and include low-angle planes, block planes, and scrub planes. Bench planes are general-purpose planes. They were the thickness planers and jointers of an 18th-century shop, used for sizing, smoothing, cutting tapers, rough-surfacing parts, or performing any of the varied tasks involved in preparing stock.

While Bailey-pattern cast-iron bench planes are the most common (many sizes are still in production), wood-bodied planes are preferred by some craftsmen for their sweet action of wood upon wood. At one time, Stanley made a line of transitional bench planes, a combination of wooden body and metal mechanical parts, which have some of the advantages of both wood and metal planes.

STANLEY NUMBERING SYSTEM

STANLEY'S PLANE numbering system has had collectors confused for decades. While it might appear orderly, some numbers seem to have been assigned as much by whim as by logic. How do you explain why a #5½ is larger than a #5, but a #5¼ is considerably smaller than both?

It all began with the first catalog of January 1870, which offered a line of cast-iron bench planes numbered 1 through 12 and wood-bottomed planes numbered

21 through 37. As new planes were developed they were generally given new whole numbers, unless they were intermediate sizes of existing planes, or nearly identical with only slightly different features (such as tilting handles). That's why we have a #4½, #9¾, and #10¼, to name just a few.

At least twice Stanley gave different planes the same number (#80 and #90), while for some reason #14 and #38 were never

used. As the first hundred slots filled, Stanley used a new numbering logic: Similar tools jumped by 100, such as routers #71, #171, and #271 (and we have a #71½, too). The Bedrock line jumped to #602, #603, #604, etc., the Stanley Victor was banished to the 1100s, and the Handyman to the 1200s. This left plenty of classy numbers such as #444 to assign to the only dovetail plane on the market. ✖

PLANES FOR CUTTING AND FITTING JOINERY

Once the stock is flattened and sized, joinery planes are put to work. We're more apt to use a table saw or a router to cut joinery today, but a cabinetmaker of the past relied on a variety of specialized joinery planes: plows for cutting grooves; rabbet and dado planes for cutting rabbets and grooves across the grain; dovetail planes; shoulder and bullnose planes for fitting tenons; and low-angle miter planes for trimming end grain. Some of these planes are still in production—and for good reason. No matter how you actually cut a joint, they are still the best tools for adjusting and fitting the parts.

PLANES FOR SMOOTHING

A third type of plane, a smoothing plane, is used after the joinery is cut. Smoothing planes have a single purpose: to plane a surface to perfect smoothness. No other tool leaves a surface with the clarity, depth, and shine of a well-tuned smoother. The best of these planes are uniquely designed for this demanding work, with thick irons to resist chatter, short massive bodies to hold the plane on the work and firmly support the iron, and narrow throat openings for the finest shavings.

Some of the most beautiful and efficient of the smoothers are steel Norris or Norris-type planes with dense rosewood or ebony infill (see the photo at left on p. 106). The #3 and #4 bench planes are also considered smoothing planes,

For plowing grooves and other joinery, every woodworker used to have a plow plane. Few, however, were as fashionable as this one of rosewood with ivory stop nuts and a set of eight irons by the Greenfield Tool Co., Greenfield, Massachusetts (c. 1872).

Before the advent of mechanical routers, craftsmen would make hand-powered ones from a worn plow-plane iron and a shapely body of beech or ebony. Stanley and competitors such as Record made an adjustable nickel-plated version (#71), which is useful for adjusting the depth of a groove or cutting a hinge recess.

As efficient as it is stunning, the Norris A6 has all the attributes of an excellent smoothing plane. This plane has soul!

A small collection of hollow and round molding planes (plus a quarter-round, ogee, and ovolo at rear) can cut a wide range of decorative profiles. Molding planes were made by the thousands until the turn of the century.

and while they work fine on well-behaved woods, they need some special tuning to produce a flawless finish (see p. 122).

PLANES FOR DECORATION AND SHAPING

The fourth task that planes perform is cutting decoration and shaping. The variety of planes and type of work this includes is enormous: spokeshaves for shaping; compass planes for cutting along curves; panel-raising planes; chamfer planes; and molding planes of every description. No other hand tools can cut such details as quickly or easily, from a small bead along a table apron to bold crown moldings.

When you consider the sheer number of molding profiles and the planes needed to cut each one—plus all the other shaping planes—this is easily the largest group of planes. Fortunately, you can do most of this work with a few spokeshaves, a dozen or so basic molding-plane profiles, and your bench planes. What you can't accomplish with these you can with easily-made profiled scrapers known as scratch stocks (see pp. 132–134).

There is one other form of plane that might be considered a fifth type: scrapers. Some look like bench planes, others resemble spokeshaves, and others are simply a piece of springy steel, yet they have all the characteristics of a plane. Scrapers smooth or shape with a high-angle scraping action as opposed to the slicing cut of a plane. They cut slowly, but they also work highly figured or difficult woods better than most other planes. They deserve separate attention (see Chapter 8).

Each of the boxwood spokeshaves in this unusually fine set cuts like a small plane, shaping curves such as the top of a headboard, a cabriole leg, or a table apron laid out with the aid of one the French curve templates (top).

Tuning Planes

Choose any type of plane—bench plane, rabbet plane, smoothing plane, or molding plane—and, while they may have different shapes or lengths (and other obvious differences), they share some basic elements. They all have a sole (flat or shaped); a chisel-like iron (also straight or shaped); a wedge or lever cap holding the iron in position; a throat (sometimes called a mouth); and a handle or some way to grip the tool comfortably and to control the cutting direction. Working in harmony, the parts add up to a tool that regulates the cutting depth and the cutting dynamics for you. The trade-off is that planes can be tricky to tune. Think of a plane as a kit, all the elements of which need to be tuned together for the best results.

I suspect that many woodworkers avoid planes because they don't understand how to tune them or fear they will ruin the tool if they try. Adding to this frustration is the expectation that a tool right out of the box is going to work perfectly—it rarely does. You can expect a new chisel to work well enough after a light sharpening (and better after a thorough one), but it's a much simpler tool than the combination of

You might not think of a hollow auger (used for cutting round tenons) as a plane, but it has many of a plane's characteristic features, including an iron held in position, a throat, and a sole. Driven by a brace and adjustable for various diameters, hollow augers were used by wheelwrights and chairmakers.

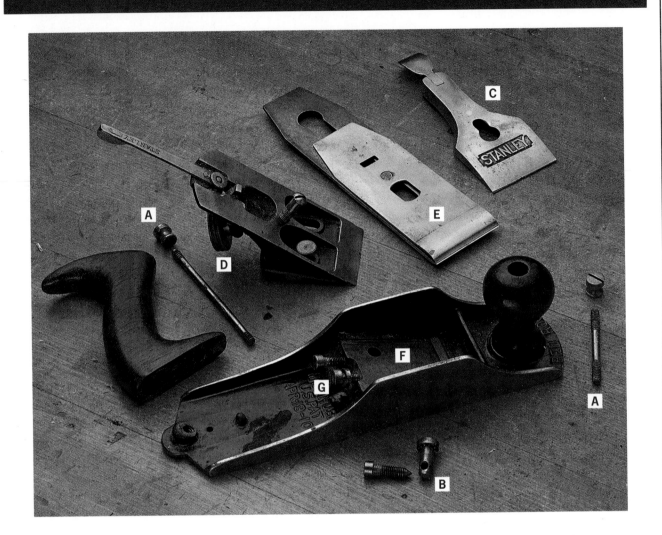

A The threaded rods that secure the rear handle and front knob to the plane can be ground slightly shorter to take up any looseness.

B Two screws or pins (as for this Bedrock plane) secure the adjustable frog to the sole; loosen them to move the frog with screw G.

C The lever cap holds the iron and cap iron (E) in position by locking down on the screw in the center of the frog. Don't tighten it too much—just enough to hold the iron but still adjust it smoothly.

D The depth adjustment for the iron should need little tuning other than a wipe of paste wax.

E Position the cap iron as close as practical to the cutting edge.

F Make sure the surface where the frog beds with the sole is flat and clean.

G Adjust the position of the frog—and the throat opening—with this screw.

parts that make up a plane. Buy any plane, other than one from a high-end specialty maker, and you will have to do some tuning; a flea-market find may require a major overhaul. Tuning is not difficult, but it can be time-consuming. The up-side is that you will understand more about the subtleties of how the tool works and be able to tune it for specific situations or trouble-shoot problems. You will appreciate the results of that tuning every time you use your plane.

How much tuning you do de-pends on what you are starting with, how finicky you are, your pa-tience, and what kind of work you expect from the plane. A rough jack plane obviously needs less tuning than a smoothing plane. Small join-ery planes that need to be accurate might fall somewhere between the two. Even in the case of a new bench plane of mediocre quality right out of the box, it's possible to turn it into an accurate and pre-dictable tool if you follow all the tuning steps (and replace the stan-dard iron with a thicker one). No matter what type of plane you're tuning, the general principles are the same—more or less.

HANDLES

Start by tuning the handles (on those planes that have them) for a quick and very satisfying improve-ment. Bench planes have two wood-en handles: a rear tote and front knob. They attach with a threaded rod through the handle into the iron casting and are tightened with a brass nut. The castings sometimes

Among the tiniest planes are the violinmaker's hollowing planes for shaping the arched back and top of stringed instruments. A tail handle that snuggles into the palm of the hand helps give the user a firm grip.

IF YOU DID NO OTHER tuning than replace your bench-plane irons with thicker ones, the results would still astound you. Whether it's in a top-of-the-line Bedrock or a low-end Handyman, a thick iron is stable and cuts far more smoothly. Thin Stanley irons are easy to hone, but they're not stiff enough for the demanding stresses of plan-ing hard woods. Many catalogs sell replacement blades and a two-part cap iron for a turbocharge of your planes you will really feel.

have a raised boss to receive the handle, giving it a more secure seat. Over time and with use the handles work loose. This can be frustrating when you are relying on the handle not only to hold the plane but also to control its direction and apply some downward pressure.

The easiest fix is to tighten the brass nut that secures the handle. This has probably been done before (and probably the nut has run out of threads). If this is the case, slip a washer under the nut (leather works well) or remove the threaded rod and grind or cut off ⅛ in. or so.

more comfortable. An occasional light rubbing of paste wax or linseed oil will polish the wood to a beautiful and protective finish.

FLATTENING THE SOLE

Very few planes—new or old—have a truly flat sole, and although they will work, they will work better with some flattening. More important than overall flatness is flatness at important points along the sole. At the very least, the area at either end of the plane and in front of the mouth should be flat. Flatness at the extremities of the sole takes full advantage of its length to guide the plane.

Understanding how a plane cuts explains why it's also critical to make sure the area in front of the mouth is flat. As a shaving is forced into the mouth against the ramped iron, the shaving is levered and bent against the forward part of the mouth (see the photo at left). This area of the sole exerts pressure on the wood fibers so splitting away (or tearout) is kept to a minimum. It can do this only if the sole ahead of the mouth is in firm contact with the surface of the wood.

The first step in flattening any sole is checking it with a straightedge. Hold the sole up to a bright light and sight under the straightedge. Depending on what you want to accomplish with the plane, it might be fine as is, or you may have many hours of flattening ahead. For a long plane such as a jointer, used for shooting accurate straight edges, expect to flatten the toe, the heel,

As the plane cuts, a shaving is bent upward against the ramp of the iron, which levers the shaving against the front of the throat, breaking it as it goes. The area of the sole in front of the throat presses down on the fibers, and the repeated breaking of the chip prevents splitting ("tearout") and curls the shaving.

You might want to replace the ugly plastic handles on new planes with rosewood aftermarket handles or shopmade ones. No handles quite compare to the beauty and ergonomic perfection of Stanley's classic rosewood styles, polished by years of handling. Unless it is a historically significant plane, don't hesitate to smooth or shape any handles (or the body of wooden planes) or strip off the varnish to make them and the area in front of the mouth to give the sole good support to cut a flat, straight surface. On planes with smaller soles—joint-cutting planes, for example—the entire sole should be close to flat. There is actually some advantage to a small amount of hollow in the sole for reducing friction. Corrugated or grooved soles supposedly slide more easily, and Japanese craftsmen purposely shape areas of their planes' soles hollow.

There are no shortcuts to lapping a sole flat, unless you are a machinist or know one you can trust to surface-grind the sole. Surface grinding is tricky, to say the least. Not only is it hard to grip the awkward shape of most planes without a lot of jigging, but the mere act of clamping can also distort the sole. It's slower but safer to stick with hand lapping on a lapping table, as shown in the photos at right.

Be sure the iron is clamped in place but pulled well back from the throat—the iron exerts pressure on the sole, which should be taken into account when lapping. If lapping seems like too big a job, just do a little. When the spirit moves you again, do some more. Give the lapped sole a wipe of paste wax for an almost frictionless glide.

TUNING THE IRON AND CAP IRON

The easiest way to improve the performance of almost any plane instantly is to replace the standard iron with a thicker one. This is especially true for smoothing planes and those

Flatten the sole on a lapping table made from ⅜-in. plate glass sprinkled with silicon-carbide powder and lubricated with oil or water (front). You can also use sheets of silicon-carbide or aluminum-oxide paper glued to the glass (rear). Retract the iron and use a back-and-forth motion with even downward pressure.

This sole needs more lapping. Much of the sole, including the important area in front of the throat, shows lap marks, but the toe and heel are still low spots.

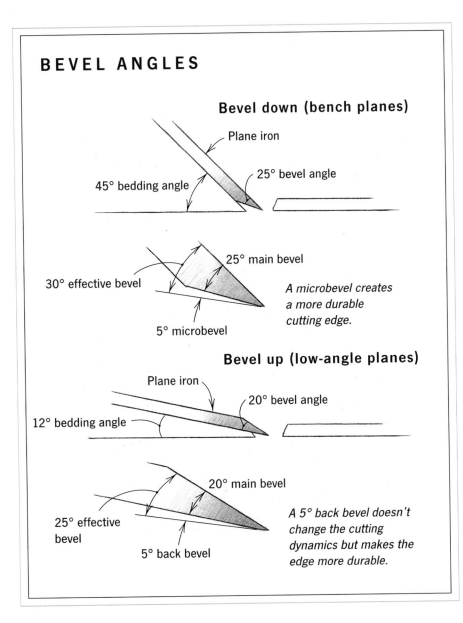

BEVEL ANGLES

Bevel down (bench planes)

Plane iron

45° bedding angle

25° bevel angle

25° main bevel

30° effective bevel

5° microbevel

A microbevel creates a more durable cutting edge.

Bevel up (low-angle planes)

Plane iron

12° bedding angle

20° bevel angle

20° main bevel

25° effective bevel

5° back bevel

A 5° back bevel doesn't change the cutting dynamics but makes the edge more durable.

For a truly sharp cutting edge, flattening the back of the iron to a polish is every bit as important as honing the bevel. Start on a lapping table for backs that are rusty or warped, and work up to your finest stone.

(see the drawing at left). For these, a 20° bevel is worth trying, or even lower (though you run the risk of chipping the delicate cutting edge). The back should be polished and flat. If you want, hone on a microbevel or a back bevel (see p. 27).

Most of the time the cutting edge is straight, but there are some advantages to a cambered or curved edge. On jack and scrub planes, a well-cambered iron cuts like a gouge for removing wood quickly. Rounding the corners slightly on a smoothing plane helps feather the strokes (see the drawing on the facing page).

Bench planes and some other planes have double irons: an iron and a mating cap iron. The cap iron supports the cutting edge and curls the shaving as it rides up the iron.

that you use on difficult woods. The thin iron typical in most bench planes, particularly Stanley and Bailey planes, is quicker to hone but entirely too flexible to stand up to the considerable stresses at the cutting edge. Remember that these planes were originally made for carpenters working soft woods, and not the hard woods typically used in a shop today. The cap iron helps stiffen the iron, but still not as well as a thicker iron. Find an old iron (old wooden planes are a great source) or buy a new thick replacement iron—it makes a world of difference.

Sharpen the iron as you would a chisel. Generally a bevel of 25° is a good compromise for most planes. (The width of a 25° bevel is about twice the thickness of the iron.) The exceptions are low-angle planes, where the lowest cutting angle possible is used for shaving end grain

IRON PROFILES

Straight iron for jointers, rabbet, and dado planes

Relieved corners for smoothing or jack planes

Cambered iron, from very slight for smoothing planes to a heavy camber for scrub planes

When you are tuning up your plane, smooth the top of the cap iron with fine emery paper and wax it. Then take the cap iron onto a stone and flatten the tip where it mates with the iron. Trial-fit the two and sight between them; there should be no gaps for a shaving to wedge itself. There need not be a lot of tension between the cap iron and iron; in fact, too much tension can curl a thin iron and cause a whole new set of problems. There should be just enough tension that the cap iron stays in place when you rap the end of the iron gently on the bench.

The most difficult part of tuning a molding plane is honing the iron to the same profile as the sole. Work with shaped slipstones, maintain a typical 25° bevel, and test the iron in the mouth to see where its shape differs from the sole.

How you set the cap iron in relation to the cutting edge depends on how the plane will be used. The closer it is to the edge, the more support it provides and the faster it can curl a shaving. A good rule of thumb is to set the cap iron back the thickness of the shavings you expect to cut. On planes doing the most exacting work—smoothing planes and some bench planes—the cap iron is quite close (if the edge has any camber you can't set the iron as close). For a general-purpose jack plane, set the cap iron and iron as much as a $\frac{1}{16}$ in. apart (see the photo at right on p. 114).

BEDDING THE IRON

The final area that needs attention is the bed of the iron—or the "frog," as this piece is called in bench planes. The frog is separate from the body casting for two reasons: It simplifies the casting of the body and allows you to fine-tune the position of the iron and, in turn, the throat opening. I don't know where the unusual name came from, but it

The multiple irons in these complex molding planes are much easier to sharpen and tune than a single, large iron.

One rule of thumb for positioning the cap iron is to set it as close to the cutting edge as the shavings you will cut. Set it extremely close for a smoothing plane (right) and with about a $\frac{1}{16}$-in. reveal for a cambered jack-plane iron (left).

Bailey-type planes have two adjusters: a lateral adjustment lever that engages with the slot in the iron and pushes it right or left, and a brass adjuster wheel that slides the iron in and out by pushing against a slot in the cap iron.

does resemble the frog of a horse's hoof (or perhaps it originates from the old saying about a frog in your throat). On well-made old planes, the frog probably needs no tuning. The frogs of newer planes (except high-end ones) probably do because expensive milling is usually kept to a minimum. A frog needs two types of tuning: one is to fit it firmly to the sole of the plane, the other to make sure the area the iron lies against is flat.

First, take out the frog and the screw that tightens the lever cap and run over the bed with a fine file. To get a solid fit between the sole and the frog, coat one side of the mating surfaces with a dye called engineer's blue. When you assemble the parts,

the color transfers and you can see where the high spots are.

File the high spots and tighten the screws carefully to avoid stripping them when re-attaching the frog to the sole. Start with the frog positioned in line with the bevel and gradually work it forward, tightening up the throat after you see how the plane performs. One virtue of Bedrock planes, Stanley's premier line of bench planes, is that you can move the frog with the iron in place, although chances are you'll set each of your planes and leave them that way.

By now you've tuned every part of the plane except the depth and lateral adjusters, and the lever cap that secures the iron. A drop of oil on the working parts of the adjusters is all they really need. The lever cap should be smooth and waxed to easily pass the shavings over it. Adjust the tension on the screw through the cap just enough to hold the iron and still adjust easily.

To set the working depth of the iron, turn the depth-adjuster wheel, either while looking at the throat (with the plane turned over) or by feeling the iron's position with a finger. Using the lateral adjuster, position the iron parallel with the sole, testing it in the same way. It's safer to start with a shallow cut and deepen it after you see how the plane performs. You'll be amazed how much a little tuning improves the way your planes feel and work.

Using Planes

The planes you'll use the most are bench planes: a #3 or #4 smoothing plane, a #5 jack, and a #7 or #8 jointer. How you use them depends a lot on what you make, but it's sure to involve the basic techniques of cutting true edges or jointing surfaces for such work as edge-gluing boards, smoothing narrow surfaces, trimming parts to exact width and length, and fitting parts together. From there, it isn't much of a leap to using joinery, molding, or other specialized planes. The best place to start is with an easy-to-handle and versatile #4. Put it to work and get a feel for the way it cuts. It's time to make some shavings.

For efficient planing you need a sturdy bench at the right height (see pp. 32-33). Planing takes effort, and you will work up an honest sweat some days; a bench just makes it easier by transferring your energy to the work (and holding it for you). If you are going to plane a lot, you'll want a lower bench to get the weight of your upper body over the plane. There is no single correct body position, but it should feel natural and comfortable. Spread your feet for stability. Think about moving your body along with the plane (when jointing a board, for example), while keeping it balanced and cutting evenly. All of this might feel awkward at first, but in time it will become second nature.

JOINTING

Trimming a drawer face to width, cutting a bevel on the underside of a drawer bottom, shooting the edges of two boards to be glued together or the four sides of a tapered leg are all variations of typical everyday jointing. Think of it as a kind of smoothing, cutting a surface (usually narrower than the width of the iron) flat and true so that two such edges can be joined together seamlessly. Smoothing larger surfaces is different and covered later.

For the most accurate jointing, use the longest plane practical. The longer the plane, the better the ability to ride over the hollows and plane off the high spots. (A shorter plane would fall into the hollows

Efficient planing can't be done without a good bench and a vise or two to hold the work while you concentrate on controlling the plane. Work at a height that allows you to get your upper body over the plane and settle into a comfortable stance.

and would have more trouble planing the surface straight.) A long plane also has more mass, which helps power the tool through the cut. This said, for cutting a beveled drawer bottom or tapered leg, where perfect flatness end to end is not vital, a #4 bench plane would be less tiring to use.

Clamp your board on edge in a side vise, on the top of the bench, or whatever way keeps it steady and well supported. Position the plane on the edge with the iron about to start cutting. The front of the sole guides the cut at the beginning, so keep pressure on it and merely support the rest of the plane with your hand on the rear handle. As you begin cutting, shift some weight toward your rear hand.

Completing the cut is the opposite, with the pressure shifting to the area of the sole behind the iron. If you put pressure on the heel of the plane at the start of a stroke and on the toe at the end, you will gradually cut a convex surface. No matter what plane you are using, keep the pressure focused over the part of the sole in contact with the wood.

There are a number of things to concentrate on all at once while jointing: You've got to balance the plane, keep your weight over the correct area of the sole, and apply some downward pressure as well. A heavy plane helps, as does the forward slant of classic plane handles. Balance comes with time. To joint an edge true, start by making it slightly hollow, since this is an easier condition to flatten than a convex one. (Even a long jointer plane will

To joint a long board, clamp it against the edge of your bench in a side vise or upon a board jack (at knee level near the far end of the board) so that the top edge is at a comfortable height. Balance the plane on the edge, extend a few fingers from your front hand to stabilize it, and walk along as you plane from end to end.

Edge-joint thin boards by folding them together and planing both edges at once. If you plane on a slight bevel, which is quite natural on such a narrow edge, it will be the same for both boards (complementary) and cancel each other out.

SPOKESHAVES are the gliders of the plane world, able to loop the loop over the curves of a headboard as easily as skim along a cabriole leg. Graceful handles—their wings—afford a good grip. With hollow, round, or flat soles (and everything in between), spokeshaves can cut along nearly any curve, in the tightest of places. Wheelwrights found them indispensable for fairing and smoothing spokes, as did chairmakers, coopers, basketmakers, and furniture makers for shaping everything from chair seats to pail staves.

Wooden spokeshaves are quite common secondhand. Their blades are shaped like a small drawknife with two tapering square tangs bent at right angles that wedge into the stock. To set the depth of the cut you tap on the tangs or blade; more sophisticated shaves have captive nuts threaded onto the tangs. Often bone or brass is inlaid in front of the mouth to prevent wear. The beauty of these simple shaves is their very low cutting angle—a noticeable advantage planing end grain—and their ability to cut easily and aggressively.

When interest turned toward tools made of cast iron in the mid-19th century, Leonard Bailey and others re-engineered spokeshaves. Their blades are steeply bedded,

Spokeshaves are small planes capable of shaping concave or convex curves. One of the author's favorites is the Stanley #53, which has a simple depth adjustment to alternate between aggressive shaping and light cuts, such as chamfering this chair spindle.

like miniature bench planes with handles. They cut with less tearout, at the cost of greater effort to power the tool. Some versions have blade adjusters. My favorites, Stanley #53 and #54, have a thumbscrew that rocks a yoke to close the mouth and lighten the cut. On nonadjustable shaves, set the blade slightly deeper on one side for the widest range of cutting options.

The trick to using a spokeshave is learning to rock it to the best cutting angle, while following the changing contour of a curve. Push or pull—the choice is yours—and skew the tool slightly for the smoothest cut. 🏵

A useful collection of spokeshaves includes some with different sole shapes: concave, convex, and flat. Close cousins to spokeshaves are scraper shaves (at rear) for a slower yet controlled cutting action shaping surfaces.

follow a convex surface, but it will cut the ends of a hollow until the surface is flat.) To do this, take a few cuts from the center only and sight down the edge to see how you are doing. If it is slightly hollow, cut end to end, and when you cut a full-length shaving, stop. Do the same thing on another edge, and with any luck, the two boards will fit together seamlessly. When I am jointing two boards, I usually take an extra shaving from the middle to hollow-joint the edges for a stronger joint.

A technique that helps with narrow boards is to joint them at the same time (see the bottom photo on p. 116). Fold them together, inside to inside, clamp them as one board, and joint them the same way. The thicker edge gives the plane better support, and any slight bevel will be canceled out. A shooting board is a jig that also helps shoot true edges, especially for jointing thin veneers (see the drawing and photo below).

When it all comes together, you'll be able to joint two edges for a glue joint superior to anything produced by machine. For one thing, a plane-cut surface is perfectly smooth and free of machine marks; it is flat and true, with fibers cleanly severed for good glue absorption. And for long boards that are always awkward to machine, bringing a plane to the work is far easier.

PLANING END GRAIN

Cutting end grain has its own challenges, although the basic planing technique is the same as for jointing long grain. Bench planes, with their

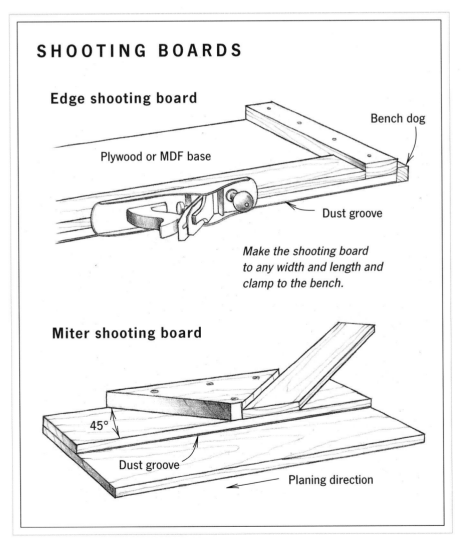

SHOOTING BOARDS

Edge shooting board

Bench dog

Plywood or MDF base

Dust groove

Make the shooting board to any width and length and clamp to the bench.

Miter shooting board

45°

Dust groove

Planing direction

Use a shooting board to accurately joint any edge, but especially thin stock such as veneer. A shopmade wooden handle turns this #7 jointer into a shooting plane and makes it easier to hold while planing with it on its side.

Shoulder planes, which are rabbet planes with low-angle irons and sides milled perfectly square with the sole, are designed for truing and fitting tenon shoulders. Shown here are the Stanley #93 (in use) and the #92 (on the bench).

Overshooting the end while planing end grain is likely to break out fibers unless you back them up with a scrap block clamped in place. Alternatives are to work from both ends toward the middle, or to cut a fine chamfer on each end.

high-pitched irons, cut end grain well—in some situations a #5 is my preferred tool—but generally planes specifically designed for working end grain are short and have low-pitched irons. End grain is tough; a low cutting angle is ideal for slicing the fibers like a knife. Tearout is much less of a concern, because the shavings are so fragile they break up, so there is no need for a narrow throat or a cap iron. And because a low pitch orients the cutting forces in line with the cutter (rather than partially against it as in a higher-pitched iron), chatter is less of a problem.

Trimming the end of a drawer face, cutting the shoulder of a tenon, and truing a mitered corner are all typical end-grain tasks. A block plane is the ideal tool for this type of work. The lower the cutting angle, the easier it will work and the smoother the surface will be. Hone

Position the iron in a rabbet plane so it is slightly proud on the working side (the side into the rabbet) and parallel with the sole. For precise cross-grain rabbets, set the nicker a hair deeper than the iron, so it will slice the fibers ahead of the cut. (The nicker is not set in this photo.)

One of the more common rabbet planes, a Stanley #78 is useful for a variety of rabbet work, such as fitting a panel to a groove (shown here), cutting a rabbet or shiplap joint between two boards, or planing a rabbet for a door.

With a minimal sole ahead of the iron, this Stanley #90 bullnose rabbet plane is a good tool for working into tight corners or for truing up small areas, such as these mitered shoulders.

a bevel close to 20°, and find a plane with a 12° bed angle for the lowest overall cutting angle. For planing longer end-grain surfaces such as a tabletop, Stanley made a low-angle jack plane and smoothing plane, basically just elongated block planes with bench-plane handles. Although it takes a little more effort, a common jack plane works almost as well.

Block planes are terrific tools, but they are useless for working into a corner, when trimming a tenon shoulder, for example. This is when you need a plane with a rabbet mouth, where the iron extends all the way to the side of the plane. Rabbet planes come in an assortment of shapes and sizes, although shoulder planes with heavy bodies and precisely ground sides and soles are the best for working end-grain shoulders. They are low angle and are tuned in the usual way, except that the iron should be positioned ever so slightly beyond the edge of the plane. This is the same with all rabbet planes. There is usually little space for moving the iron laterally, so you'll have to keep the edge honed square to do this.

No matter what plane you use, it's easy to split away the end grain fibers by overshooting an edge. The simplest way to overcome this is to chamfer the edge slightly. Clamping a block against the edge does the same thing; the block splits out but not the workpiece (see the top right photo on p. 119). A shooting board or bench hook is useful for planing end grain because it holds the work and backs up the fibers. A light cut,

SPIERS PLANES are one of Britain's best-kept secrets. By about 1845, at least 15 years before the better-known Thomas Norris set up shop, Stewart Spiers in Ayr, Scotland, was devising the building methods and patterns for some of the most exquisite planes ever made. Besides dozens of styles and sizes of smoothing and bench planes, he made specialty planes, such as a shoulder rabbet and thumb plane, as well as custom planes to any pattern a client desired. The enduring quality of Spiers planes is in the dovetailing that joins the sides and sole, so expertly done that the joints are often invisible.

Norris readily copied Spiers methods and designs—right down to the shaping of the sides, screw cap, and rosewood infill. Why then are Norris planes so eagerly sought after and not those of Spiers, the more prolific, and according to many opinions, the better maker? It all comes down to one feature—a single lever depth and lateral adjuster for the iron—that Norris fitted to his planes after 1914. American craftsmen accustomed to Bailey bench planes and their easy-to-use adjusters naturally prefer adjustable Norrises. Spiers planes never went out of favor with British craftsmen, who appreciate their impeccable performance and a price tag often half to two-thirds that of a Norris.

Shoulder planes such as the four shown here are typical of the work of Stewart Spiers, an early maker of stuffed planes. Two of the planes have unusual double irons for two cutting positions.

skewing to slice the fibers for the least amount of pressure against them, also works. Working from both sides toward the middle avoids the problem entirely.

A shoulder plane and block plane are two basic planes that should be in any well-equipped shop. For real versatility, look for a Stanley #90, #92, #93, or #94; they all break apart into useful chisel planes, and can cut tenon shoulders and small rabbets (see the top left photo on p. 119). Block planes fit your hand just right for many trimming tasks, not all of them end grain. They also make great little smoothing planes with only minor adjustments.

SMOOTHING SURFACES

Machines have taken over many of the mundane tasks of working wood once done by planes—quite thankfully. They do their work well, too. But no machine can match the surface cut by a smoothing plane. The flat plane and cleanly sliced fibers cut by a sharp iron have a clarity and brilliance that is unsurpassed. If this weren't justification enough to start using planes to finish surfaces, consider how efficient they are. It takes just minutes to plane all of the parts for a modest

Sight over a pair of winding or "winking" sticks to tell if a surface is flat—the sticks are parallel—or twisted (in "winding"). Two straight scraps work, but it is easier to sight differences if you make them from contrasting woods or inlay holly sights.

(although you do somewhat), but smooth it to a polish.

My favorite smoothing planes are the stunning planes made by a man named Stewart Spiers in Ayr, Scotland, before 1900 (see the sidebar on p. 121). Many of his designs were continued by the better-known Thomas Norris. All of these planes combine a steel body dovetailed together with rosewood infill for the handle, front knob, and iron bed, which adds mass to the tool. With irons two or three times as thick as a standard Stanley iron, they are perfectly suited to their task.

Tuning a plane for smoothing is so specific that you should think about using a dedicated plane just for this task. Buy the best plane you can afford; if you are like me, you will use it plenty to make it worth the cost. Wood-bodied smoothers, often made of beautiful tropical or fruit woods with thick irons, make great smoothing planes. Flatten the sole with another plane and inlay a throat plate into the sole to narrow the opening as much as possible. Similarly, adjust the throat on a cast-iron smoother as narrow as possible and keep the cap iron close to the cutting edge. Find the thickest iron that will fit in your plane. Hone it with the slightest camber or round the corners to feather the smoothing strokes seamlessly together.

In all woodworking there are surfaces to smooth. Use the same basic planing technique as for jointing with a few minor changes. Take a very fine cut and plane parallel with the grain as much as possible.

cabinet door or a small tabletop to a finished polish.

Stanley #3 and #4 bench planes are considered smoothing planes and they will smooth some woods, but the best smoothing planes are designed and tuned specifically for this demanding work. You want a plane with lots of mass to give the iron rock-solid support. The thicker the iron, the more stable it is, especially against the extreme cutting pressures of figured hardwoods. A long plane isn't necessary, because you're not trying to level the surface

TO STORE their planes more compactly in a chest, joiners once removed irons and wedges. I store my planes in drawers or on shelves with the irons set, ready to go to work—just as I rest one on my bench while working. To protect the exposed iron, either lay a plane on its side or raise the toe on a scrap of wood. For that matter, it's good practice to lay any cutting edge—saw, auger, chisel, or file—propped on a piece of wood and out of harm's way.

Complex molding planes such as the two shown here were too expensive for most 18th-century joiners (who made do with hollows and rounds). Their wide irons, sometimes as wide as 5 in. or 6 in., were tricky to tune, but they could quickly cut yards of identical moldings.

Skewing the plane often leaves a better surface and is an advantage around areas of difficult grain. Start cutting at one edge and plane to the opposite edge in one stroke; stops and starts leave noticeable marks. Overlap strokes as you move across the width of the surface so that they blend together. If you have to start or stop mid-stroke, glide in or out slowly. If things are working right, you'll be sending up billowy light shavings and leaving a surface that you can almost see your reflection in.

Smoothing beautiful surfaces—or any planing really—is easily the most satisfying part of working wood, but not the most easily mastered. Only experience can teach you how to read the grain or which tool to choose for a particular situa-tion. This chapter offers just the barest hint of the possibilities of planes; for more detailed informa-tion on all types of planes, see *The Handplane Book* (The Taunton Press, 1997). Finally, there is no better way to learn about planes or gain more confidence using them than by picking one up, tuning it, and mak-ing some shavings.

SCRAPERS,
Files, and Rasps

More mystery surrounds scrapers than any other hand tool. The tools themselves are not unusual; they resemble spokeshaves or planes, and the simplest is no more complicated than a rectangle of thin and springy steel. There is no confusion in what the tools are capable of—cutting gossamer shavings from the most figured and challenging woods. The mystery surrounds the sharpening: how to burnish on the tiny hooked edge that allows a scraper to perform its magic.

Files and rasps are also scraping tools, but they cut with hundreds of little teeth that shave the surface like tiny planes. Files will sharpen the metal cutting edges of some hand tools, or smooth curves and flat surfaces in wood. Rasps cut more aggressively, like coarse sandpaper. 🐾

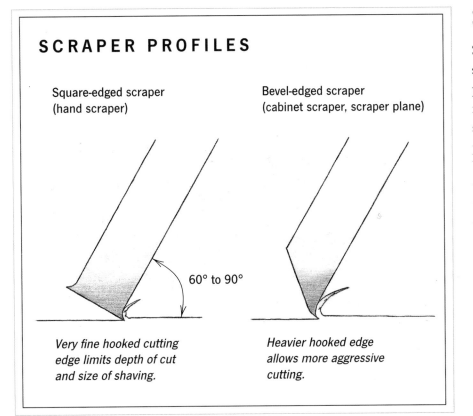

SCRAPER PROFILES

Square-edged scraper
(hand scraper)

Bevel-edged scraper
(cabinet scraper, scraper plane)

60° to 90°

*Very fine hooked cutting
edge limits depth of cut
and size of shaving.*

*Heavier hooked edge
allows more aggressive
cutting.*

Pieces of a heavy hacksaw blade make excellent scrapers, stiffer and easier to use one-handed than a flexible hand scraper. Bevel one edge and sharpen as you would a cabinet-scraper blade.

Scrapers

Scraping is such an unflattering description of the finesse and precision possible with a hand scraper. We're not talking here about tools for scraping off old varnish or peeling paint from the hulls of wooden boats—although scrapers are certainly capable of this. Rather, we're talking about finely tuned tools with minute cutting edges for curling up delicate shavings.

These tools are classified as scrapers because they cut with a high cutting angle, a different sort of cutting dynamic than the slicing cut of planes. Yet scrapers are also planes, in a way, and are just as versatile for cutting anything from small moldings to finished surfaces, although they cut slowly due to the nature of the cutting edge. When it comes to working highly figured woods— something scrapers excel at—that same feature causes less tearout than a plane. A smoothing plane is still my preferred tool for creating a nearly polished surface, but I usually finish the job with a few strokes of my hand scraper to smooth out the small amount of tearout that is inevitable.

Most planes demand special tuning and adjustment to work well. They are complex tools. A hand scraper is the simplest of the lot, and handled scrapers, known as a cabinet scrapers and scraper planes, aren't far behind. Sharpening aside (this is the crux of making any of these tools perform), using scrapers couldn't be easier. Once you get the right cutting angle—by feel alone—a scraper can work into the tightest corner to scrape out some dried glue, skew over the most contorted figure and leave the wood almost polished, or fair a tight curve to a smooth and finished surface. When you get the hang of it, the versatility of a hand scraper is unmatched by any other hand tool.

CABINET SCRAPERS AND SCRAPER PLANES

If a simple hand scraper is so useful, why use a spokeshave-like cabinet scraper or scraper plane? The main advantage of both of these tools is that they have soles (like a plane) that help level a surface, and the tool holds and tensions the scraper blade so it is less tiring to use when smoothing large surfaces. With a hand scraper, your hands become the holder and the sides of your palms the sole, which makes it easy to change orientation or cutting angle but also makes this task fatiguing. Heavy scraping also builds up heat, which conducts right to your thumbs. A cabinet scraper or scraper plane eliminates this problem.

The most common cabinet scraper is the Stanley #80, although Stanley made a number of versions and so did other manufacturers (see the photo on p. 128). Some have wooden soles, others are cast iron. Stanley also made four scraper planes, three of which are among the most sought after of the Stanley line. All will take a toothed blade for "toothing" veneers (to give them

This sleek ebony spokeshave scraper with comfortable handles, a thin scraper blade, and a microscopically fine throat will smooth and fair curves.

A chairmaker uses a few sizes of specialized shaves, or "devils," for smoothing round parts such as spindles and legs. Placing a few fingers under the spindle helps to stabilize it and damp out vibration.

Cabinet and scraper planes have the advantages of a flat sole for scraping a true surface, comfortable handles for good control, and a blade held in position at an effective working angle. From the top: a bronze Lie-Nielsen based on a Stanley #212; a Sargent cabinet scraper with rosewood sole (like a Stanley #12½); a Stanley #112 scraper plane; and a wooden holder for a hand scraper (which keeps the edge stiff and less likely to dish a surface).

a good glue bond) or for leveling ornery woods (much like a scrub plane). The main advantage of a scraper plane is a long sole and a bench-plane handle or two for comfort and control. (If you invest in a good smoothing plane and learn to use other scrapers, however, a scraping plane isn't essential.)

The blades in both a cabinet scraper and a scraper plane are heavier for more aggressive scraping, and the blades are beveled like a plane iron to help burnish on a larger hook. A minor disadvantage of cabinet scrapers and scraper planes is that instead of four usable edges as in a hand scraper, you have at best only two, or even just one edge that you can sharpen (requiring more frequent sharpening). The angle of the bevel is not critical: 30° to 45° works well.

SHARPENING AND USING SCRAPERS

The cutting edge of a scraper is a fine hook that feels slightly smaller than the burr you naturally hone onto a chisel edge when sharpening (before removing it on a finer stone). A scraper will work as well without the hook—with a square but sharp edge, in other words—but the edge will not last as long. The larger the hook, as typically used on cabinet scrapers and scraper planes, the more aggressive the cut and the larger the shaving. A small hook works fine, though, and leaves a very smooth surface.

The sharpening process is essentially the same for all of the scrapers, with some small differences between a hand scraper—in some ways the hardest of the lot—and a cabinet scraper or scraper plane. Sharpening is like filing a saw—you don't have to go through every step each time. If it isn't very dull, you can begin part way through and end up with a nicely sharpened edge. The concept perhaps hardest to grasp is that you can burnish down the hook on a scraper and then roll up a new cutting edge. But let's start at the beginning with either a brand new scraper or one ready for a totally new edge.

Sharpening hand scrapers

Hand scrapers are usually rectangular, although I have about a dozen filed to various curves, including a few commercial "gooseneck" scrapers with a variety of edge shapes (all great for fairing moldings). Sharpening is the same, but for the sake of

simplicity let's stick with a typical hand scraper.

The first step is jointing the two long edges with a fine file (and the short edges, too, if you want to sharpen all four sides). An 8-in. bastard mill file is commonly available and works well. The goal is to shape an edge square with the sides and straight, although a slight convex shape is fine. Clamp the scraper low in a machinist's vise with soft jaws (or in a side vise at your bench) and lightly file the edge from end to end. Try to cut the edge square to the sides, using the vice jaw as a visual guide. If this seems too difficult, run a saw kerf in a scrap just big

SCRAPE, PLANE, OR SAND?

WHAT'S THE difference in the final surface depending on whether you scrape, plane, or sand? All three techniques can smooth a surface that feels and looks polished, yet there are subtle and distinct differences. A planed surface has the most depth, clarity, and shine. A scraped surface has nearly as much, and a sanded surface—even one sanded with a fine grit—can appear slightly dull. A finish helps hide these differences, but they will still be there.

Under the ideal circumstances of a perfectly sharp iron and working with the grain, a smoothing plane cleanly slices the fibers and cuts a flat surface. It has clarity

and shine due to the consistent way it reflects light. An ideally sharp scraper cuts as cleanly, although in reality the fine hook edge degrades quickly due to the high-angle cut, and some fibers get torn rather than sliced as a result. The wood feels smooth, but it doesn't have the consistent radiance of a surface cut by a plane.

Sanding combines a little of both: It tears fibers while cleanly slicing them, too. Unfortunately, as the sandpaper dulls, a lot more tearing goes on. The finer the grit, the smoother the wood feels, but the surface is still irregular enough that it doesn't reflect light with quite as much sparkle. 🌋

A gooseneck scraper has curved edges of different radii to scrape moldings and shaped parts. It's faster than sanding, cuts a more consistent profile, and leaves a smoother surface.

The first step in sharpening a new or dull scraper is filing the edges straight and square, either freehand with a bastard mill file or with a shopmade jointer (made from a scrap with a file-sized saw kerf in it).

Hone the edges on a fine stone to polish them. Either work upright with a zigzag motion, or flat on a board against the side of the stone. Only when the edges feel very sharp (they should curl up a fine shaving) are you ready for the next step: burnishing them with a triangular or oval burnisher (foreground).

Lubricate the burnisher with a couple drops of oil, lay it flat on the scraper, and wipe it up and down to draw the metal out slightly and work-harden the edge. Use modest pressure and do all four sides.

The magic in a scraper is the tiny hooked cutting edge burnished onto it. Work with a light touch; stroke the burnisher from end to end starting at 90° to the edge and gradually lower it to 80° by the third pass.

enough for a file, slip in the file, and use this as a jointer (see the top photo at left).

Hone the edges next, to polish them straight and square. It's easiest to hold the scraper upright and hone back and forth on the stone, although this can wear a groove in the stone if you are not careful (especially a soft waterstone). Use light pressure and work from a medium through a fine stone. Hone the flat sides of the scraper, too. Another method is to hone the edge of the scraper against the side of each stone, guiding the scraper by sliding it along a flat board. This is a sure way to hone the edge at 90°, and by varying the thickness of the board, you won't wear a groove in one place. Hone a curved scraper the same way, except roll it perpendicular to the stone.

At this point the edge should feel sharp, and it should be sharp enough to curl up a fine shaving. Try it out on a piece of hardwood. Grip the scraper in both hands, thumbs behind tensioning and curving the flexible blade into an arc, tip it slightly forward, and push. You should be able to feel subtle differences in the way the tool cuts by tipping the blade forward, or angling it more upright. If you are scraping up dust, then the edge is still not sharp; hone it some more.

This is called a hookless edge, and it is fine for delicate scraping work—leveling inlays or smoothing veneered surfaces, for example. Putting a hook on the edge makes it longer-lasting and more aggressive. To create the hook you'll need a burnisher, a polished steel rod that can be triangular, round, or oval in cross section. A round or oval burnisher is easiest to learn to use, because it glides along the edge and disperses the force over a wide area. On edge, a triangular burnisher applies a concentrated force.

The first step to produce a hooked edge is to draw out the steel that will form the hook. Apply a drop or two of oil to the burnisher, and with the scraper flat on a board and the burnisher flat on the scraper, stroke back and forth along the edge a few times. Keep the burnisher flat on the surface of the scraper (resist the temptation to tip it down). Do both sides of each long edge (for four working edges). This step does two things: It work-hardens the edge ever so slightly, and it draws out the metal to be formed into the hook. If your scraper is only slightly dull, this is where you can start the sharpening process, by burnishing the edge to lay down the old hook in preparation for the new.

The trickiest part of sharpening is the next step, actually turning up the hook. Hold the scraper in one hand, the burnisher in the other, and stroke along the edge with light pressure. Slide the burnisher as you stroke the scraper so you don't wear it in one place. Make your first stroke at 90° to the edge, the next one at 85° or so, and the third one at 80°. You can roll up a more obvious hook by tipping the burnisher even more, but you will then have to tip the scraper well forward for it to cut—and risk burnishing your knuckles while you scrape. The

Hone the beveled edge of scraper-plane and cabinet-scraper blades as you would a chisel, then burnish up a hook along the edge with slightly more pressure than for a hand scraper. Start along the bevel angle and finish at about 15° to 20°.

smaller the hook, the easier it is to renew without having to file and hone. When you finish one edge, roll up the hook on the next.

If you have been successful with sharpening, using a hand scraper is a pure joy. The tool will amaze you. You can scrape in any direction, although working with the grain (and at a skew angle) leaves the smoothest surface. It doesn't take a lot of pressure or tension to bend the scraper into a tight curve in your hands. Curving the scraper

stiffens the cutting edge and lets you concentrate on scraping small areas with precision. The more relaxed the curve, the wider area you can scrape in each pass.

Experiment with different cutting angles; often a lower angle is less aggressive but not quite as smooth. As with a smoothing plane, try to glide in and out of each stroke to minimize noticeable cutting marks. The only thing to be aware of is scraping the surface out of level, so go at it carefully and check with a straightedge, scrape large areas around knots or tearout with long strokes, and switch to a cabinet scraper or scraper plane if you are worried about keeping the surface absolutely flat.

Sharpening cabinet scrapers and scraper planes

Sharpening a bevel-edged scraper is much the same as sharpening a square-edged hand scraper. File and hone the beveled edge and the back face of the blade (the way you would a chisel or plane iron) and work-harden the edge with a burnisher laid flat against the back of the blade. Turning the hook is nearly the same, except that you use a little more pressure. Stroke first along the bevel and then two or three times more, so that you finish about 15° to 20° from perpendicular (see the photo on p. 131). In the #80 Stanley scraper, the bed for the blade is fixed, but in many of the other cabinet scrapers and planes it is adjustable. A fixed bed means that the hook angle can't vary much from 15° to 20° or the tool won't cut well—a small disadvantage over a versatile hand scraper.

To set the blade at the correct depth, slide a piece of paper under the sole ahead of the blade, then clamp the blade in place. In the #80 scraper, tension the wing nut behind the blade to set the depth: more tension pushes the blade into more of an arc, making it cut deeper. In other cabinet scrapers, cutting depth is changed by rocking the movable bed forward (for a deeper cut) or backward (for a lighter cut). The threaded arm that adjusts it locks against a post with two nuts (see the photo on p. 128). With any of these tools, take a light cut for the smoothest finish.

Scratch stocks are versatile scraping tools for cutting anything from inlay grooves to small moldings. They are no more complicated than a profiled blade secured in a simple wooden holder that also functions as a fence.

SCRATCH STOCKS

In a family of unusual tools, scratch stocks stand out. Furniture making can be challenging enough; any little tricks or tools that make things easier are favorites with me, and these tools are among my favorites. Scratch stocks essentially are reverse profiled hand scrapers with a fence of some kind to guide the cut. Stanley made a cast-iron version, the #66 beader, with a dozen different cutter profiles. Scratch stocks cut with the same gradual scraping action, so they aren't the best tools for cutting large moldings. But in figured woods, around curves, or for minute details, they shine. The ease with which one can be fashioned only adds to their appeal.

Any piece of old hacksaw, hand scraper, or bandsaw blade works for the cutter. Hacksaws and bandsaw blades are hard, so you have two choices if you want to work with them: either soften them and file the profile, or grind and hone them to shape. Filing is usually faster, but for the most durable edge, you'll have to reharden the blade. Don't bother with this unless you expect to use a specific profile a lot. Soften the blade by heating it red hot with a torch or stove burner, then cool it slowly. Needle files work well for shaping the profile. Reharden the blade by heating it red hot again and quickly quenching it in water.

To cut well, the sides of the blade (the cutting edges) must be honed square and polished, similar to a honed hand scraper ready for burnishing. Use slipstones for the curved edges. You can bevel the edge and even turn up a small hook, although it will work fine if you don't. Stick with sharp square edges and the scratch stock will cut in either direction—a real advantage in figured woods where the grain is apt to change orientation.

Cut a saw kerf in a scrap of wood for the fence and drive the cutter into it. This lets you tip the cutter forward for the best cutting angle (or backward while pulling the scratch stock). The flat sole of the #66 beader is nice for guiding the depth of cut, but it is not as versatile as this simpler version.

To make a scratch stock, start with a scrap of old hacksaw, plane iron, or scraper blade. Heat it red hot and cool it slowly to soften or anneal the steel so you can file the profile. (For shallow profiles you can grind the hard steel to shape and bypass this step.)

Needle files or chainsaw files work well for filing the profile, in this case a series of five reeds first marked out on the steel with dividers. File straight across to create square edges. (A small machinist's vise fastened to a block and clamped in a side vise is a secure way to hold the small blade.)

Hone the flat faces of the blade with a benchstone and the profile with slipstones, creating polished and square edges. For a fence, saw a scrap with a kerf slightly smaller than the thickness of the blade, and drive the blade into position.

The scratch stock cuts smooth and consistent reeds along the curved leg of a Regency chair in a matter of minutes.

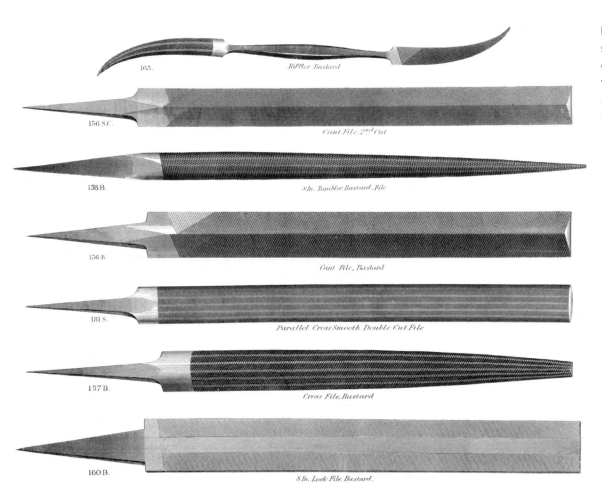

163. *Riffler Bastard*

156 S.C. *Cant File 2nd Cut*

158 B. *8 In. Tumbler Bastard File*

156 B. *Cant File, Bastard*

181 S. *Parallel Cross Smooth Double Cut File*

157 B. *Cross File, Bastard*

160 B. *8 In. Lock File, Bastard.*

Files have uses for sharpening metal cutting edges and tuning tools but also for shaping curves or smoothing small parts like knobs and pulls. Their teeth vary from extremely fine to aggressively coarse.

Files and file handles come in all styles and sizes. The shop-made split handle (center) has enough spring to grip the tang—no ferrule is needed.

The key to unlocking the potential of scratch stocks and scrapers is no different than with other tools: good sharpening technique. You'll know when you get it right—when you feel the slightest resistance against the cutting edge and see the lightest of shavings curling up.

Files and Rasps

Files and rasps are a scraper's handy cousins when it comes to shaping wood or metal. While the primary use of files in a woodshop is for tuning the metal parts of hand tools and sharpening saws and other cut-

Among these file-smith's tools are a hammer with an ergonomic head for working close in to the body, two chisels for cutting files, and a pointed punch for rasp teeth. The hand-cut rasp (by Thomas Brammall, dated 1787) has random teeth, which cut more smoothly than the more ordered pattern of a machine-cut rasp.

ting edges, a fine-toothed file can also cut flat or curved wood surfaces, and do it surprisingly well. The teeth are cut at an angle across the file, so almost any way you hold the tool it will cut with a clean shearing action. Rasps are simply coarse files with random teeth, for aggressive shaping or smoothing. Somewhere between the two are floats, with their large file-like teeth and smooth cutting action, and cabinet files that cut faster than common metal files.

The variety of files and rasps is staggering, with hundreds of combinations of shapes, patterns, tooth designs, and lengths. It's easy to be-

come confused about which ones to use where. It doesn't have to be confusing, however, because a small kit of a number of common files and rasps will do nearly every task you will face (and will save you from having to find a specialized tool dealer).

Over the years I have collected a number of files and rasps at flea markets, where I always seem to find at least one dealer selling surplus files with a few good rasps mixed in. While I can't tell you the names of most of them, nor does it really matter, I do know how aggressively each cuts and the finish to expect. After a little bit of experi-

ence and a good look at the teeth, you'll know the same thing about any file or rasp.

FILES

The most common shop file is the mill file, so named by the sawyers that used them for filing lumber-mill saws. These are the files you are likely to find at any hardware store, 4 in. to 16 in. in length (excluding the tang), flat with square sides, and tapered gradually toward the tip. Other common patterns are triangular files for sharpening saws, and half-round and round files for shaping curves. The teeth on any of these files can be uniformly angled

FILEMAKING was once a specialized trade, allied with similar metalworking trades such as saw and edge-tool making. With special hammers, chisels, and punches, a filemaker would sit at an anvil and punch-form the teeth at about 80 per minute, making 20 files in a day.

A file blank was first prepared from high-quality steel by rolling and forging it to shape. The steel was left soft so it could be worked and so the faces could be ground as flat as possible for the most uniform teeth. Holding the file against an anvil with leather straps looped under his feet, the filemaker punched up row after row of teeth with a special hammer and a wide chisel similar to a cold chisel. It took angling the chisel at just the right angle (close to plumb) and giving it a blow only learned by experience.

By guiding the chisel against the ridge of the last tooth, the filemaker found the position for the next cut. The heavier the blows, the higher and farther apart the teeth, and the coarser the file. Round and half-round files were made with many rows of straight cuts, while rasps were created by chopping one tooth at a time in a random pattern with a chisel-like punch.

Hardening the file to make it useful demanded equal skill. To protect the vulnerable edges of the teeth in the heat of the fire, the file was first dipped in a sticky mixture, such as beer grounds, and then salt. When the salt melted, the file was withdrawn from the furnace and quenched in water, using a different technique for each file pattern to prevent warping. Today, the process is done by machine, but the quality of the finished file still depends on the same process, from preparing the blank to hardening and quenching.

A filemaker hunches over a small anvil, a file blank held in place with two leather straps looped under his feet, as he punches up row after row of skewed teeth. He uses no guide other than his eye and the previously cut tooth.

in one direction, known as *single cut,* or they can have another set of teeth crossing it, known as *double cut.* To complicate things further, each file pattern or shape—of which there are dozens—comes in a range of grades (from coarsest): coarse, bastard, second-cut, and smooth. Furthermore, a longer file of the same grade has coarser teeth.

Naturally, the finer the tooth pattern, the slower the file cuts and the smoother the surface. But fine teeth clog easily, especially on wood and nonferrous metals. Single-cut files clog less quickly than double-cut, and they cut faster, but they wear out faster, too. Both leave an equally good finish.

Files, floats, and rasps were once made in far greater variety of tooth patterns and cuts than you are likely to find today, as shown in this catalog from the mid-1800s. The larger the teeth, the more aggressive the cut (and the more space for holding and carrying off sawdust).

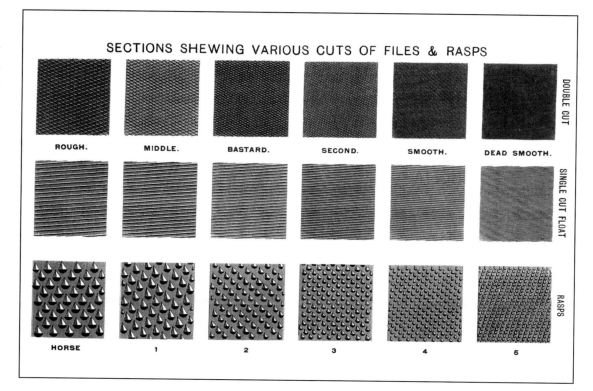

SECTIONS SHEWING VARIOUS CUTS OF FILES & RASPS

DOUBLE CUT

ROUGH. MIDDLE. BASTARD. SECOND. SMOOTH. DEAD SMOOTH.

SINGLE CUT FLOAT

RASPS

HORSE 1 2 3 4 5

No file (or rasp) is going to cut well or leave a very good finish unless the teeth are kept clean of the small pieces that inevitably clog them. I dislodge them by rapping the file flat against my wooden bench every few minutes, or I use a file card or brush with short stiff bristles (but soft so they don't damage the teeth). A toothbrush or brass brush also works. What material remains you can pick out with the point of a small nail. Files (and rasps) will last longer and stay sharp if you store them hanging up or in a shallow drawer with dividers, so they don't bang together and knock off the brittle cutting edges.

Every tanged file should be fitted with a handle for two reasons. First, the tang can be quite sharp, so covering it with a handle protects your

hand. Second, a handle extends a file's usable working length, while giving you more control over the tool at the same time. The farther apart your two hands are when filing, the more precise you can be. The handle doesn't need to be elaborate—a scrap of pine with the corners planed off works as well as a turned rosewood handle with

SOME FILES have edges with no teeth (known as safe edges). This feature lets you cut right up to a corner without also filing into the corner. An auger-bit file has two safe faces on one end, and two safe edges on the other, specifically for the tricky work of filing the spur and cutting lip of an auger bit, but not at the same time. ᛟ

a brass ferrule—although a nice handle only adds to the joy of using a file. (See pp. 200-201 for more about making and fitting handles.)

Using a file properly is not as easy as you might think. Like a chisel, all of the control over the tool comes from good hand-eye coordination, plus the little bit of guiding the length of the file provides. Because the teeth cover most of each face of a file, it cuts continuously, despite small shifts in your hand or body position.

Filing a truly flat surface is the hardest task, mainly because the joints of your arms and hands want to rotate and not remain stiff. For flattening wood, a plane is a better choice, anyway. There is a subtle way a mill file (the best choice for flattening) is made that also helps.

The center is slightly thicker so that even if it warps during heat-treating, both faces will be a bit convex in their length. This is a better shape to use for flattening, rather than a concave face, which would cut the outer edges more aggressively.

The natural rotation of your arms and wrists is an advantage in shaping or fairing curves with a half-round or round file, or a rasp. With either tool, the smoothest cut is a combination of a slightly skewed forward stroke (to give your file the widest bearing) with some downward pressure and a rolling action (to prevent clogging the teeth). Filing straight across tends to chatter and rip the fibers and concentrates the cutting in only one place. Instead, file with a skew motion into each stroke as you slide the file along the curve to fair it. Sensitivity to the way the tool cuts will guide you to a comfortable and natural motion.

RASPS

The variety of rasps is much narrower than that of files, but the two tools are similar. Whereas a fine file might be my first choice for smoothing odd surfaces, such as the top of a chair leg or relieving the sharp corners of a drawer opening, a rasp is a better tool for rough shaping. While the individual teeth of a rasp scrape, they also tend to tear the fibers. The same could be said of some files—cabinet files, for instance—that are nearly as coarse as a fine rasp. The most important idea is not what the tool is called but whether the fineness or coarseness of the teeth suits the work you want to do.

Because rasps are most useful for shaping curved surfaces, half-round and round rasps are the most com-

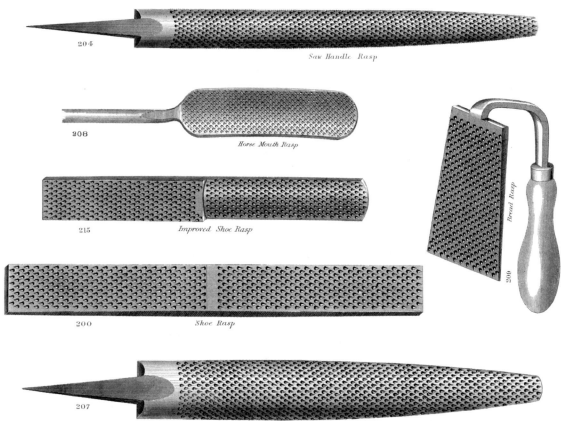

204
Saw Handle Rasp

208
Horse Mouth Rasp

215
Improved Shoe Rasp

200
Shoe Rasp

207
Last Makers Rasp

Bread Rasp
209

Many trades relied on rasps, from saw-handle makers to "last makers" shaping curved wooden shoe lasts (forms). Even cooks used rasps—for scraping the burned crust off the bottom of a loaf of bread.

mon shapes. Nicholson pattern-maker's rasps #49 and #50 (slightly finer) are two readily available and versatile rasps. Hand-cut rasps have an enduring appeal that has lingered despite the reality that most rasps are now cut by machine. The allure is the randomness of their teeth for the smoothest cutting action. Rif-flers are small curved and double-ended rasps (sometimes they have file teeth) for working in tight places and for carving.

Use a rasp like a file, with the same forward and rotating motion. The more downward pressure, the more aggressive the cut. To protect my fingers from the sharp teeth and to give me a comfortable place to grasp the tip, I always wrap it with a few layers of masking tape. Then, if I am working a flat surface (such as filing proud dovetails), the tip rides along on the tape and doesn't dig in. Use a half-round rasp for cutting or fairing a curve. Cut close to the line and then switch to a cabinet or finer file. For the smoothest surface, finish with that most versatile of hand tools—a hand scraper.

One of the best rasps still on the market is the #50 patternmaker's rasp made by the venerable Nicholson File Co. of Providence, Rhode Island. It's the ideal tool for making light, controlled cuts, such as filing away high spots to fit a tapered leg to its mortise.

Somewhere between a plane and a rasp are Surforms, with their individual razor-sharp teeth that cut like miniature planes for aggressive shaping and smoothing. They never need sharpening—you merely replace the blade.

BORING TOOLS

Not long ago a brace and bits could be found in every tool kit

in every woodworking shop, because every trade had a need for drilling holes. A carpenter drilled holes for cutting mortises and pinning their tenons; a shipwright bored holes for the long treenails that joined planking and ribs; a wheelwright drilled the holes for spokes and reamed tapered holes in the hub, all by hand with augers, braces, and an ingenious variety of bits.

Electric drills and drill presses bore holes quickly and accurately and have largely replaced augers and braces. I appreciate and take advantage of these tools. But for drilling holes at compound angles, for working with maximum sensitivity and control, or just for the pure pleasure of using the tools, I still prefer my classic Miller's Falls brace and hand drills. 🐝

Augers, Braces, and Drills

Many tools bore holes—augers, braces, hand drills, push drills, and bow drills, to name several. They supply the rotational energy needed to penetrate wood, and some of them provide considerable mechanical advantage for cutting large holes. The bit is what actually cuts the wood. Bits are as different from one another as a small screw hole is to a tapered bung hole in a whiskey barrel. While the bits evolved in a logical way from simple sharpened points to sophisticated and accurate twist bits with multiple cutters, the same can't be said for the boring tools that power them. Typical of many hand tools, augers, braces, and various kinds of drills evolved to meet the needs of specific trades in an interesting but not always linear way.

Boring is both simple and complicated at the same time. Boring a small hole is not difficult—the rather blunt point of a nail makes an adequate drill that wears its way through the wood as much as it actually cuts. Twisting a chisel-pointed bradawl into the wood cuts and divides the fibers, making a crude but entirely adequate hole.

Drilling larger, more accurate holes is more complicated. It takes more power to remove a greater volume of wood. And with every revolution the bit is cutting long grain half the time and end grain the other half. The bit must be able to cut cleanly in both situations, while also cutting straight, despite knots and irregular grain. Clearly the design of the bit is important, balanced with the speed and power of the brace, drill, or auger.

AUGERS

Augers are the simplest boring tools. They are no more complicated than a handled bit. They range in size from a large shipwright's auger, with its long wooden handle that fits through an eye forged at the top of the bit (and interchangeable with other bits), to tiny gimlets used to make pilot holes for nails and screws. Each clockwise turn of an auger handle spins the bit a single revolution. Augers don't cut very fast, but they are powerful enough to handle the largest holes. Wheelwrights, carpenters, and shipwrights were just a few of the many trades-

---

BORING WITH BRADAWLS

THE SIMPLEST and quickest way to pierce a hole is not with a drill bit but with a bradawl. This small, screwdriver-like tool has a round blade with a chisel point. Merely pushing the awl into the fibers and giving it a half twist makes a pilot hole for nails or screws.

A similar tool with a tapered, pointed blade and square cross section can cut a hole quite close to an edge without danger of splitting the wood. This square-pointed version is also known as a birdcage awl for its use in boring the holes for the wire framework of a birdcage. 🐦

The chisel tip of this bradawl severs—rather than just parts—the fibers as it is pushed and twisted into the wood to drill a small hole for a screw or nail.

men who relied on augers for boring and reaming.

You can add a handle to any drill bit to make an auger, which might lead you to believe that augers were the first boring tools, evolving just behind early copper or bronze bits. Interestingly, Egyptian and Roman craftsmen used far more complex bow drills for the simple reason that augers are frustratingly slow for drilling small holes—at least with the crude sharpened point bits then available. A bow drill has all of the advantages of rapid speed, forward and backward.

Eventually bits became larger and more sophisticated, with lead screws on some and cutting lips that both pulled the bit into the hole and improved cutting performance. Adding handles was a logical step, to deliver the greater power necessary to turn larger bits. With its many styles of handles and bit shapes, augers became the most important boring tools for centuries.

Many years ago, I built a house from an old barn I took down, repaired, and moved. There weren't many nails holding the barn together, but each joint of the massive frame was a variation on a mortise-and-tenon joint, pinned together with wooden treenails. When I rebuilt the barn, I cut many more such joints, some with mortises 8 in. deep and 2 in. wide. I could have rented a generator and a powerful electric drill to waste the wood from the joints, but instead I used an old wood-handled auger. It was hard work and I got a lot stronger

To drill out mortises and peg holes in the heavy frame of a barn, bridge, or house—or for any strenuous drilling—a carpenter would once have used (and still might) a large T- or crank-handled auger. With the slick he would pare tenons and pegs to fit.

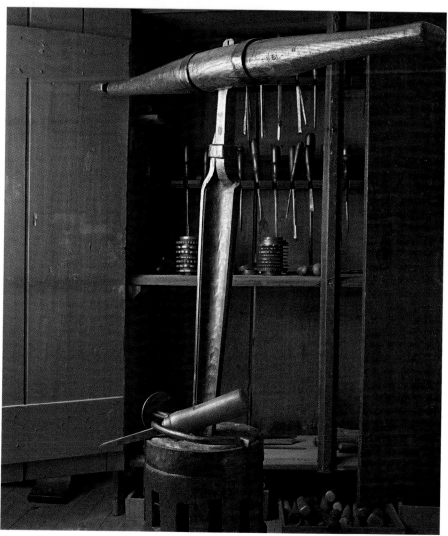

This 17th-century reamer, with a large T-handle bound with two iron rings to stand up to hard work, would have been used by a wheelwright to taper the inside of a large wheel hub to fit snugly onto an axle spindle.

The diminutive cousins of T-handled augers, gimlets are ideal for drilling small holes or starter holes for screws, especially deep in barely accessible places. Various bits fit into the large T-handle for both drilling a hole and cutting a countersink.

Ancient yet sophisticated in concept, a bow drill (top) uses the sawing action of a bow to rapidly spin a pointed bit forward and backward to drill small holes. A push drill (center), this one made by Goodell Bros. of Greenfield, Mass., works on the same principle, only with an internal spiral screw in place of the bow.

that summer, but it was quite amazing how quickly the auger hogged out a hole, quietly, and without any electric cords to get tangled.

GIMLETS

Augers have all but disappeared, but gimlets, their tiny cousins, have survived. Gimlets are versatile and practical for everything from drilling small holes in awkward places to boring quick pilot holes for screws. With a superior twist-bit design and small screw feed, a gimlet bites into the wood and carves out a hole. Bell hangers once used gimlets as long as 36 in.—as a phone lineman today uses extra-long twist bits for installing phone lines—and brewers and vintners used gimlets for making small holes to taste wine or vent beer kegs.

When making and repairing furniture, there are plenty of times I want to add a small screw after assembly—usually somewhere difficult to reach. Other drills might work as well (a push drill for instance), but not as simply as my old gimlet with its worn and polished applewood handle. A few turns of the wrist are all it takes.

BOW DRILLS

The complexity of Egyptian furniture is all the more amazing when you consider how basic craftsmen's tools were three or four thousand years ago. When drilling holes for inlays and typical joints held together with wooden pins, for example, they relied entirely on bow drills. The bit was simple enough—a sharpened and flared point—but the drill itself was quite a sophisticated idea. The bow supplied power and rotation to the bit by back-and-forth "sawing" of a string wrapped around it. Meanwhile, the craftsman held the bit shaft by its head, which spun freely, in order to guide and apply pressure to the bit.

BRACES

Hints of the modern brace and contemporary hand drills first appeared in a variation of the auger known as a breast auger. It looked no different than any other handled auger, except that it had a large and loose head for leaning against, hence the name. The idea originated with shipwrights, who not only needed to drill large holes but also worked in tight places. The loose head let a shipwright get the weight of his upper body against the tool, while still being able to turn the handles. At around this time—late in the 10th century—bits were shaped like a gouge and needed considerable pressure to cut a hole of any size.

Logically, a simple brace should have preceded the more complex bow drill, but it didn't. Just by adding some sort of crank arm to an awl or pointed bit, such a brace would have allowed continuous drilling motion as opposed to the backward and forward motion of a bow drill, and the stops and starts of an auger. But such is the history of braces: What seems obvious to us today actually took until the 15th century to develop. But when it finally happened, braces had the

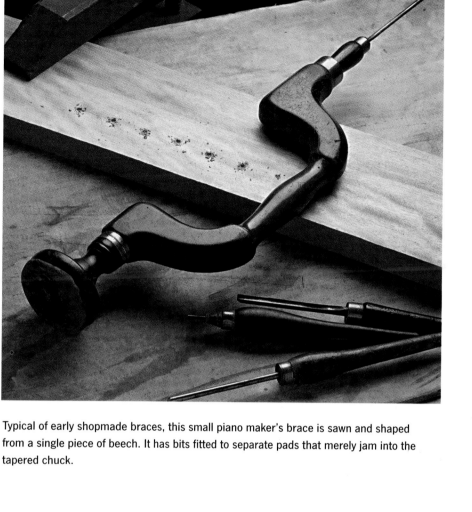

Typical of early shopmade braces, this small piano maker's brace is sawn and shaped from a single piece of beech. It has bits fitted to separate pads that merely jam into the tapered chuck.

NOT ALL DRILLS bore round holes. A passer drill can bore a square, diamond, or any shape hole, much like a modern-day router. Power is provided by a bow, which twists the bit—two steel rods welded together at one end with flattened cutting tips at the other—within a template pierced with the desired hole shape. The springy legs of the bit follow the outline of the template and rout out the hole. One of the drill's uses was to rout diamond recesses for decorative rivets on try squares.

important elements of a loose head and a cranked arm.

The chuck that we take for granted today—the piece of hardware that holds a wide range of bits securely in the brace—was also a long time in coming. Attempts to perfect a chuck parallel the trials and errors that planemakers were going through in the first half of the 19th century, as they tried to improve the mechanics of wooden and cast-iron planes. Many ingenious minds were at work.

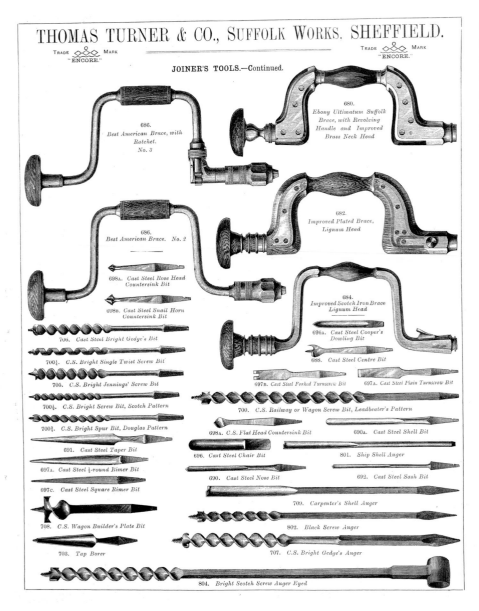

Advertised alongside a selection of bits and fancy English braces with three different chuck designs (from top: push ring, button, and lever) are streamlined American steel braces (top left), which eventually dominated the market due to their positive shell chucks and ratcheting drives.

was different, so that each set of bits had to be fitted individually.

Many other solutions were tried, but none were as successful as the "shell" design patented by William Barber in 1864. This is the chuck you will undoubtedly find on any new brace, and quite likely any one made in this century by Miller's Falls or Stanley, the two biggest manufacturers. The two internal jaws that hold the tapered rectangular shank of the bit are forced together by a threaded shell that screws over them (hence the name "shell"). By simply screwing and unscrewing the shell, bits of different sizes could be slipped into place and held securely.

While Americans were tinkering with better chucks and designing clever braces that could drill around corners, in tight spots, or with ratchet drives, British makers were refining the brace into a high art. A typical craftsman still worked with wooden braces—or metal ones for trades such as coachmaking, where the tools got hard use—but for the master furniture maker there was the grandly named "Ultimatum." William Marples was only one of many makers of these exquisite braces, which, typical of

The simplest chuck solution, one adopted by chairmakers who needed a limited range of bit sizes, was to fit the bit permanently in the brace. Because braces were wooden and shopmade anyway, a chairmaker merely made additional braces. For workmen who traveled to the job site, a far better solution was to have one brace and individual bits fitted to wooden pads that either wedged into the tapered chuck or had a

wooden spring similar to a clothespin that locked the pad in place.

The problem was never holding the bit while drilling—downward pressure kept the pad in place—but preventing the pad from falling out when retracting the bit to clear the shavings. A later variation had an internal spring (with a button to release it) that engaged with a notch filed in the end of each bit. The only problem was that each brace

Compared with stripped-down, mass-produced American versions, this fancy English gentleman's brace—with its shapely head, incised lines on the bulging handhold, and chamfers along the frame—displays the kind of art and elegance that often went into handmade tools.

Drilling holes in tight corners or around obstructions is never easy, although many designers tried innovative solutions. From top: Stanley corner ratchet bit brace with a flattened head to lie tightly against a wall or floor; a right-angle corner brace with a universal joint by Dumont Tool Co., and a Miller's Falls brace with a detachable cornering handle and gear.

British tools, combined exotic woods, such as ebony, rosewood, or boxwood, with a metal frame (usually brass) and other details, such as an ivory ring inlaid in the head. Ultimatums once cost as much as the best smoothing planes—about a week's wages. American braces were far less beautiful, but their ingenuity and effective chucks won over workmen throughout the world.

Brace basics

Braces have so few moving parts that they last a long time. Any tool shop or flea market is bound to have at least a few classic braces, both wood and metal. Stick with a metal brace: it's stronger and will have a better, more user-friendly chuck. Barber's shell chuck is still quite common, although you might find a Spofford brace with a split chuck tightened with a wing nut on the side (see the photo on p. 149). This is a good design that fits the tapered tang of most bits.

While there are subtle variations in details, the most obvious difference between braces is the length of the cranked arm. The larger the sweep—the diameter of the circle the arm makes—the more power you can deliver to the bit. Watchmakers used braces with tiny sweeps, and carpenters ones in the range of 4 in. to 14 in. Ten inches is a good compromise—a brace big enough to turn a large bit without bumping into your chest if you happen to lean over the tool while you

Before cordless and electric drills, egg-beater and breast drills such as these Yankee drills by North Bros. Mfg., Philadelphia, Pa., did all the small to modest drilling jobs—boring screw holes, countersinking, and even driving screws. Their workaday chucks hold modern brad-point, twist, and countersink bits.

Among these unusual hand drills is one in the shape of a pistol made by Ruger Manufacturing Co., an Archimedean double-screw pump drill, and a T-handle that converts an ordinary twist bit to a small auger (here with a depth stop).

work. Another feature to look for is a head with ball bearings for the smoothest boring action. (In this type of brace, there will be a small oil hole under the head to lubricate the bearings.) Before you buy any brace, take the chuck apart to check if any internal parts are worn or missing, and to see how they work together. There should be two jaws, a spring between them, and an outer shell. Before using a used brace, be sure to clean and oil everything.

Along with the chuck came another invention: a ratchet mechanism for drilling in tight spots. The ratchet has three positions. The center one is for positive drive both clockwise and counterclockwise. To either side of this is a position for all clockwise or all counterclockwise ratcheting rotation. This is a nice feature for drilling large holes, where you can get maximum leverage by short, ratcheted swings.

HAND DRILLS

Braces are ideal tools for boring modest to large holes, but what about small holes for screws, nails, wooden pins that lock joints, and all of the light drilling tasks typical in a shop? Hand drills or egg-beater drills, as they are sometimes called, are invaluable for this sort of work. Most have a lightweight cast-iron frame with gears and shapely rosewood handles. They are light, have an easy-to-use and positive three-jaw chuck, can turn slowly or fast enough to drill metal, and can drill in tight places. Often the side handle is removable for just this purpose.

Not all hand drills are small. I have one made by Miller's Falls that has a breast plate, ratcheting gears, two speeds, a large chuck, and enough mechanical leverage to drill a fair-sized hole. (It's essentially a hand-powered drill press.) Stanley made more than a dozen different models, as did Miller's Falls, including a combination of brace and hand drill. Portable electric drills can drill circles around hand drills and have largely replaced them, yet a hand drill is still my preferred tool for drilling extra slowly, or when I need maximum precision and control.

PUSH DRILLS

A push drill is another small drill for light drilling tasks, similar to a Yankee screwdriver, with an interesting mechanical system that transforms pumping action into rotation (see the bottom photo on p. 144). It works with an Archimedean screw, a spiral-fluted shaft, and a nut in the hollow handle that engages with it, so that every push and release turns the shaft. The advantage of this design is that there are no handles to turn, so it will drill a hole in the tightest space.

Push-drill bits are unique, similar to straight router bits with two cutting flutes, except that one flute cuts on the push, the other on the release (when the shaft turns in the opposite direction). Push drills are quick, not very powerful, and best used for small screw and nail holes.

Bits

The best brace or drill is worthless without a collection of bits, the business end of the tool, so to speak. Straight and clean holes—and twist-bit designs that eject the shavings effortlessly—are easy to take for granted. Such improvements, however, are relatively modern. For centuries, craftsmen had to make do

Bits have evolved from sharpened points to sophisticated cutting tools. Shown here (from left to right) is a reamer for enlarging and tapering holes, a countersink, early nose and shell bits similar to spoon bits, a center bit with single spur and cutting lip, a single-twist auger without cutting spurs, and a double-twist auger with cutting spurs.

with less efficient bits that demanded considerable pressure for effective cutting. They cut roughly, or had to be withdrawn frequently to clear shavings.

Early bits were spoon-shaped, with a round tip to start the cut and sharpened sides to enlarge it. The more pressure applied, the faster the shavings curled up inside the hollow center. The design has survived, and for good reason. Unlike bits with a lead screw, you easily can change direction when drilling with a spoon bit by starting a hole perpendicular to a surface and gradually shifting to an oblique angle. This is a technique common among Windsor chairmakers. Because spoon bits can cut slowly or rapidly, and along their sides as well as at the tip, they don't split out the backside of a hole (the way a twist bit might). They are also the only bit that will cut a pear-

shaped hole—a further subtlety of locking the parts of a Windsor chair together.

An 18th-century carpenter had an interesting variety of other bits to choose from. Among them were nose bits, which resembled spoon bits, except they had a flattened end sharpened into a single cutting flute; shell bits with a gouge end; and pod bits with a gimlet's twist or two at the end. This small twist at the end of a pod bit, used on long pump augers for drilling out logs for water pipes, helped the bit cut fast and straight. Without any lead screw, nose and shell bits were hard to position without first gouging out a depression, much as we center-punch a hole before drilling.

Where today we use Forstner bits, an 18th-century craftsman would have used a center bit to drill a flat-bottomed hole. A center bit

Although they express beauty beyond their function, every detail of the shape and cutting edges of these large gimlet-point and Scotch-eyed augers is designed to cut wood fibers and spiral the chips away.

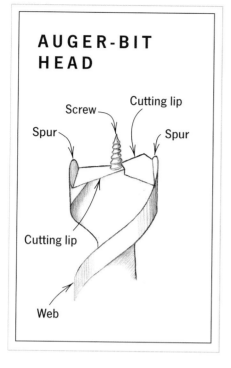
was also used to drill holes at modest angles, and for drilling in thin wood where its point is less apt to split the wood than the wedging action of a lead screw.

Today, the most useful and common twist bits have the improvements of a lead screw to pull the bit into the cut, cutting spurs and chisel-like lips that score and pare a shaving, and a spiral shank to eject the shavings. A drill bit might seem like a fairly simple cutting tool, but it is actually quite sophisticated—it combines different types of cutting actions simultaneously.

As with other hand tools, many creative minds worked on perfecting the design, each contributing some improvement. Russell Jennings was one who made a seemingly small change in the mid–1800s, yet it established the design of twist bits since (including modern brad-

DOING THE TWIST

THE PROCESS of forming the spiral shape and cutting edges of a twist bit by hand and machine is an interesting bit of manufacturing history. A bit starts as a blank of hot-rolled cast steel, forged flat for the twists and round for the shank. To eliminate confusion through the rest of the process, the tang is stamped with the bit size. (The standard marking is a number, 7 for instance, for a $\frac{7}{16}$-in. bit.)

The twists were once formed in a hand-cranked lathe with the steel red hot, and later with dies, rugged molds that shape the hot steel under the pounding of a very heavy hammer in a process known as drop forging. The cutting head is formed in a separate die, the drill is heated and annealed, and then machined to cut the threads, cutting lips, and spurs. All of the forging and pounding of the steel increases its density, and careful annealing in small batches eliminates stresses, making a more durable bit. ✦

In a process once done by hand, auger twist bits are now formed in dies or molds and drop-forged to shape. First a blank of cast steel is twisted into an accurate spiral, and then the cutting lips, spurs, and center screw are forged to shape. After hardening and tempering, the cutting edges and screw are precisely ground and filed to sharpness.

Whether powered by hand or machine, brad-point drills (left and right) are a woodworker's first choice for small holes. For easy shopmade depth stops, use a snug block twisted along the shank into position, make a loose sleeve out of wood to the correct length, or wrap the bit with a piece of tape.

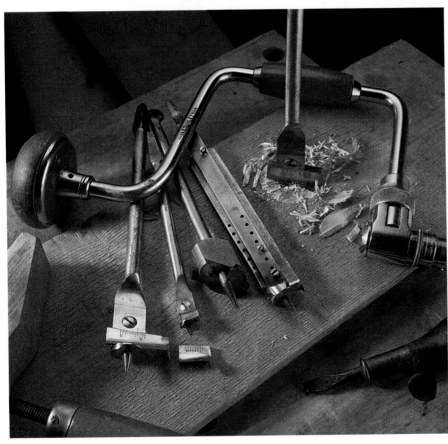

Jacks-of-all-trades and masters of none, many expansion-bit designs have been devised to cut a range of small to large holes, although none do it very easily. All have a large center screw to pull the bit into the work, and one or more adjustable spurs and lips to score the fibers and pare them out.

point bits). Instead of placing the spurs in line with the cutting lips, where the lips were thinnest and weak, he pushed the spurs back. The result was a stronger spur and one that didn't interfere with the cutting action of the lips.

A "Jennings pattern" bit is what you are likely to find new, although a look through a box of old bits at a flea market will turn up quite a variety of other designs. Some of these bits might have a single twist in the shaft, with a single spur and lip, while others have double twists and two spurs and lips. You can find twist bits with coarsely threaded lead screws for rapid drilling into softwoods, or ones with fine screws for hardwoods. Irwin, the largest modern bit manufacturer, still makes another variation, a solid center bit with a single twist for rugged drilling. A subtlety of most of these bits is that the spiral—or "web" as it is known—is slightly smaller than the width of the cutting lips, to give the drill clearance.

While twist bits are the best choice for holes larger than about ½ in., two similar types of bits—brad points and common metalworking twist drills—work better for smaller holes. Brad-point bits have spurs and cutting lips, plus a sharp center point in place of a lead screw. Twist drills have two cutting lips and no center point or screw, and were designed for drilling into metal, although they also work well with wood. While both are designed for a drill press that could turn the bit quickly, they cut more slowly but just as cleanly in a geared hand drill. Just be careful using a hand drill, because it is easy to wobble just a little and snap a fine twist drill in two.

At the other end of the spectrum, adjustable "expansion bits" are used for large holes. Augers are an alternative, of course—this is the work they are designed for—but with a single compact expansion bit you can cut any hole up to 3 in. Most expansion bits have a simple design—a single spur and cutting lip adjustable for different diameters. I find them awkward to use; they feel unbalanced and don't drill accurately in anything other than softwoods. They also need a brace with a large sweep to deliver the considerable power required for all but the smallest holes.

SHARPENING BITS

If you can sharpen a chisel, sharpening a boring bit is no more challenging. The cutting edges all are variations on the familiar chisel edge. Understanding the physics of how the bit cuts also helps with sharpening, but so does looking at the bit closely and simply tuning what's there, at least as a start. Bits other than twist drills are soft enough that they can be filed easily. Auger files are designed just for this task, with two tapered ends and safe edges on two sides and two faces so you can safely file one cutting bevel at a time. Needle files also work.

Twist bits are ideal for learning how to sharpen, because they are big enough to work on and their cutting edges are obvious. Watching how the bit cuts explains a lot about

To better understand sharpening the various parts, twist an auger bit into a piece of softwood to see how the lead screw pulls the bit into the wood, the spurs score around the hole, and the cutting lips chisel out the chips.

Sharpen the lips as you would a chisel, at about a 25° bevel angle, using small needle files or a special tapered auger file. File or hone the underside if possible.

File the cutting spurs as little as possible to prolong bit life, and only file on their inside face or you will change the cutting diameter of the bit and cause it to bind. The lead screw should need no tuning.

153

Useful for more than just drilling holes, braces can turn hollow augers, such as this one by A. A. Woods, used for cutting the round tenons on the ends of the bowback on a Windsor chair.

To help drill straight, Stanley at one time made a bit level that pinches the drill shank, or you can sight against a square (or two) placed on the work. Slip a piece of paper between your work and a waste block and you'll know you're through when you see bits of paper in with the chips.

Drill at a compound angle by sighting against a square and bevel gauge set to the required angle. A ruler establishes a sighting plane against the square, to keep the bit angled yet plumb. Steady yourself by planting your feet, leaning against the bench, and locking your upper body.

sharpening the various edges: As the lead screw pulls into the wood, the spurs are the first to cut (see the top photo on p. 153). They score around the hole, the horizontal cutting lips pare some chips, and the twist of the web spirals them out of the hole.

The spurs are the widest part of the bit, establishing the diameter of the hole. File them on the inside only, or you may alter the clearance of the bit. The spurs should be the same length and sharp on their leading edges. Both lips should cut equally, too. Turn the bit into soft wood to see that they start cutting at the same time. File the lips along the top bevel, being careful not to cut into the lead screw or spurs.

The back of the bevel is harder to sharpen; work it with a small file or a slipstone. Think of it as a small chisel, and file as little as possible to extend the life of the bit. A properly sharpened bit should work smooth–

ly, sending up consistent chips with clean round edges. Unless you use a bit often, you might go years without having to resharpen.

Learn to sharpen a twist bit, and a spoon bit or gimlet isn't much harder. Avoid any filing and instead hone the outside and inside edges that you can reach with a slipstone. The technique with both bits is to roll or rock them across the stone. Sharpening a spoon bit is similar to sharpening a gouge, except that you have to hone the rounded tip at a higher angle to the stone. Look at a teaspoon for the proper shape.

Using Braces and Hand Drills

Don't think of braces and hand drills merely as tools to bore holes. While this is what they do best, a brace is also a powerful tool for setting large screws or removing them, countersinking or reaming holes, cutting round tenons with a special tenon cutter, and even pointing their ends. As for drilling a few holes, a brace or hand drill is a pleasing alternative to an electric drill. It is not much slower and offers a lot more control. Learning to drill straight, on the other hand, takes practice.

Securing a bit in a brace might seem like a basic place to start, but it is not quite as simple as it appears. For the longest time I shoved bits into the chuck and just tightened down the outer shell, only to have the bit loosen after a few turns of

While a simple piece of tape or a wooden sleeve works for a depth stop (see the top photo on p. 152), Stanley manufactured two positive versions that clamp to the bit: the #47, which clamps to the drill shank, and the #49, which clamps to the spiral web.

Dowels make a quick and fairly strong joint, but the mating holes must be accurately drilled. This Stanley #59 doweling jig clamps square to an edge and holds various sizes of hardened bushings and drill bits. A shopmade alternative is to drill a length of hardwood (center) and use it as a guide.

Driven with a brace or by hand, dowel pointers cut like a pencil sharpener (which also works) to bevel the ends of dowels or any round part, such as a turned leg.

The simplest and quickest way to make dowels is to rough blanks through a dowel plate, a thick piece of steel with various sizes of holes drilled through it. Point the blank first with a dowel pointer or pencil sharpener (at center).

the brace. The trick is to pull the bit up so that the squared tang engages in the grooves of the jaws, and then tighten down the shell. In a pinch, a brace chuck will hold bits with smooth shanks, although a three-jawed chuck common in hand drills is more positive.

Drill bits vary in size so much (most twist bits are actually $\frac{1}{64}$ in. oversized) that drilling a test hole is always a good idea for the most accurate work. With an expansion bit it is vital. A properly sharpened bit should take only modest pressure to cut in long grain but far more into end grain. If more force is required, you can lean over the head of a

brace, pressuring it with a chest or thigh, or whatever works in some of the awkward positions you may find yourself when drilling holes in difficult places.

Start slowly, letting the spurs score the hole for a clean start. If you can, clamp your work to a bench or use a vise so you can concentrate on drilling. Back up your workpiece with a scrap, if possible, not only for a cleaner exit hole, but also for a place for the lead screw to bite into to finish the cut. Put a piece of paper between the two and when you see bits of paper in with the chips, you'll know you're through. Or you could drill until the point just pokes

through and finish by drilling from the other side.

Drilling straight with a brace or hand drill is challenging, but it's no more difficult than with an electric drill. I find it easiest to drill perpendicular when working vertically. Try to set your work up and stand so that you can see in both planes, and set up a square or bevel gauge on the work to sight against. Stanley made a little level that clamps onto the shank of a drill that helps, or you can make your own (see the top right photo on p. 154). For accuracy when drilling deep holes, drill from both sides toward the middle, if you can.

Sometimes I need to drill an accurate hole at an angle—a pocket hole for a screw, for instance—or a perpendicular hole for a knob and lockset on a door already hung. A hole drilled in a scrap at the right angle (best when done with a drill press) becomes an accurate jig when clamped to the work to guide the bit. Doweling jigs work on the same principle, only with hardened bushings for guides (see the bottom photo on p. 155). Drilling a series of holes in a piece of hardwood works as a doweling jig for one-time operations such as drilling a row of dowel holes in mating parts.

Dowel pointers are designed for easing the ends of dowels (on table-leaf pins, for instance) or round tenons. The pencil-sharpener action of a dowel pointer works best with a few slow and careful cranks using a brace (see the photo at left on the facing page). I find that countersinks work best this way, too, especially when countersinking holes already drilled. An electric drill simply cuts too fast and often with lots of chatter.

Countersinks come in a variety of patterns, from roseheads with multiple cutting flutes, to clean-cutting metalworking countersinks with a single cutting edge formed ingeniously by drilling an oblique hole through the head. This latter design also works well for counter-boring holes for plugs. Reamers are similar tools turned by hand or by brace, still used by chairmakers for tapering or enlarging holes to an exact diameter.

Chairmakers use round, tapered tenons and mortises for the leg-to-seat joint for a snug fit that tightens under pressure (but can be disassembled for repair). A reamer pares the mortise to a consistent taper and also can fine-tune the leg angle.

Most countersinks make dust rather than shavings and cut less than perfect holes. This unusual design, used mainly by machinists, cuts very cleanly and quickly no matter the speed or rotation and will counter-bore for a plug.

Use a hand drill or brace for reaming, boring, countersinking, or turning in a row of screws, and you will quickly appreciate its slow speed and the control you will have over the tool. Of course, electric drills and drill presses have their own advantages, earning them a place in any shop. Hand boring takes practice to master and can be slow, but then there are plenty of times when working a little slower suits me just fine.

10 SAWS

Before the advent of water-powered and electric saws, cutting wood to size was sweaty, hard work. Imagine the labor involved sawing logs into boards with a heavy 7-ft.-long pitsaw, one man on top and the other below under a steady rain of sawdust. Cutting the boards to size required rip and crosscut handsaws, or a large frame saw to shape them into chair seats, headboards, and curved wheel felloes. Joinery called for fine-toothed, brass-backed saws, and a host of specialty saws were used by carpenters and other tradesmen.

Even with contemporary machines, there is still a need for handsaws. Make a chair, join a curved apron to a leg, or cut a complex joint and you'll quickly see the versatility of sawing by hand. There's no better choice than a handsaw for superior control when making the most complicated cuts.

Before routers, the recesses in stair stringers for treads and risers were cut by hand with a stair saw and chisel. A hole the same diameter as the tread nosing gives a place to saw into. The beech body of the saw (top) by E. C. Atkins stiffens the narrow blade and acts as a depth stop. The saw in the foreground is blacksmith-made from a piece of old scythe blade.

While the physics of saws has changed little in 4,500 years, the variety of sizes, shapes, and functions has grown enormously—from the tiniest fretsaws to large ripsaws and specialized salt saws with noncorroding zinc blades.

THOMAS TURNER & CO., SUFFOLK WORKS, SHEFFIELD.

Bygone Saws

Unlike many other hand tools, saws haven't changed much in 4,500 years. There aren't many Bronze Age saws around to compare with a modern handsaw, but enough to see the similarities. Both have thin metal blades, the teeth are only slightly different (even allowing for millennia of deterioration), and the bronze blade is curved like a pruning saw and narrower than the straight, wide blade of a steel handsaw.

The bronze saw even has some of the subtleties of later saws, such as finer teeth filed into the toe of the saw to help start a cut. Likewise, to overcome the weakness of the thin blades, ancient saws cut on the pull stroke, like Japanese saws. Early saws probably didn't cut all that rapidly, but all of the physics were there.

Bronze is a sufficiently malleable material to form into wide, thin sawblades, but this wasn't the case with iron, a superior material, until the metallurgy of steelmaking was mastered. The difficulty was forging a blade strong and stiff enough to cut on the push stroke without buckling. Pushing lets you get your body behind the stroke, and it's a big advantage for holding the work simply and firmly—against a sawhorse, for instance. (Remember, this was before fancy benches and vises, when lashing a board to a tree was one holding strategy.)

One solution to overcome the buckling problem was to forge a narrow blade and tension it in a wooden frame. Eventually, master smiths in places like Sheffield, England, developed the means to make sheet steel for flexible and strong handsaws in many shapes and styles. There have been only minor changes since, such as refining the shape of the teeth for more efficient and rapid cutting.

HOW SAWS CUT

For all their numerous variations— from coarse-toothed pitsaws to tiny coping saws—handsaws cut wood in only two ways: either along the grain (ripping) or across the grain (crosscutting). How they cut depends primarily on the shape of the teeth, and to a lesser extent on the fineness of the teeth. A ripsaw will cut across the grain, but not very efficiently, just as a crosscut saw will rip. You can file a saw to cut both ways modestly well (as I explain later). This is useful for joinery, for instance, where you might make a rip cut one minute and a crosscut the next.

To see the differences between the teeth of a ripsaw and crosscut saw, you have to look closely. Because cutting with the grain is no different than planing or chiseling along the fibers, ripsaws have the same chisel-shaped teeth, square

Saws cut wood in one of two ways: along the grain (ripping) or across the grain (cross-cutting). Chisel-like rip teeth (bottom) pare curly shavings, whereas the beveled knives of crosscut teeth (top) score and cut the ends of the fibers into a fine dust.

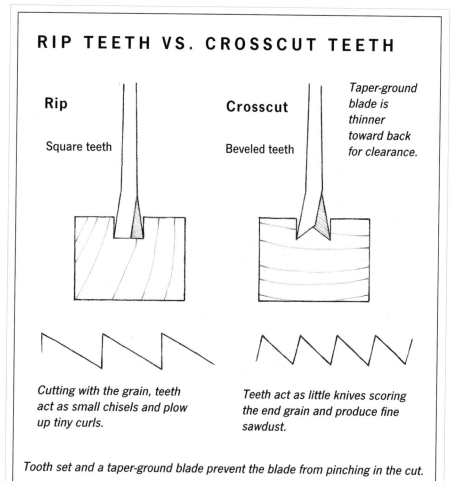

RIP TEETH VS. CROSSCUT TEETH

Rip

Square teeth

Cutting with the grain, teeth act as small chisels and plow up tiny curls.

Crosscut

Beveled teeth

Teeth act as little knives scoring the end grain and produce fine sawdust.

Taper-ground blade is thinner toward back for clearance.

Tooth set and a taper-ground blade prevent the blade from pinching in the cut.

The coarseness or fineness of a saw is measured in the number of tooth points per inch, always one more than the number of complete teeth per inch. The fewer the teeth, the quicker and rougher the cut.

Setting, or bending the tips of the teeth alternately outward and slightly wider than the thickness of the sawblade, creates the necessary clearance to prevent the blade from binding.

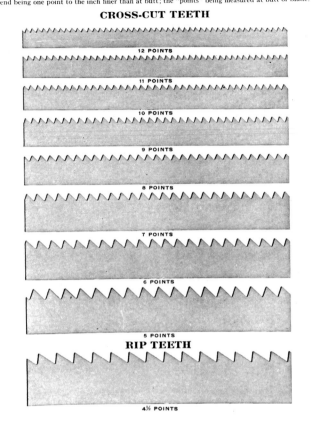

ORDER ALL HAND SAWS BY THE NUMBER OF POINTS TO THE INCH

The following cuts are full size of the respective number of teeth and points per inch which they represent. It will be noticed that in one inch space, there is **one tooth less** than there are **points.**

Rip Saw Teeth six points and coarser are graduated from butt to point of blade, the narrow end being one point to the inch finer than at butt; the "points" being measured at butt of blade.

CROSS-CUT TEETH

12 POINTS

11 POINTS

10 POINTS

9 POINTS

8 POINTS

7 POINTS

6 POINTS

5 POINTS

RIP TEETH

4½ POINTS

with the direction of the cut. They plow up little curls—miniature shavings—quite different from the fine sawdust from a crosscut saw. Rip teeth cutting across the grain cut roughly, tearing up the fibers much like a rabbet plane without a nicker. Crosscut teeth are filed into little knives that score the fibers on each side of the cut. The bits of weak grain between them break away and are swept out by the teeth. The "gullet" or valley between each tooth holds the sawdust. In a fast-cutting pulp saw, the gullets are large and special raker teeth clean the sawdust out of the saw cut, or kerf, as it's called.

In addition to the shape of the teeth (and there are many variations of the basic shapes), saws are further distinguished by the number of teeth—more specifically, the number of tooth points per inch (which is one point more than the actual number of complete teeth found in one inch of blade). This number can range from as few as 2 points in a ripsaw to as many as 25 points in fine dovetail and coping saws. (The number of points is often stamped on a handsaw blade below the handle.) Large coarse teeth cut quickly, especially in softwoods, whereas in hardwoods more teeth per inch are desirable for a smoother cut.

If the teeth were merely filed onto the bottom edge of the sawblade, the saw would bind in the cut after a few strokes. My father, who understood little of the subtleties of saws, used to liberally swab a saw with oil before using it, in order to prevent binding. So did pit sawyers. It's a messy solution to a simple problem: The teeth don't have enough "set," or slight outward bend, which allows them to cut a kerf slightly wider than the thickness of the blade. You need a lot more set sawing green wood than dry hardwood; in fact, fine dovetail saws work best with almost no set at all.

Some saw manufacturers added a further refinement to their best handsaws that also prevents binding: They taper-ground the blade thinner toward the back and the tip. In

Sheffield, grinders pressed sawblades (backed by a flat board) against huge water-powered stones all day, flattening and taper-grinding them. Not only do such handsaws work sweetly with a minimum of set, but in musical hands such saws can also be "played" to sound like a violin.

Whether for playing or cutting wood, no single saw, or even two or three, will do it all. You could get by with one set of chisels or a single brace, but you will need more than a couple of saws because there are just too many different ways to saw wood—crosscutting or ripping boards to length and width, cutting curved parts, or cutting joinery, inlays or fretwork, to name just a few. There are special saws for every woodworking task, varying in size, shape, and tooth pattern, as well as quite different Japanese saws that have become increasingly popular. Depending on what kind of work you do, you might need specialized saws such as veneer and flush-cutting saws. Machines can do a lot, but so far they haven't replaced all of these saws.

Types of Saws

There are easily dozens of types of saws, and dozens of variations within each type. Some variation is purely the result of different saw designs for different cutting tasks; for example, huge pitsaws and crosscut saws—yesteryear's sawmills—compared to tiny backsaws for cutting fine joinery. Other differences can only be explained as regional tastes or the preferred saw styles of certain trades. American and British craftsmen loved backsaws; Continental craftsman preferred bowsaws. Between the two groups dozens of variations of both types of saws evolved, however subtle in their differences, to suit the work exactly.

PITSAWS AND CROSSCUT SAWS

Sawmills have replaced the pitsaws that once cut every board and plank by human power alone and with tremendous effort. Today, from our machine-dominated perspective, it's

Only slightly exaggerated, the two Japanese sawyers in this print by Hokusai Katsushuka (1760-1849) rip boards from a balk resting on a trestle with huge, coarse-toothed *maebiki-nokogiri*. Two men pitsaw, while another man sits at a stump filing and setting their saws.

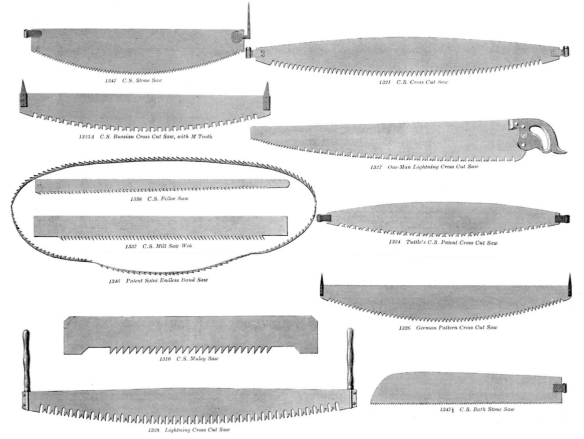

Loggers once felled and cut trees to length with one- and two-man crosscut saws, yesteryear's chainsaws. Given colorful names such as Lightening, Lumberman, and Great American, each saw had a different tooth design to cut more quickly or smoothly.

1347 C.S. Stone Saw

1321 C.S. Cross Cut Saw

1323A C.S. Russian Cross Cut Saw, with M Tooth

1327 One-Man Lightning Cross Cut Saw

1338 C.S. Felloe Saw

1337 C.S. Mill Saw Web

1324 Tuttle's C.S. Patent Cross Cut Saw

1346 Patent Solid Endless Band Saw

1326 German Pattern Cross Cut Saw

1310 C.S. Muley Saw

1347½ C.S. Bath Stone Saw

1328 Lightning Cross Cut Saw

hard to appreciate the importance of the pitsaw and its partner, the crosscut saw, for felling trees and bucking them to length. Yet these are some of the most important tools of our woodworking heritage, tools that in one sense made all other woodworking possible.

Not all lumber was sawn over a pit, but it certainly was a common and not overly complicated way to work logs into usable lumber. Besides boards and planks, shipwrights pitsawed large curved futtocks (ribs), knees, and stems, and wheelwrights felloes and wagon parts from crooked logs. All that was needed was a 6-ft.-deep pit 12 ft. to 14 ft. long, with a couple of logs across the top for support. Roll a log on,

snap a few chalklines down its length to mark the cut, and saw away.

Early pitsaws were of the framed type with a narrow blade, 4 ft. to 5 ft. long—the only shape possible with the limited knowledge of iron metallurgy. Later versions resembled long handsaws, up to 10 ft. in length, with coarse teeth, a tiller handle on one end, and a removable box handle (so it could be slid into or out of the log) for the pit man to grab. (A pitsaw's other name, "whipsaw," gives a sense of the narrowness and flexibility of the blade.)

Nathaniel Dominy of the well-known Dominy family of craftsmen was probably typical of 18th-century furniture makers in that he owned a pitsaw with others and shared its

use. Eventually, water power replaced manpower and single pitsaws were ganged together to slice a log into many boards at once.

Axes and crosscut saws were the tools of the logger for felling trees and sawing them to length. Used by one or two men, crosscut saws (sometimes as long as 16 ft.) improved upon the shape and design of pitsaw teeth to work faster, to clear the kerf of sawdust more easily, or just to cut more sweetly. These tools live on at lumberjack contests, where savvy contestants know to start sawing on the shaded side of a log or risk breaking off the sharp points of their saw teeth on the sun-hardened side. Both pitsaws and crosscut saws also survive in the poorest and most remote areas of the world, where there is a need for lumber and no sawmills to supply it. Chainsaws are rapidly replacing these venerable old tools.

FRAME SAWS

Once the lumber was sawn from the log, smaller versions of the framed pitsaw were used to cut it to shape or to resaw it into thinner stock (for drawer bottoms, for instance). The frame design is ancient, originating with the Romans. The blades are narrow and thin, the frames rigid enough to tension the blade to keep it running true and make it less apt to buckle.

A thin blade was an advantage for sawing veneers, where less of the valuable wood was wasted in sawdust. For curved parts commonly used by chairmakers, wheelwrights and a whole host of other trades, a narrow blade was used for cutting along a tight radius. From large chairmakers' saws to smaller bowsaws, these were the bandsaws of a hand-powered shop.

Once the technology needed for producing high-quality steel plate for handsaws was mastered, British and American craftsmen adopted the handsaw, and its many variations, over frame saws. Continental craftsman continued to use framed saws of some kind, and still do. I understand why. It's partly a matter of custom and the conservative nature of woodworkers clinging to the tools they learn with and know, and partly the efficiency of the tools themselves. There is not much cut-

Essentially a hand-powered bandsaw, a turning saw was the choice of chairmakers and wheelwrights for cutting curved seats and wheel felloes. Just like a deep throat on a bandsaw, the large ash frame allows plenty of maneuverability, while the ram's-head nuts maintain blade tension.

ting resistance with a thin blade. It will cut straight lines as easily as it will cut curves (something handsaws don't do as well). I've seen dovetails—waste and all—cut in one continuous motion with a bowsaw. I still use a bowsaw for curved work too large or awkward to carry to a bandsaw.

For sawing smaller logs into veneer or thin boards (for drawer bottoms), or for extra thick parts such as bed posts, craftsmen used a frame saw. The thin blade held in tension in a stiff frame cuts a thin kerf, wasting less wood and cutting more easily than a thicker blade.

A framed bowsaw can cut dovetails as easily as it can follow a curve. Steady the blade against a fingernail to start, shift to sawing with both hands on the front handle, and use smooth, full-length strokes.

ASK A HUNDRED woodworkers if they know what a table saw is, and you can bet that all will describe the stationary machine found in workshops everywhere. But through the last half of the 19th century, a table saw was a handsaw—an enlarged version of a compass or keyhole saw—with an open handle and a long, narrow blade. The "hand-table saw" is no longer in use, and there remains some confusion about what it was actually used for. Some believe that it was for cutting round table tops, while others think that it was used in fitting the mating surfaces (or "tables") of a scarf joint. 🐾

Think saws and classic rip and crosscut handsaws likely come to mind. Among the more unusual (left to right) are a saw with a shapely handle carved in the profile of a panther, a Disston combination saw complete with level, plumb, square, and awl, and a Disston practical double-sided saw—two saws in one.

You could build a bowsaw quite easily, in a style and size that suits your needs, and get a great amount of enjoyment doing it. A simple design has loose mortise-and-tenon joints to join the stretcher with the sides. The blade is attached to turned handles that rotate for cutting at different angles and is tensioned with a simple toggle and twisted cord. You can buy narrow blades or make your own by refiling a piece of a bandsaw blade.

HANDSAWS

In the English tradition, handsaws rather than bowsaws are the tools that most quickly spring to mind when imagining a saw. With flat blades tapered heel to toe and shapely handles so comfortable you can almost forget you are grasping them, classic handsaws are elegance

Among the rarest of the rare and prized by every saw collector is a panther saw by Woodrough and McParlin Saw Company of Cincinnati, Ohio (c. 1880). Flowing from the shapely lines of the handle and incised decoration is the head of a growling panther.

itself. Before power saws, handsaws were the most used saws in any shop. They were used for ripping boards to width, crosscutting them to length, and, with an unusual variation called a table saw, for cutting around modest curves as well.

"Handsaw" is quite a general term for saws that vary from 1 ft. to 2½ ft. in length, some with coarse teeth and others with fine teeth. What distinguishes them from other saws is their wide, thin blades unsupported by any frame or thickened back, and a single handle with a closed or open grip.

As ancient as saws are, the design is relatively modern, able to be made only after it was possible to manufacture large and flexible sheets of steel. The earliest (and for a long time the best) handsaws came from makers such as Spear and Jackson in Sheffield, England, with its long tradition of making high-quality edge tools and superior cast and spring steels. Henry Disston learned the

DISSTON

WARRANTED REFINED CRUCIBLE STEEL, PATENT GROUND AND TEMPERED, HAND, PANEL AND RIP SAWS

Refined Crucible Steel, Highly Polished Blade, Warranted, Apple Handle. Carved and Polished, Brass Screws.

America's largest saw manufacturer, Henry Disston & Sons, improved on English designs to produce a skewed-back hand-saw for a lighter, more flexible, and grace-ful saw. It was just one of hundreds of different saws offered in their catalog of 1914, and, in this age of handsaws, sold by the dozen.

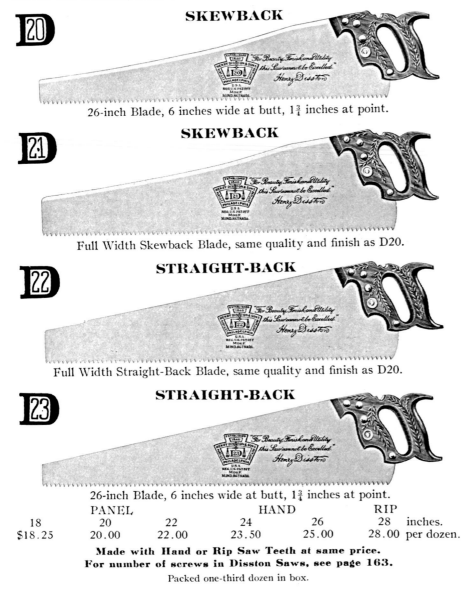

SKEWBACK

26-inch Blade, 6 inches wide at butt, 1¾ inches at point.

SKEWBACK

Full Width Skewback Blade, same quality and finish as D20.

STRAIGHT-BACK

Full Width Straight-Back Blade, same quality and finish as D20.

STRAIGHT-BACK

26-inch Blade, 6 inches wide at butt, 1¾ inches at point.

PANEL			HAND		RIP	
18	20	22	24	26	28	inches.
$18.25	20.00	22.00	23.50	25.00	28.00	per dozen.

Made with Hand or Rip Saw Teeth at same price.
For number of screws in Disston Saws, see page 163.

Packed one-third dozen in box.

> HANDSAWS come in many different lengths—24 in., 26 in., and 28 in., to name a few. Why so many sizes? One obvious answer is that small tasks require smaller saws, but there is more to it than that. Each of us has an optimum saw length related to the distance of our natural sawing stroke. Use too short a saw, and it will jump out of the cut. Use one too long, and you won't use all of the blade, wearing the teeth unevenly as a result. Pretend you are sawing and measure a comfortable stroke to determine the best saw length for you.

and can cut quite aggressively without tearing out the fibers. I use a 4-point ripsaw infrequently, but it's the best saw for timber framing or for ripping a valuable board that is too awkward to cut with a bandsaw. It cuts a narrow kerf, and the wide blade guides the cut. On the other hand, I have a number of crosscut saws—with 6, 8, and 10 points—and I use them often for cutting boards roughly to size, or for cutting long or heavy parts to length at my bench. Numerous machines can do the same thing, but it is often easier to reach for a saw, mark out the cut, and quietly start in.

trade at Spear and Jackson, emigrated to America with his knowledge, and in 1840 started his Keystone Saw, Tool, Steel, and File Works. Disston grew to be the largest maker of saws in the world, producing almost 200 different types of handsaws in a typical year. More than likely, any used saw you find will be a Disston.

Other than the shape of the teeth, there is no difference between a rip and crosscut handsaw. Ripsaws generally have fewer points per inch, since they are cutting with the grain

WHAT'S THE PURPOSE of the little nib on the end of fine handsaws? Is it there for decoration, as some suggest, or is it a place to secure a cord to tie on a saw guard? Is it a special tooth for starting a cut? If it's important to the function of the saw, why do some saws have it and others do not?

While a nib is useful for holding one end of a saw guard (a slotted cover, usually wood, that protects the teeth), its origins go back to the earliest handsaws. Late-17th-century Dutch handsaws had quite fanciful decorative curls where we find a nib today. Less elaborate nibs must have been on English saws at about the same time, because Moxon, one of the earliest writers about various trades and tools, illustrates one in 1683. Disston and others carried on the tradition. ✺

The little nib on the end of fine handsaws has sparked much curiosity about its function and origins. It's a vestigial decoration dating back to the 17th century.

Outwardly, modern saws don't look much different from classic Disstons. The teeth might have a more aggressive shape influenced by Japanese saws, they might be impulse-hardened (electrically made extremely hard but unfileable) to hold up to manmade materials, and the handle may be plastic rather than wood.

Some cut easily, but using them is nothing like the experience of an older saw. For one thing, the balance feels different. Disston's skew-back saws—some of the most graceful—feel light even though the blade is long. Taper-grinding further lightens the blade, giving it flexibility and a sweet cutting action with minimum set. The handles are beautifully polished apple, beech, or figured maple that conform to the hand with a place for every finger. Every detail of an older saw speaks of a tool designed to be used day in, day out.

BACKSAWS

Backsaws, a variation of handsaws, will never become obsolete in any shop doing challenging high-quality work—or in one where you enjoy working quietly by hand. For cutting joinery or any fine sawing task, a backsaw is versatile and accurate. A backsaw has much finer teeth than a typical handsaw, along with a thinner blade stiffened with steel or, on the best saws, a brass rib folded

For cutting joinery accurately, a backsaw combines the virtues of fine teeth and a thin blade, which is stiffened by a brass or steel rib folded over the top edge. A snug-fitting wooden sleeve protects the blade from getting bent and the delicate teeth from getting damaged.

Possibly the oldest dated tool in England, the dovetail saw at top is dated 1756, though it is no different from a good modern saw. Below it is an uncommon table saw with a long flexible blade, and a long carcase saw for sawing large joinery.

over the top edge. The rib prevents the saw from cutting very deeply, but it is a perfect design for cutting a narrow kerf right to a line.

At a minimum you will want to have at least two different sizes of backsaws: a 12-point tenon saw, 12 in. to 16 in. long with a handsaw-type handle either open or closed; and a smaller, finer dovetail saw (15 or more points per inch), with a straight-turned handle known as a "gent's" handle. Unless you are cutting thin wood, it's not an advantage to have finer teeth on your dovetail saw; they cut more slowly, giving you more chance to wander off your line.

For exacting work, I have a bead-saw with extremely fine teeth. This kind of saw can be used for slicing inlays, or for sawing around a shoulder of a dry-fit mortise and tenon to fit it exactly. A shop of a century ago would have had a number of other sizes of backsaws: a carcase saw, sash saw, and long miter saw used in a miter box. These saws vary only in length, blade width, and in the fineness of their teeth.

Cutting the cheek of a tenon is a rip cut; cutting the shoulder is a crosscut. Because these two joinery tasks are common, the backsaw you use will be more useful if you can file it to do both types of cutting. This certainly is a subtlety, considering how difficult it is to file the small teeth of a backsaw anyway, and it doesn't improve the quality of the cut, just the cutting speed. Nevertheless, I explain this along with filing and setting fine-toothed saws later in this chapter.

Among the author's collection of everyday joinery saws are fine-toothed dovetail saws with both closed and turned "gent's-style" handles, a half-backsaw with a blade flexible enough to be used for flush cutting, and unhandled bead saws with very fine teeth.

The extremely thin blade and unset teeth of a Japanese flush-cutting saw allow you to flex it flat to saw off screw plugs, proud tenons, or pins locking a joint, without marring the surface. The wooden-handled version in the background has teeth set only on the top side for the same reason.

FLUSH-CUTTING AND VENEER SAWS

First cousins to backsaws are flush-cutting saws—useful for cutting off proud through-tenons, screw-hole plugs, or pins locking a joint—and veneer saws. In most variations of these saws, a thin flexible blade has a partial back to stiffen it, and the teeth are set on one side only (sometimes, as with Japanese saws, they have no set at all). This allows a flush-cutting saw to cut flat against a finished surface (unset side down) without scoring it.

When trimming veneer to size, a veneer saw is usually guided against a straightedge. The unset teeth against the straightedge will not dull, or wear the straightedge. Uneven set has another advantage: The saw cuts toward the set side and away from the straightedge, or finished surface, in the case of the flush-cutting saw. Because the blades are thin and flexible, they most often cut on the pull stroke.

JAPANESE SAWS

At one time all saws cut on the pull stroke, for the simple reason that the blades were not strong enough to resist buckling and bending if they were pushed. As soon as it was possible to make flexible steel for saw-blades, Western saws got turned

It's safer to cut veneer with a saw guided against a straightedge than with a knife that can follow the grain. A veneer saw has fine teeth set on only one side to avoid dulling them against a steel straightedge.

Japanese saws, designed to be pulled, are very different from their Western counterparts. A pulled blade is in tension, which means it can be thinner, less flexible, and the steel can be tempered harder. Add in complex tooth bevels, and you have saws that work easily and stay sharp a long time.

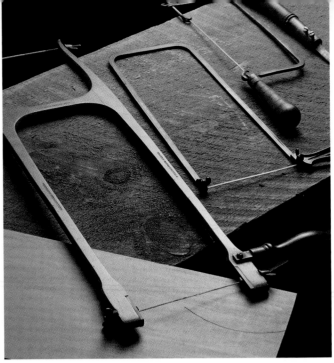

Call them fretsaws, coping saws, or jigsaws (front to back), they are all small frame saws with fine and narrow blades for cutting along tight curves, coping a joint, or cutting inlay and marquetry. A key-hole or pad saw (rear), a close cousin, has a wider, stiffer blade.

around so that almost all of them cut on the push stroke. The Japanese, on the other hand, never gave up pulling their saws. One explanation is that Japanese craftsmen work from a sitting position, in which case pulling is more powerful. On the other hand, sawing from a standing position allows the whole upper body to power the push stroke.

Whether used sitting or standing, the advantages of Japanese saws are compelling enough that many craftsmen who use no other Japanese tools are likely to have a *dozuki* or *ryoba*, two common types of Japanese saws, for cutting dovetails and joinery.

A blade that cuts on the pull stroke can also be very thin, since it will be in tension and not subjected to the buckling forces of pushing. A thin blade cuts with less effort than a thicker blade, removing less wood to cut as deeply. For both reasons Japanese sawblades can be tempered harder than Western saws. Hard blades mean hard teeth, which stay sharp longer. Japanese saws also have more sophisticated tooth shapes, with different patterns depending on whether you are cutting hardwood or softwood. You can now buy Western saws with Japanese-style teeth, diamond-cut and sharpened.

For someone learning to saw dovetails or tenons, there are definite advantages to using Japanese

saws. Right out of the box they are generally better tuned and thus more accurate than a new Western saw. Pulling feels quite natural—that is, unless you have pushed a saw all your life, as I have. Once you get the feel, controlling the blade right to a line is not difficult. Particularly nice is the fine kerf they cut. The only disadvantages are that you cannot sharpen your own saws (unless you are a *metate-shokunin,* a master saw sharpener), and the hard teeth are brittle and quite easy to snap off.

COPING, FRET-, AND COMPASS SAWS
When it comes to coping saws and fretsaws, both framed saws with very fine blades, the debate over pushing

versus pulling still goes on. Sometimes I push; other times I pull. It all depends on how fine a blade I am using and whether I am cutting horizontally or vertically.

Coping saws and fretsaws are simply small bowsaws, sometimes called jigsaws. Their blades are fine-toothed, in the range of 14 to 30 points, and so narrow that it is easy to cut around curves—the most important function of these saws. Blades can be removed easily so you can shift from pushing to pulling, or start a piercing cut within a drilled hole.

As with other framed saws, the frame gives the blade stability by holding it in tension. The blade in a coping saw can swivel 360° so that you can saw in any direction and not have the frame in the way.

A fretsaw has a fixed blade, but often a much deeper throat.

Whether you push or pull, the side you are cutting toward may splinter out slightly. This can obscure your line. Coping two moldings or cutting out the waste from a set of dovetails—typical uses for a coping saw—I can see my lines clearly if I push, and it feels natural to me.

Really thin blades break or don't track well when they're pushed, so I pull them and try to saw vertically, handle down. I support the work flat on my bench, overhanging it just enough to work the saw. For delicate work, such as cutting out decorative fretwork or marquetry, I clamp a board with a V-cutout in my vise to support the work. Sawing on the pull stroke (within the V), I can see the line clearly.

Pad or keyhole saws were often shopmade from a piece of broken sawblade fitted to a handle. A Japanese keyhole saw (on the bench) that cuts on the pull stroke gives good control cutting delicate keyholes or working into tight places.

Compass, pad, and keyhole saws are all names for similar long and narrow-bladed saws without any frames. They will also cut around curves, although not as well as a coping saw or fretsaw. They can cut anywhere with just a drilled hole to get started in. Because the blade is tapered, you can saw tighter curves and reach into very small openings (such as keyholes) by using just the tip. The handle of a pad saw is hollow, so just as much blade as you need can be exposed. The teeth on all of these saws are quite coarse, and the blades are too thick (so they don't buckle) to cut a smooth hole. But when you need one, there's no other choice.

The fine, narrow blade of a coping saw allows you to change direction easily, when sawing a tenon and haunch in one continuous motion, for example. The blade pivots in the frame (note the levers front and back) for even more maneuverability.

Usually the first step in tuning an old saw is cleaning off surface rust with emery cloth and fine steel wool to restore the blade close to its original shine. An occasional wipe of paste wax (on the blade and the handle, too) will keep your saws working sweetly and prevent rusting.

Saw Maintenance

Other than sharpening—no small feat to master—most saws need little maintenance or tuning. Any saw works best with an occasional waxing, the handle bolts must be kept snug to keep the handle secure, and the inevitable kinks should be straightened out. When it comes time for a sharpening, the details of which are explained on pp. 175–181, once you learn the basics you can sharpen nearly any saw you own.

TUNING

The brightly polished steel blade of any saw will rust, especially in a damp shop or in one that experiences large swings in temperature (because the steel will sweat). Most secondhand saws have some rust. I would avoid buying one that's pitted, although you can restore it to usable condition with fine abrasive paper and steel wool. Keep your saws rust-free and working sweetly by giving them an occasional wipe with paste wax. Wax or oil the handle and other wooden parts.

Saw handles can break or work loose. You can't control a saw with a loose handle. Making a new handle is fun and not very difficult—and it's a perfect place to use that exotic scrap you've been saving. Chapter 11 includes some patterns for beautiful and comfortable handles (see p. 200).

Special two-part bolts secure the handle to the saw (one part screws into the other for a flush finish on the handle); a high-quality handsaw has four or five bolts. Tighten the

The bolts that secure the handle to the blade screw into one another. To eliminate any handle looseness, tighten each bolt with a thin-bladed screwdriver. (They sometimes bottom out before they are snug, so file the bolt shorter if necessary.) A small carriage bolt makes a good substitute for any missing handle bolts.

A kinked blade will not saw straight. Sight down the blade to find any kinks, mark them with chalk or tape, and then bend them out against a hard edge such as your bench, using concentrated pressure with your thumbs and slightly less with your palms.

SHARPENING

Sharpening a saw is tricky and time-consuming but no more difficult than tuning a plane or sharpening a chisel. I find that the hardest part isn't jointing, setting, and filing the saw but simply seeing the teeth, especially on fine saws. So start with a 5- or 6-point handsaw whose teeth are clearly visible, but don't use your best saw until you get the feel for sharpening.

If you protect your saws with blade guards when not in use, and keep them from running onto hardware, they will stay sharp a long time, and you won't need to file them very often. In the 20 years I have had the same dovetail saw, I have sharpened it just twice. Not everyone will want to sharpen their own saws, but if you do they will cut effortlessly and accurately.

A couple of caveats: You can't sharpen Japanese saws (at least most

bolts with a screwdriver (older ones use a special slotted screwdriver). Unfortunately, missing bolts are not easy to replace without stealing some from another handle, and even then they are likely to be a different size. A small carriage bolt makes a serviceable (though not elegant) substitute.

Sometimes a saw binds, flexes too much, and kinks. It can happen because the saw is dull, there is too little set to handle the damp wood you're sawing, or because you are working too aggressively. Even stiff backsaws will kink. Sawblade steel is flexible enough to take some bending, but bad kinks can crack a blade

(and, with Japanese saws, break off a few teeth).

However bad the kink, as long as the blade is not cracked, you probably can work it out (and will have to or your saw will not cut straight). First, find and mark the kink by sighting down the blade. Bend the saw over the edge of your bench to straighten a mild kink. You'll need to hammer out a severe one. In this case, lay the saw on your bench or anvil and flatten the kink with a ball peen hammer. Unfortunately, any kink weakens a saw just enough that it will likely kink again in the same place. The best you can do is keep it properly set and sharp.

SAW STEEL is spring steel, with a certain amount of elasticity. For the same reason that a frame saw holds its blade in tension, and Japanese saws are pulled (tensioned) as they cut, a traditional handsaw will work best if the cutting edge is in tension. Saw doctors (the specialists who make and tune saws) use hammers with slightly crowned faces to tension the blade. By spreading the steel in the center of the sawblade, putting it in compression, the edge is put into tension. Circular saws work in a similar way: As the blade heats up and expands, a slight amount of tension along the edge helps keep the cutting edge stiff. ✺

Careless sharpening results in misshapen teeth of different heights, so that no matter how sharp they are, only some are cutting. It's time to joint the teeth level, file them to a consistent shape, and set and sharpen them.

of us can't, because the tooth geometry is too complicated). Nor is it worth your while to file a coping saw—just replace the blade. First, I'll describe a method that works for any saw up to about 12 points per inch, and then another method for fine-toothed saws that speeds up sharpening considerably and creates a combination tooth suitable for both ripping and crosscutting.

Sharpening a saw is similar to tuning a hand scraper (see pp. 129-132). Just as you can burnish down the edge of a scraper blade and roll it back up again without going through the whole process of jointing and honing, the same is true with a saw. File the teeth lightly and stay away from nails, and you can delay a complete overhaul. This involves jointing the teeth so all the points are the same height, reshaping them to the same size with the proper angles, setting them, and then filing them sharp.

To do any sharpening, you'll need a saw vise of some kind (you can make one from two boards clamped in a side vise), good light, a mill file for jointing, and a double, extra-slim, tapered saw file (one 6 in. to 7 in. long for handsaws and one 4 in. long for fine-toothed saws).

The key to the whole sharpening process is good light. You have to be able to see each tooth clearly and the glint from the sharpened bevels. For me, this means natural light, morning light if possible, against the far side of the saw. If you rely on electric lights, a clip-on light shining right where you are working helps greatly.

The key to sharpening is good light—bright natural light against the far side of the blade is ideal—along with a sturdy saw vise, such as this shopmade one with wooden screws, cushioning leather washers, and holes for storing files.

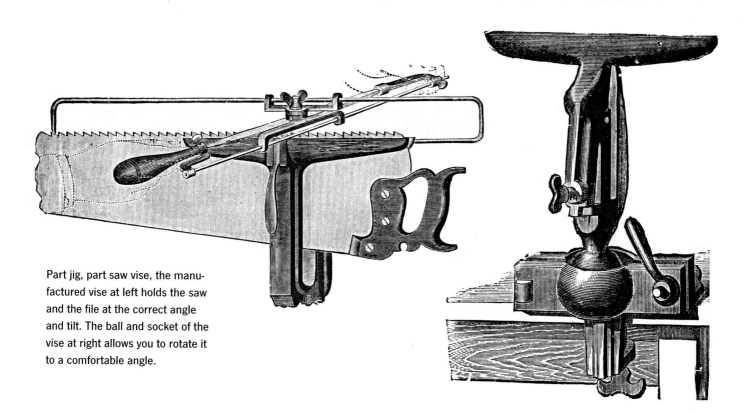

Part jig, part saw vise, the manufactured vise at left holds the saw and the file at the correct angle and tilt. The ball and socket of the vise at right allows you to rotate it to a comfortable angle.

The first step in sharpening is to joint the teeth to a consistent height, leaving the edge slightly crowned end to end. With a manufactured jointer or a simple shopmade one, file just enough to create a small flat at the top of each tooth.

Jointing the teeth

Assuming you have worked out any kinks and your blade is straight, the first step is to joint the teeth to an even height. I always make a light jointing pass, even if I am just filing the teeth. Even teeth cut smoothly.

The same wooden block with a groove for a mill file that you use for jointing a scraper works for a saw (see p. 130), or you can use a manufactured jointer. Good saws have a subtle crown to the cutting edge, just enough to be noticeable when you sight down the blade. Run the jointer over the teeth from end to end, crowning it by working the ends slightly more, until you just see a bright flat spot at the top of each tooth.

Shaping the teeth

The next step—shaping the teeth—is definitely the trickiest part of sharpening. Even careful filing cuts more off one tooth than another, until after a couple of filings the teeth are not identical. They don't really have to be, but your saw will work noticeably better the closer they are. The best guide is to follow the existing tooth shape. (Go by the ones near the handle; they are the least used and sharpened.) This is also the time to fine-tune the angle of the teeth for a more aggressive hook, if you want.

It's no accident that a sawtooth gullet is a 60° notch, the same angle as a triangular file. Running the file in the gullet you can cut both the back of one tooth and the front of another. Ripsaws and crosscut saws have different tooth shapes, which you will need to keep in mind during this step. Rip teeth slant backward about 3°, and crosscut teeth about 15° or more. The angles are approximate and a matter of preference, although the smaller the angle the more aggressive the tooth. To help maintain this angle, I make a simple guide from a softwood scrap with the appropriate angle marked on it, which I drive onto the tip of the file. If I keep the guide level, I know the front angle of the teeth will be the same.

The saw should be in a vise for this step, with the teeth just above the jaws. Grab the file in both hands, one hand on the handle and the other at the tip guiding the cut, and hold the file in a horizontal position. Feel the gullet with the file and stroke across. By pressuring the file forward, backward, or down, you can cut more off one tooth than another to shape each one. The flats jointed on the tops of the teeth also guide you. Try to leave an equal flat on the top of each tooth and the gullets an even depth.

Setting the teeth

The next step is setting the teeth. Traditionally this was done with a saw wrest, a steel tool with different-width slots slipped over the tooth and levered to bend it. Another method is to use a special hammer and anvil, bending one tooth at a time. A pliers-type set (available new) is the easiest to use and is very consistent.

How much set you bend into each tooth is a matter of experience and knowing what kind of work you will be doing with that saw. You need a lot of set to saw green wood, but in dry hardwood only the smallest amount is required. A good

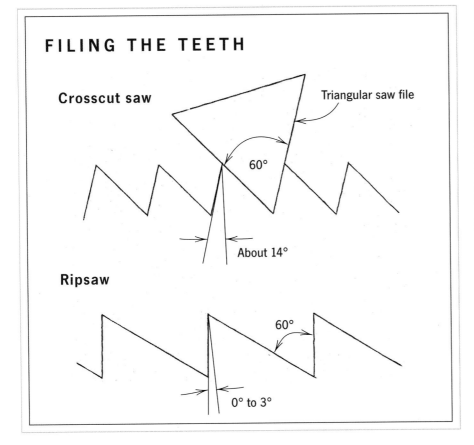

FILING THE TEETH

Crosscut saw

Triangular saw file

60°

About 14°

Ripsaw

60°

0° to 3°

Traditional methods of setting saw teeth include slotted saw wrests (at right) that slip over each tooth to bend it over slightly, H. Aikens patent (1830) anvil set struck to bend each tooth (bottom), or a wooden saw-setting block with a plunger hit with a setter's hammer that works on the same principle (top).

Each squeeze of the handles of this pliers-type saw set presses the top third of a tooth between a small plunger and a beveled anvil, bending it a uniform amount. The anvil adjusts up or down for more or less set and for larger or smaller teeth.

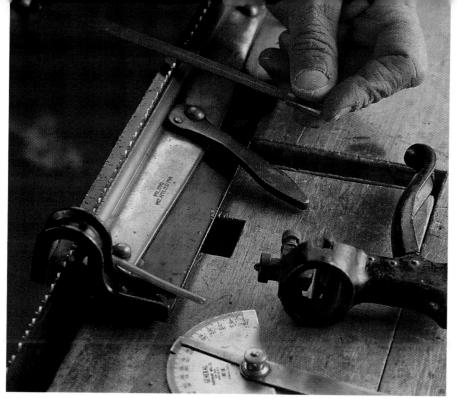

File the back face of a tooth set away from you and the front face of one set toward you—straight across for a ripsaw and at an angle of 60° to 75° for a crosscut saw. Lock your wrists to keep the file face cutting a rip tooth vertical and a crosscut tooth slanted back 12° or more. File every other tooth, then turn the saw around to file the rest.

rule of thumb is an overall set equal to 1½ times the thickness of the blade.

Bend just the top half or third of each tooth. I like to hold the saw in my lap while setting, so that I can easily move it to get the best light where I am working. Follow what is there and work from one end to the other setting half the teeth one way, then back to the other end to set the other half.

Filing the teeth

If your saw is only somewhat dull, you can skip all of these steps and go right to filing the teeth sharp. Sharpening is similar to shaping the teeth, with distinct differences between filing a ripsaw and a crosscut saw. The front edge of a ripsaw tooth is nearly vertical and square across. A crosscut tooth, on the other

The final step in sharpening a saw is to lightly run a stone flat along the side of the blade to even out the set and hone off any burrs created by filing.

Hacksaws, which come in a range of tooth sizes, make accurate patterns for reshaping fine backsaw teeth. Clamp the two blades together; the harder hacksaw blade will keep your file cutting a consistent depth and shape.

Keep an eye on the jointed flat and the faces of each tooth, and pressure the file forward or backward to maintain tooth shape. At most, file only half of the flat away. File down one side of the saw, turn it around and file back the other way. The best technique is to file each side twice, just creeping up to sharp points. This helps keep the teeth evenly shaped.

Finish sharpening by running a stone flat against the teeth from end to end on both sides of the saw. This evens out any teeth with too much set. If you've done well, your saw will cut smoothly, with just a whisper.

SHARPENING DOVETAIL SAWS

The most challenging part of sharpening a dovetail saw is seeing the small teeth. I'll explain a couple of tricks that help. I usually don't worry about shaping the teeth, jointing them to a uniform height, or setting them (filing creates enough set), but focus on filing the points sharp. Most dovetail saws are so inexpensive that you can replace them after a few filings if things get way out of tune.

Hacksaw blades have fine teeth perfectly cut by machine in a range of point sizes. They make good guides for either refiling a dovetail saw with fewer points (10 to 12 points are an advantage for faster cutting) or for shaping existing teeth. Clamp the two sawblades together with the gullets lined up. Use the hacksaw as a pattern, which is hard on your file, but foolproof.

Clamp a dovetail saw between two boards with beveled top edges both to hold the saw and to keep track of where you are filing (and how deep). Each file stroke should leave a consistent mark in the wood. Tap a wooden block onto the end of the file as a guide to maintain the same tooth angle.

hand, is slanted back 15° or more, and beveled at an angle of 60° to 75° rather than straight across. The more square to the saw you file, the smaller the tooth bevels and the longer they will last in hardwood. Use a greater angle for saws used mostly for cut-ting softwoods. You can also use the same wooden guide for sharpening as you did for shaping.

Starting at the handle end, file the back face of a tooth set away from you and the front face of one set to-ward you, and file *every other* gullet.

The key to filing fine teeth is having a pair of wooden jaws clamped right at the bottom of the gullets. Each file stroke leaves a groove on the wood that helps you keep track of position, cutting depth, and filing angle. I use a wooden guide on the end of the file for maintaining the angle of the front of the teeth, just as I described for handsaws. With these aids I can see where I am working without having to actually see each tooth.

Because I am aiming for more of a rip tooth, I try to keep the front face of the teeth slanted backward about 5° or so. I create a small bevel by filing at an angle of somewhere between 5° and 10° across the saw. Use a single stroke in each gullet to cut the teeth evenly. Otherwise, the filing process is no different: up the saw filing every other tooth and back down filing the remaining ones.

On very fine-toothed saws, which include dovetail saws, the burr formed on the tooth from filing creates enough set. A new saw probably has too much set to begin with. To find out, make a cut 1 in. deep in a scrap and then turn the saw on end and insert it in the kerf. Quite likely there will be a lot of slop.

To remove some of the set, lay the saw on a flat surface and with an oilstone (harder and less apt to be scored than a waterstone) lightly hone a stroke or two flat along both the sides of the blade and teeth. The idea is to hone away some of the set, which has the additional benefit of sharpening the teeth noticeably. Make another cut and try the saw in it. Hone again if necessary, until the saw cuts a kerf just barely snug against the blade. Now you're ready to go cut some dovetails.

To get started in the cut, hold the blade to the line against a thumbnail and pull the saw back to create a small kerf. Use a few light half-strokes until the saw is engaged in the cut.

A new dovetail saw is likely to have far more set than you need, which only lets the blade wobble around in a wide kerf. The three trial cuts show (from left) an untuned saw, partially tuned, and tuned so that the saw just fits the kerf.

Lay the saw flat on a board and hone off some of the set with a fine oilstone (a soft waterstone would get scored by the teeth). Take one or two light passes on each side and make a trial cut. Honing the teeth also sharpens them noticeably.

Using Saws

There is no one right way to saw, but it should feel natural, and your arm, shoulders, and body all should be relaxed. Think only about guiding the saw, not pressuring it into the cut, and let it cut at its own pace. A few careful strokes to get started straight is far easier than fighting the saw to your line for the next dozen strokes. To help get started, visualize how the stroke of your arm and the saw (as an extension of your arm) aligns with the cut. You can hear when a saw is cutting well; when everything is right, it sings. When it's not, it will chatter and squeal in a most unmusical way.

you can. Saw only the lines you can see, not the back side you cannot. Turn the work around to complete the cut.

I like to use the fingernail of my thumb as a rub block for getting the cut started right to a line (see the top photo on p. 181). Go easily or you risk having the saw jump out of the kerf. Draw the saw back, then ease it gently forward. Use full strokes once the kerf is started. To reflect some added light onto tricky sawing, clamp a piece of white paper in the vise sticking up above the jaws a few inches and creased away from you work. For precise work, leave a little of the line to plane or chisel away. For difficult or repetitive cuts such as miters or bevels, a shopmade or manufactured miter box is quicker to use and more accurate than sawing freehand.

Hand-powered miter boxes such as this classic Stanley might be slower than motorized chopsaws, but they are ideal for working high up on staging when mitering large cornice moldings, or for quietly cutting accurate frame miters back in the shop.

No matter the saw or the task, clamp your work in a comfortable position, one that lets you see your lines. Holding strategies can be as simple as clamping a board in a side vise, using a pair of bench hooks to hold work flat on your bench, or working on a pair of sawhorses and clamping the work with your knee. The more comfortable you are, the more you can concentrate on sawing accurately. Crosscut saws are designed to cut best at an angle of 45°

to the surface, and ripsaws at a higher 60° angle. But use them at any angle or hand position that works, including sawing backwards when you need to.

For careful work, such as sawing the cheeks of a tenon, clamp the work upright in a side vise and position yourself to see two of your lines at once. Saw vertically if possible. Over time, working with any tools, you develop an internal plumb, so take advantage of it when

Miter Boxes and Trimmers

At one time, large crown moldings and all manner of house trim were cut with long backsaws guided in wooden and iron miter boxes. Today, chopsaws rule. Tilting-arbor table saws and radial-arm saws also have pushed classic miter boxes aside, but not entirely, at least not yet.

A miter box is a simple solution to a timeless problem: cutting accurate bevels and miters. Without a chopsaw, there are plenty of times I need to cut a large molding either deeper than my table saw will handle, too awkward to cut safely, or while I am working on staging. For

Simple wooden miter jigs or miter boxes (rear) are easy to build and make sawing identical cuts or at specific angles quick and accurate.

very small parts, such as fine strips to secure glass in a rabbet (which are hard to cut by machine without splintering) or for slicing inlays where every millimeter counts, I make special miter boxes for my finest backsaws.

A miter trimmer works on the same principle as a miter box, only with a knife and guillotine action. The knife shears as it cuts, slicing off the thinnest shaving much like a plane, cleanly and without splintering. For mitering small moldings, picture frames, or cockbeads around a drawer, or for miters at odd angles, no machine matches the accuracy and efficiency of a miter trimmer. Fortunately, there are plenty of tasks where the same could be said of handsaws. Any tool that has survived more than 4,000 years with few changes must have earned its keep along the way, and likely will continue to do so.

For the greatest accuracy sawing small parts or precious inlays where the width of every saw kerf counts, make a wooden miter block to hold the work snugly, or a one-sided jig for cutting miters (foreground).

The shearing knife cut of a miter trimmer cuts a face as perfect as if it were planed by the Stanley #9 miter plane in the foreground. This hand-powered machine is the ideal tool for cutting small or delicate parts likely to splinter on a table saw.

11

Making and Restoring
HAND TOOLS

Bill Carter saws and files away in a little shed at the end of his garden, cutting dovetails to join together another of his exquisite planes (photo facing page). Fifteen years ago he hadn't made a single tool—never even thought about it— and today he's one of the best toolmakers around.

You too can make beautiful tools; maybe not dovetailed planes to start, but simple tools like a marking knife or a square. If you don't feel up to making tools, consider repairing them. Flea markets are full of orphaned tools in need of repair. Shape a new iron and heat-treat it or make a shapely handle that fits your hand perfectly, and you're on your way to more complicated repairs. You may even decide to make a tool. For people who love tools, making your own is merely the next step. ❧

Coachmakers often made many of the unusual tools their work required, such as these tools for routing grooves, planing a V-groove, or cutting a small cove around a curved coach frame.

Over the years, the author has made a number of special-ty tools (for inlay work, for example) which he couldn't find new or second-hand. Among those shopmade tools are tiny chisels and wooden gauges with small scrapers for cutting the grooves for string inlays.

Toolmaking

All tools were once made by hand—often by the same hands that used them. Two hundred years ago, a carpenter or joiner wouldn't have given much thought to making a jack plane or frame saw. For the iron or sawblade—or for an ax or drawknife—he would have gone to a local blacksmith. A craftsman could also order special tools or those of the highest quality—a brass-ribbed backsaw, a fancy brace, or a set of carving chisels—from long-established toolmaking centers such as Sheffield, England.

Through the 19th century and into the 20th, toolmakers such as Stanley, Sargent, and Miller's Falls grew to dominate the world tool market by producing catalogs of tools to suit every need or desire. For the most part, craftsmen stopped making their tools and bought them instead. Why make a tool that you could buy inexpensively, made of cast iron and more durable than one you could produce yourself, made of wood?

When toolmakers mastered cast iron, it became the favored material for parts of tools or for the entire tool, such as Stanley's line of planes. Steel replaced wood in braces, saws, marking gauges, and rules. The strength and durability of these new materials allowed innovations in design: new patterns, and tools that were lighter, easier to use, and easier to adjust. But while a small shop could make wooden tools, as many continued to do, cast iron and steel required complex manufacturing methods.

English toolmakers didn't immediately embrace cast iron, although they had long accepted the advantages of metal for plane bodies. To avoid the complex technology of casting planes, they devised hand methods of dovetailing flat plate sides and soles together. These methods survive today—the only machine Bill Carter uses is a grinder. Otherwise he works with a hacksaw and files, cutting dovetails much as you would to join two pieces of wood. You can make a great variety of planes this way, as handsome and functional as you could ever desire, with the hand tools you already own. If you can cut dovetails in wood, cutting them in metal is easier, because you can spread the metal to fill any gaps.

Over the years I have made a number of tools, from planes to small forged hammers. Some, such as scratch stocks, took hardly any time to make (see pp. 132–134). Other tools I have made because I couldn't find them—for inlay work, for instance—or because the one I found didn't suit my needs as well as something I could make. Still others I've made simply because of the challenge of making them and the satisfaction of using them. Toolmaking is a lot less difficult than you might think. Sometimes finding a

ENGLISH planemaker Bill Carter makes exquisite planes entirely by hand using common shop tools. He employs his woodworking skills to lay out, cut, and fit the dovetails that join the brass sides and steel soles of his small miter planes. He uses a ball-peen hammer to spread the metal into gaps between the tiny dovetails, securing the joint (photo below).

The old Spiers jointer plane (at top in the photo at right) is constructed with dovetails. The dovetail sample (foreground) shows a small bevel filed in the dovetail.

When the metal is peened and spread to fill the beveled area, the joint appears as though it is dovetailed on both sides.

"INNOVATION IN TOOLS" might be their motto, but "we can do it" is easily the motivation behind Veritas, the woodworking arm of Lee Valley Tools of Ottawa, Canada. It all started in 1979 when Leonard Lee, the company's inspirational leader, couldn't find some framing chisels or a broadax for a log addition he was building. He believed that there must be a need for at least one Canadian supplier of such tools, so he started one himself. Since then, Veritas and Lee Valley have grown enormously by redesigning some familiar old tools, developing new ones, and winning design awards for their efforts along the way.

Leonard Lee's long experience using hand tools and his keen observations of how they work or might work better (he has written *the* book on sharpening) is often the beginning of a project for one of Veritas' team of engineers. Inspiration is just as likely to come from a customer's suggestion, Lee's gene pool of old tools he's collected over the years, or something he's found at a flea market or among the 50 tons of salvage hardware he just purchased.

Some Veritas designs are inspired by a desire to overcome the limitations of a user's skills: jigs to help solve the problems of sharpening, honing, and using cabinet scrapers. Other designs are new takes on old tools: a chisel plane that's simply a plane body with a bench chisel for the iron, or a set of scribing dividers with bubble levels and articulating arms. The engineers make and test prototypes, and Lee challenges them at every step along the way.

A typical problem Lee tackled involved Japanese handsaws. He understood the advantages of their thin kerf and razor-sharp teeth, and how cutting on the pull stroke helps some novices saw more accurately. These saws work amazingly well in softwoods and fine in hardwoods, at least until the teeth start breaking. So Lee went to Japan, first to learn how the saws were made, and then to work out a tooth redesign that would hold up to cutting hardwood. He ended up with a new line of saws and satisfied customers.

No design challenge is too big—so far. The next frontier is bench planes, and already Lee and his engineers have been collecting planes with interesting designs, including ones from eastern Europe and the Paragon line of planes Veritas once made. How can they make a plane easier to use or more accurate, to improve upon a design essentially unchanged from Leonard Bailey's clever ideas of well over a century ago? Judging from their successes so far, this modern-day Leonard just might. 🎴

At Lee Valley Tools, the process of designing and refining the prototype for a new chisel plane involves drawings, wooden models, and plenty of close inspection of older tools such as this Stanley #97 and an anonymous cast-iron plane for inspiration. (Photo by Ray Pilon.)

good iron or a beautiful chunk of rosewood inspires the rest.

With only modest woodworking skills—and ideally a tool to copy—you can make the wooden parts of almost any tool. Tempering useful blades and the metalworking side of toolmaking is not as familiar to most woodworkers. For this reason, I have only lightly addressed the woodworking aspects of toolmaking in this chapter. Instead, I focus on metalworking techniques.

No matter what tools you make, you'll need to have the right tools at hand, suitable materials, and an understanding of heat-treating the cutters. If you find your interest piqued, there are books about every aspect of toolmaking, from making wooden planes to forging chisels (see the Bibliography on p. 214).

TOOLS FOR MAKING TOOLS

A well-equipped woodshop has all the tools you need for making your own tools. Ideally, you should have a separate area for metalworking so that the mess of metal filings doesn't dirty your woodworking bench. A machinist's vise is the most versatile way to hold everything from small parts to entire tools. Attach one to your bench or to a platform that can be clamped in a side vise and adjusted to a comfortable height (see the bottom photo at right).

I have a small vise attached to a maple block that I clamp in my side vise for delicate work, such as filing a cutter for a scratch stock. Metalworking vises have an anvil behind the jaws for riveting and flattening

Isolate the dirt and mess of toolmaking on a separate bench, preferably with a metal top, a large metalworking vise, a grinder, a buffer, and the necessary hand tools nearby.

A small machinist's vise is handy for holding metal parts. Mount the vise on a sturdy wooden platform and clamp it in a side vise or in the jaws of a larger metal vise at a comfortable height.

Shears are quicker than a hacksaw for cutting hand scrapers, durable patterns, or tool parts from thin-gauge metal. Modern shears often have leveraged jaws, which are considerably easier for cutting tough materials than these antique shears. (Also shown is an early metal rule that pushes into a revolving cup inside the case.)

A small bench anvil is a handy work surface for flattening parts, peening rivets, or bending sections around the round horn. An assortment of needle-nose pliers and nippers is useful for bending, holding, and cutting.

parts. A pin vise for holding small parts and a bench anvil are also useful, as is a large floor anvil if you decide to take up forging.

You'll need a hacksaw, various files (especially needle files for fine shaping), pliers in assorted shapes and nose configurations, nippers, shears, taps and dies for metal, punches and countersinks, a few cold chisels, a good assortment of twist drills, and at least one ball-peen hammer. Many of these tools you may already have. If not, they are readily found. Taps and dies (for wood threads) are not as common. I have found a few smaller sizes (⅜ in., ½ in., and ¾ in.) useful in toolmaking—for making small clamps or locking screws on marking gauges—as well as for securing knobs in my furniture making (Peugeot Freres made some of the best). Always buy a matching set of tap and die.

One other tool that you are not likely to have is a set of letter and number punches. Not only are they useful for stamping your name, initials, date, and any other revelation that might occur to you (Bill Carter stamps "Diana" and "Carter, Plane-maker to the Gentry" on his planes), but it's also a good way to keep track of parts and their position. A stiff whack with a hammer makes a clear mark in end grain or soft steel that won't be mistaken. On many British planes, the cap irons, irons, and infills are stamped with the same number, so as the parts are made they will find each other during assembly.

MATERIALS

Wood is a perfect material for fashioning tools. Take away the steel cutters, brass wear plates, and a few other small metal parts and, for many tools, all you will have left is familiar old beech, birch, rosewood, or perhaps even apple. Beech is the favored wood for many tools because it is tough, fine-grained, and works easily, although any stable hardwood is just as good. I prefer the beauty and polish of rosewood, ebony, and boxwood.

Working steel into cutters and blades is not as familiar to woodworkers as making the wooden parts of tools. But you don't have to be a metallurgist to make blades for common tools (and you can even buy some of them new from catalogs). To make your own cutters, you first need to find good steel that can be hardened and tempered to an edge that will hold its sharpness. High-carbon steel, sometimes stamped "cast steel," is what you should look for.

Old plane irons, chisels, handsaws, worn-out bandsaw blades, heavy hacksaw blades, and files are all made of good steel. I know black-

Taps and dies cut consistent wooden threads and mating nuts for such tools and tool parts as clamps, saw vises, and locking screws. An older hand-cut tap is at top; a modern continuous thread is in the foreground.

With a set of number and letter punches, you can impress your name (or any other inscription) into the wood or soft metal parts of a tool.

The high-quality steel in old rasps and worn files can be forged or ground into practical new tools, such as rugged timber-framing chisels (with rasp teeth clearly visible), a lathe tool, a burnisher, and a drawknife.

Early tool steel, known as blister steel, was made by heating pure Swedish bar iron with charcoal in a closed chest, where only the outer layer of the bar absorbed carbon (visible in the engraving). Depending on how it was forged, the steel was then used for making everything from shears to chisels.

Double Shear Steel

Single Shear Steel

Hoop L Blister Steel

Steinbuck Blister Steel

GL Blister Steel

Blister Steel, Melting Temper

Blister Steel, Shear Temper

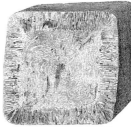

Blister Steel, Spring Temper

Tool Steel in the Ingot

Punch Steel

Chisel Steel in the Ingot

The simple wooden details of these gauges—sliding arms that lock in place with wedging keys or a wooden thumbscrew (top)—lock positively, are easily made, and are worth keeping in mind when designing more complex tools.

A lucky find—a Sheffield spokeshave cutter—inspired the author to make a boxwood shave with a horn wear plate (at rear). The ebony scraper, with a blade cut from a hand scraper, is a copy of a traditional tool.

smiths who forge tools from old leaf springs. You can also buy flat ground stock in a wide range of widths and thicknesses specifically for toolmaking. And if you want to go that far, there are special alloys such as A11 or M4 for making cutters with incredibly long-lasting edges. They are available through steel retailers, who can tell you the specifics of each.

Just by looking in flea markets, junk shops, and tool shops, I have found a complete inventory of toolmaking supplies: brass stock, bits of ivory or bone for wear plates or other details, cast-steel irons of every vintage, knurled knobs, ferrules, and parts from other tools. And these are good places to get inspiration, to see tools that work well or construction details that might come in handy someday. If you get serious about toolmaking, you'll need to have more than just the materials. You'll need a basic knowledge of metalworking techniques, including riveting and, even more important, heat-treating.

Some modern toolmakers make complete (and working) tools only an inch or two long. Among these miniatures by Paul Kebabian are an ebony plow plane, an ivory bow saw, a brass and ebony Ultimatum brace, and tiny coachmaker rabbet planes.

HEAT-TREATING

Nearly all woodworking tools (rules and squares being notable exceptions) have a cutting edge or edges. Hardening and tempering those steel edges give them durability. You can make tools without heat-treating them—by careful grinding you can make new blades from old ones and preserve the original temper of the steel. But it's a lot easier to soften or *anneal* the steel first, and then saw and file it to shape. Restoring the steel to a harder state then requires

heat-treating. Not all steels heat-treat, so make sure you start with high-carbon steel, a known alloy, or old blades. The best way to learn is to experiment.

Beyond the physical composition of the steel, which is out of your hands, the durability of an edge (and its ultimate usefulness) depends upon heat-treating. This involves heating the finished blade until it is red hot,

quenching it rapidly to make it very hard, then drawing some of the hardness out by heating it to 350°F or so. Commercial heat-treating is done in special ovens, with scientific control for predictable results.

Japanese tools are testimony that a small forge and experience can do the job just as well, if not better. Sometimes I use a small riveter's forge, especially when I also want to

The first step in making a marking knife (on the bench anvil) is to anneal or soften the blade so it can be filed to shape and drilled for the rivets. Heat the blade red hot and let it cool slowly. Harden the finished blade the same way, only quench it rapidly in water. (Photo by Jon Binzen.)

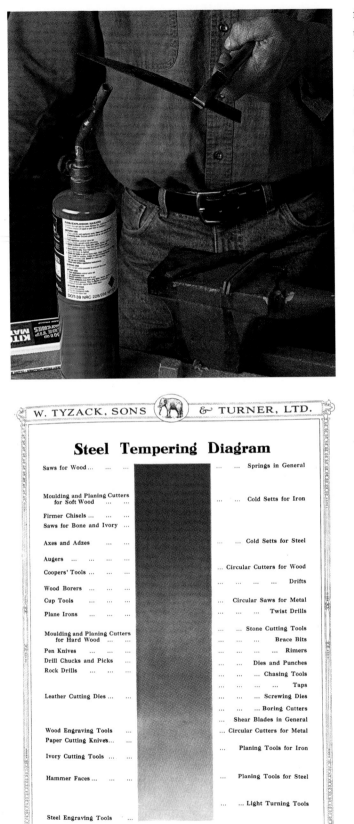

Each cutting tool has an optimum tempering range, visible by the color the steel turns as you apply heat. The more heat you apply, the darker the steel colors and the softer the resulting tempered edge. A softer edge will also be less brittle.

W. TYZACK, SONS & TURNER, LTD.

Steel Tempering Diagram

Saws for Wood...	... Springs in General
Moulding and Planing Cutters for Soft Wood	... ... Cold Setts for Iron
Firmer Chisels	
Saws for Bone and Ivory ...	
Axes and Adzes ...	... ... Cold Setts for Steel
Augers	
Coopers' Tools	... Circular Cutters for Wood
	... ... Drifts
Wood Borers	
Cup Tools	... Circular Saws for Metal
Plane Irons ...	... ... Twist Drills
Moulding and Planing Cutters for Hard Wood	... ... Stone Cutting Tools
	... ... Brace Bits
Pen Knives	... ... Rimers
Drill Chucks and Picks ...	... ... Dies and Punches
Rock Drills	... ... Chasing Tools
	... ... Taps
Leather Cutting Dies	... ... Screwing Dies
	... ... Boring Cutters
	... Shear Blades in General
Wood Engraving Tools ...	... Circular Cutters for Metal
Paper Cutting Knives... ...	
Ivory Cutting Tools	... Planing Tools for Iron
Hammer Faces...	... Planing Tools for Steel
	... ... Light Turning Tools
Steel Engraving Tools	

· 1921 ·

forge a tool, but otherwise a propane torch works for heat-treating all but the heaviest irons.

The first step in making a cutter is annealing it to a soft and ductile (workable) state. If the blade has any sort of profile, such as a new molding-plane iron, annealing the steel allows you to file it to shape easily. Play the torch over the business end of the blade until it is uniformly bright red, then bury it in a can of warm ash or fine sand, allowing it to cool slowly.

It helps to work in subdued light, as "smithies" often do, to see the subtle color changes of the steel as it heats. Sometimes I throw a blade into a dying fire in my wood stove with just enough heat left to get it to red hot, letting it cool as the coals burn out. If a file cuts the steel easily, it's annealed. This is the time to complete all of the forming and shaping of your cutter. But annealed steel is useless as a cutting edge until you take it through the next step of hardening it once again.

To harden it again, heat the steel to cherry red and quench it rapidly, edge first, in a pail of warm water. Agitate the steel in the water to shake off any steam bubbles clinging to the surface that prevent it from cooling quickly. The internal structure of the steel is now frozen, you might say. It's hard and brittle, quite different from its "relaxed" state while annealed. Water is the easiest and safest liquid to quench in, although some steels require oil. (Any steel alloys you buy will be noted "W" for water hardening,

Screws are best for adjustable or replaceable parts, such as the throat plate fitted to the smoothing plane and the sole of the spoke-shave (foreground). Rivets can be nearly invisible, such as those through the wear plates of the marking gauge, and they can hold steel cutters in wooden handles securely (see the reamer at left). (Photo by Jon Binzen.)

Two brass rivets hold the finished blade snugly in place. Work on a stable, flat surface like this bench anvil, and tap the rivet carefully to mushroom a head on both ends without splitting the wood. (Photo by Jon Binzen.)

"O" for oil hardening, and "A" for air hardening, which requires a special oven.)

If you ever overheated a cutting edge while grinding—and who hasn't?—then you already understand a little about tempering. Any part that turned blue will no longer hold an edge very well; much of its hardness has been tempered out. If you reheat the blade in a controlled way, you're tempering it, or drawing out just enough of the hardness to make the edge tough. Any shiny area of the blade will show a progression of colors from light straw to blue as the steel heats. Apply heat well back from the edge,

along the entire width of the blade, and watch for the colors as they run toward the edge.

Where you stop and quench is a matter of experience, but as with most things it's a compromise and depends on how the tool will be used. Apply just a little heat and the edge will be very hard yet brittle (good for a cold chisel). More heat will leave a tough edge, but one that will not hold its sharpness as long (good for an ax or adze). Temper woodworking edges to light straw, at least as a place to start. Test your blade, and if the edge chips in use, soften it slightly by retempering it with a bit more heat.

RIVETING

If heat-treating mystifies you, riveting is a piece of cake. Rivets are a metalworker's nails, available in nearly as many sizes, shapes, and materials. Nails themselves even make serviceable rivets. To join metal to wood—brass wear plates or the handles of a marking knife, for instance—rivets are strong, easy to make and, in some situations, nearly invisible. You can make a movable "knuckle joint" between two wooden parts with a rivet.

Rivets are also great for joining pieces of metal together. While not as strong as welding or soldering, they avoid any potential problems of

ONE OF THE LAST in the long tradition of making hand tools for the world's tradesmen, Footprint Tools carries on in Sheffield, England. As the largest privately owned manufacturer, their production includes wood and cold chisels, auger bits, hammers, joiner's tools, and planes.

The day I paid a visit to Footprint Tools, two 20-ton drop hammers were vibrating the entire factory (and probably everything else for blocks around). Each deep thud shaped a 2-lb. ball-peen hammer head. Smashed between matching molds or dies (drop forging, as it is known), the red-hot round stock was roughly shaped with one whack, and another whack in an adjacent die refined it. A third thud sheared off the glowing head; a neighboring ancient machine punched out the eye for the handle as easily as you'd core an apple. Finally, the hammer faces were heat-treated and ground smooth.

Everywhere in the factory were cart loads of tools in various states of manufacture. Men at smaller mechanical forges worked each woodworking chisel, much as they would have a century ago. Nearby, finished chisels were tempering in special ovens, and the woodworking shop was turning out dozens of plane and saw handles. 🕸

Two whacks of a 20-ton drop hammer and the red-hot round stock is neatly forged in matching molds, or "dies," into the shape of a ball-peen hammer head.

As the eyes for the handles are punched out, the red-hot heads fall into a metal bin to cool.

Woodworking chisels begin as Swedish steel bar stock forged to shape in dies. The chisels are then hardened, tempered in ovens, finish-ground, and finally fitted with handles.

Dozens of knobs come off lathes, are lacquered red, and are then fitted to block planes.

heat. Modern glues are certainly another alternative, although I put more trust in the mechanical connection of a rivet or screw.

Why rivet and not screw? Screws are best for parts of tools that will need to be disassembled, replaced, or loosened to make adjustments—fences and depth stops, for instance. The problem with screws is that, over time, the threads lose their grip on the wood, so that the connection is no longer as secure. You always can tighten a rivet, however, with a few taps of a hammer. Rivets also are smaller than screws and less apt to weaken the narrow cross sections typical of many tools.

Whether you use nails, brass rod, or commercial rivets made of steel or copper, the rivet must be annealed so you can peen the metal into a head. (Anneal brass by heating it dull red and quenching.) The hole for the rivet must be no smaller than its diameter, and hardly any bigger. To set a rivet flush (making it invisible, if the materials are the same), countersink the hole slightly. Securing the rivet is then a matter of forming a head on both ends with many light blows using a ball-peen hammer.

One method is to cut the rivet long, clamp it in a vise, and peen one end into small head. Tap the rivet into place (into the wood side first, if you can), cut it off just proud of the surface, and peen a head on the other end. Work both sides and back up the work on an anvil. Be especially careful of the side set into the wood to avoid splitting. The connection will be stronger if you

Any woodworker with modest skills could restore these flea-market finds with some basic repairs, such as shaping a new handle, replacing a missing wedge, or piecing in the charred heel of the round plane.

use a small washer under the rivet head (as you commonly see on old knife handles).

If you countersunk the hole on the metal side of your joint (or on both sides) and peened the rivet to fill it completely, you can then file the surface flat and have an invisible connection (or repair). Whether you are trying to hide a rivet or true a metal surface flat, proper filing technique is critical. It's no different than using a rasp or file on wood, as explained in Chapter 8.

Restoring Tools

Restoring some venerable old tool to usable service can be just as challenging and satisfying as making a new one. Make a new blade or a new handle, and you're using all the same skills. At least with an old tool you have something to start with, even if it's hidden under years of dirt.

A stiff brass brush, fine steel wool, and a mixture of boiled linseed oil and beeswax will clean and polish both wood and metal surfaces.

CLEANING

If you buy many secondhand tools, you'll quickly become adept at cleaning. Beneath typical paint spatters, grime, and surface rust there's probably a beautiful tool just waiting for you. Exactly how much to clean is an ongoing debate among collectors and users. This is not a problem with common tools—manufactured ones such as molding planes or Stanley tools—but if you are overzealous in cleaning a rare or historically significant tool, you risk irreversible damage.

You might remove tool marks that indicate how it was made, the patina of years of use that make it so appealing in the first place, almost certainly devaluing it considerably. Old tools have a soul that too much cleaning only diminishes. My guide is to clean a tool to a condition to be used—to make it look the way it would if I had found it on a past owner's bench.

The first step in cleaning a tool is to take it apart so you can get into every crevice filled with grime. Everyone has a secret formula for cleaning: a solvent (such as kerosene or turpentine) and a gentle abrasive. I use 0000 steel wool, a small scraper, and a fine brass or steel brush—all gentle enough to clean surfaces and protect the patina. For stubborn gunk I use 00 steel wool, and for surface rust I sometimes reach for 400-grit wet-and-dry paper (or coarser if necessary).

Work as little as possible on gunmetal parts to preserve the beautiful color that only time can produce. A good rubbing with paste wax (I mix beeswax and boiled linseed oil) brings up the shine and prevents rusting. Nothing polishes a tool better than using it. (The same wax or thinned boiled linseed oil is a good universal finish on any wood.)

REPAIRS

While it can be tricky to repair the wooden parts of some tools, the skills involved are not beyond the means of any capable woodworker. Add basic metalworking skills to your repertoire, and you might succeed with a more complicated repair: drilling out a sheared-off bolt and retapping for a larger one, restoring damaged threads by some delicate filing, or fabricating a missing part. This is all part of the thrill of making a tool whole again, especially if you can buy it for a bargain price. But when it comes to repairing cracked or broken cast iron, you have to be careful.

If you work with old cast-iron tools, you are bound to drop one, as I have done more than once. Cast iron is tough but brittle. If you are lucky, a dropped tool might only chip or crack, but it could also split in half. Tools become rare for this reason alone. It's also why there is a lively market for tool parts. I've seen some ingenious handyman repairs on cracked tools, with rivets and plates that are not much to look at but that saved an old friend from an early demise.

Really good repairs—gas welds that are almost invisible—are expensive, and sometimes more than the tool is worth. Brazing is another option and often less expensive. (You could even try a tough, modern epoxy, although it won't be as durable a repair.) Most repairs are noticeable, which is not usually a concern for a tool that's going to be used, but the alignment of the repaired handle or the flatness of a

Cast-iron tools are tricky to repair. The gas weld to the Bedrock #604½ (top) is very good, a similar repair to the block plane (middle) is utilitarian, and the brazing on the #78 rabbet plane (foreground) left the front part of the sole twisted.

Any of these traditional handles would be a good model for making your own, for repairing a broken handle, or for fitting a new one to a file, rasp, or chisel.

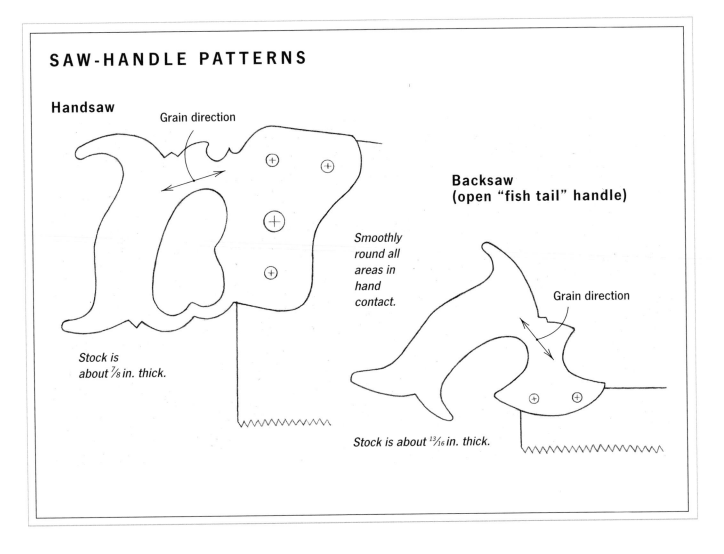

SAW-HANDLE PATTERNS

Handsaw

Grain direction

Stock is about ⅞ in. thick.

Smoothly round all areas in hand contact.

Backsaw (open "fish tail" handle)

Grain direction

Stock is about ¹³⁄₁₆ in. thick.

plane's sole with a repaired side might never be the same. Certainly don't go looking for broken cast-iron tools—at any price—but when you drop a favorite tool, think long and hard about your options. Your old friend might end up with just a scar—or a limp.

Making handles

One of the easiest repairs is to make a new handle for a chisel, saw, draw-knife, or any number of other tools. Considering how long most wood-working projects take, making a handle is quick and satisfying. Of course, it takes longer to shape a saw handle than to turn a round one on a lathe, but either handle will be better than anything you can buy, and it will fit your hand comfortably.

Rosewood, boxwood, beech—any hard and fine-grained wood can make a stunning handle. I save scraps of exotic or wildly figured woods just for handles. Every round handle needs a ferrule to keep the wood from splitting where the tang enters, and for heavy-duty framing chisels and other tools apt to be hit often and hard, a steel hoop on the opposite end is a good idea. Flea markets are good places to look for brass and steel tubes of various diameters and thicknesses, and you may even find old ferrules with special details, such as knurling or cap ends. You can also find orphaned handles at flea markets for a few dollars at most.

A lathe is the simplest way to shape round handles. You can also use a plane, rasps, and scrapers, with the advantage that you can cut an oval handle just as easily as a round one. For a fine gent's backsaw or a rasp—tools you tend to hold in the same orientation to the work—an oval handle provides a more positive grip than a round one. You can also plane a round handle into an octagon for a comfortable grip (and to prevent the tool from rolling off your bench).

On the lathe, size the wood for a snug fit for the ferrule and hoop, and flush with the rest of the handle. Tap either into place with another piece of pipe of similar diameter. Drive the hoop lower than the top of the handle so that the wood can mushroom out and hold it on. If you planned well, the lathe center will be the start of a hole for the tool's tang. For more tips on drilling the handle and fitting the tang, refer back to pp. 87-89.

Making a new saw handle is more time-consuming, but you'll appreciate the results every time you grasp it. Apple, curly maple, and cherry are my favorite woods for saw handles. For a pattern, use either of the ones shown on the facing page or another favorite handle; just make sure to plan for the saw bolts. If you have them, measure the length of

Cut out a new saw handle with a bandsaw or coping saw, and refine and smooth it with rasps and files. All three handles on the bench were turned on a lathe and fitted with old ferrules. (Photo by Jon Binzen.)

TO HELP determine the diameter or length of a handle, measure other handles that feel particularly comfortable. I prefer simple shapes, with a bulging center section and tapering ends. A dip and then increased diameter just above the ferrule gives a nice place to get a thumb and finger behind for extra leverage when pushing, for tools such as paring chisels and carving tools.

your saw bolts to determine the thickness of the handle. Pay attention to the grain orientation to give the fine tails of your handle maximum strength.

I like to rough out the shape, saw a kerf for the blade with a tenon saw (or whatever saw you have that cuts a properly snug kerf), and fine-tune the handle's position before getting too caught up in the shaping. Cut the details with either a bandsaw or a coping saw, and then rasp and scrape the edges into comfortable and flowing curves. Embellish with some carving.

To transfer the location of the holes for the saw bolts, hold the

blade in the correct position on the handle. If you are lucky enough to have the right bolts, measure them for the proper counterbore to sink them flush. If you don't have any bolts, soft copper rivets work nicely. Who knows, your handle might be so comfortable it will encourage you to use a saw more often.

Whether you make just the handles or entire tools, the tools will certainly become favorites. Getting started is the hardest part, and there is no better way to get inspired than by looking at old tools. The next chapter explains where to look and what to look for.

BUYING USED
Hand Tools

Twenty-five years ago I didn't know a Bedrock from a Bailey, a Sargent from a Stanley, but secondhand tools were cheap and I bought plenty. I was a carpenter, I needed tools, and these were far better than anything I could have purchased new. Every detail—from shapely rosewood handles to sturdy parts—spoke of quality, of tools designed to work day in and day out. After I found my first Norris smoother at a flea market for $125, I was hooked.

Until the recent renaissance of quality toolmaking, buying secondhand was the surest way to build a shop of good hand tools. For unusual tools it still is. Even if you rarely buy anything, looking is half the fun—the thrill of hunting through boxes at flea markets, haggling with dealers, or feeling a tingle of adrenaline counter-bidding at an auction. 🪰

Where to Look

You never know where you'll find tools besides all the places you would expect: yard sales, tool auctions, antique stores, and, of course, flea markets. A couple of years ago I met a woman at a church supper, and in passing I mentioned that I was a furniture maker. Recently, she called to tell me that she was selling her father-in-law's house, and he had some tools I might be interested in. Knowing almost nothing about tools, she described worn wooden bench planes and some iron tools bought at auctions over the years.

Ever curious, I went to investigate. But no, this story doesn't end with the find of a rare early patented plane among that jumble of iron,

As beautiful as Christmas tree ornaments, finely turned plumb bobs are common finds at flea markets. Every carpenter once had one in his tool kit.

No matter where you find used tools, look them over carefully for cracks, damaged or missing parts, and rusted cutters or adjusters. Even the best price is no bargain if the tool is unusable.

although it could have. Instead, I found a clean Stanley #53 spokeshave and a small bench anvil—both of which I put right to work.

I've heard plenty of stories, though, of similar outings ending in great finds: a Spiers miter plane found in a bucket at a country auction for $4 (value $1,000), a going-out-of-business sale at a hardware store where a Stanley #164 was thrown in with a lot of junk (value more than $3,000), and the earliest marked wooden plane found in Maine for $12 (value at least $10,000, if not more).

It might seem that with more interest in collecting tools and more education about them through price guides and books, these sorts of lucky discoveries are a thing of the past. They aren't. The lure of the unexpected and the minor triumphs along the way keep the hunt interesting.

FLEA MARKETS

Nowhere is the hunt more unpredictable than at flea markets, yard sales, and secondhand stores. You never know what might turn up, but there's a good chance you can find some bargains. The drawbacks are that the hunt takes time, and you have to wade through a lot of junk—sometimes entire boxes of rusty tools and hardware—for the chance of finding a complete tool in restorable condition.

Wherever you look for tools (but especially at flea markets, auctions, and tool dealers), knowledge about what you are buying is critical. It doesn't matter how great a bargain you get if the tool is missing important parts, or if it's entirely wrong for the work you want to do. Just looking a tool over very carefully is a good start. Experience is still the best teacher; expect to make a mistake or two along the way. Buy a reprint of the Stanley #34 catalog (1915 edition) or other catalogs and learn what you can about tools that interest you (see the Bibliography on p. 214). How else will you know that the rusty piece you found is a rare beader for a Stanley #72 chamfer plane?

DEALERS

Dealers are a more reliable source for tools. Some have entire stores filled with classic hand tools of every sort, which you can examine and even try out before buying. Many put out catalogs several times a year, with each tool photographed and fully described, or they might have a Web site updated more often. Woodworking catalogs are another source (although more limited) for new tools in classic patterns. The only disadvantage of buying from dealers is that you'll pay the market price. But for this you also get a number of benefits.

The best dealers have a love and respect for the tools born from a long history with them—as collectors and users—and a ready knowledge of their details that they are glad to share. They are the inside circle of the tool market, connected to its ebb and flow and to each other. This network can find any tool, especially the rare ones not easily found other ways. They'll answer your questions, sometimes even take tools you no longer need in barter, and, of course, they will dicker. You will pay more than flea-market prices, but you get the assurance (and sometimes a guaran-

You never know what treasured tool you might find in amongst the old crockery, tinware, and common household junk at a flea market.

The three golden planes and a handsaw mark the modest shop of tool and book dealer Roy Arnold in Needham Market, Ipswich, England. Over the years, many of the best British tools have passed through his hands.

Inside Roy Arnold's shop there's everything from a Holtzapffel engine lathe to hundreds of new and used books about the once-common woodworking trades, and workaday tools just waiting to be tuned and put back to work.

Harrisburg International Tool Auction

Imagine a huge hotel ballroom filled with row after row of dealer tables. Some are piled high with usable tools of every sort—planes, handsaws, braces, sets of chisels—with more filling shelves and boxes on the floor. Spread over other tables are levels and boxwood rules, old tool catalogs, rare Stanley planes, British tools (including many gleaming Norrises and Spiers), hammers, and axes.

Four 50-ft.-long tables are spread with more than a thousand tools ready for auction, with the most valuable and smallest guarded in glass cases. Then there are the buyers, two or three deep, filling every aisle. Such was the busy scene for the dealer show and preview of the Saturday auction. The action at this event continues late into the night over dinner, in hotel rooms transformed into tool shops, and anywhere two tool lovers chance to meet.

tee) of a complete tool in working order. Buying from dealers might not be as exciting as attending auctions or prowling junk stores, but they are dependable sources for excellent tools.

AUCTIONS

If you are willing to pay the price, you could buy a whole shop's worth of tools in just a couple of days at a large regional sale. Dealers and collectors congregate from all over for the same reason that attracts you: the chance to see lots and lots of tools in one place. There are a number of regional sales in this

country and abroad, in addition to organizations such as the Midwest Tool Collectors Association, which gathers twice a year to sell tools and swap stories.

In researching this book, I headed off to Harrisburg, Pennsylvania, where the rare, the unusual, the pristine (sometimes in an original box)—in short, the best of the best—are on the block. And then for a comparison to this granddaddy of the domestic auctions, I went to a most prestigious auction in England (see the sidebar on p. 209).

WHY ARE THERE so many more inventive tool designs found in the United States than in England? The answer lies partly in the conservative nature of English craftsmen, working with familiar tools. English guilds stifled change by their strict control over every aspect of a trade, including its methods and tools. Guilds and tradition were much less important in colonial America, where ingenuity flourished.

The key to success at any auction is to read the catalog and carefully preview the tools. Make notes, narrow your focus, and set your highest bids before the action begins.

Even the best catalog description doesn't tell you as much as a hands-on inspection of a tool that interests you. Disassemble a tool if need be to see all its details.

Bud Brown started this auction in 1983; Clarence Blanchard, a down-home Mainer with a long history of collecting Stanley tools, has run it out of his home since 1997. It takes a full year to put together, to find everything from entire collections to consignments of a single high-ticket item such as a Thomas Falconer coachmaker's plow plane, the highlight of the 1998 auction that I attended (the plane sold for $22,500).

Also up for sale were almost three dozen Scottish planes—unusual and beautiful examples of the plane-maker's art—from the collection of Ken Roberts, an early collector of hand tools and a prolific writer about them. And among the 762 lots were the usual selection of Stanley tools, plow planes, molding planes, and unique tools from many trades.

Clarence gathers a cross section of tools that will appeal to a wide variety of collectors and users, and then writes a catalog enticing them to come and bid. A tool might not look like much, until you read in the catalog where it was made, by whom, and other details that set it apart from similar tools, as well as information about what trades used it, its condition, and an estimate of its value. Many bidders never appear, instead submitting bids by mail based on the thoroughness of the catalog alone.

In the tool world, this is certainly an auction for the big boys, drawing collectors from all over the world.

The rare and unusual tools at any auction attract all the attention, which leaves plenty of common tools for the alert (and prepared) buyer to snatch up for a song.

Every chair is taken, every catalog open, and every eye follows the action at the start of the 15th Annual International Auction in Harrisburg, Pa., the granddaddy of domestic tool auctions.

The centerpiece of any collection and, at $22,500, one of the highest-priced hand tools ever sold, an extremely rare Falconer's plow plane was on the auction block for less than two minutes.

variety that are on offer at auction. And no museum will let you handle and take apart its tools, to see the details of how they were made and how they work. I doubt I'll ever see another Falconer plow, but I'll remember the way this one felt in my hands as I imagined cutting a groove along the sinuous curve of a coach. I might think back to the details of the cutters someday, perhaps when I need to make a tool for inlaying along a curve.

The big event is choreographed, orchestrated. Beginning with the auction preview, bidders plan their strategies, trying not to look too interested in tools they desire. Catalogs are out, and everyone is scribbling notes in the margins. I had my eye on a couple of Scottish planes, but seeing a constant knot of admirers handling them, I gave up hope of owning them. I might have a chance with one later in the sale, an old beauty covered with a century of grime, which would be a discouragement to others. Or at least I hoped.

No matter what type of tool you're buying or selling, ones in top-notch condition with the name of the maker clearly marked, always bring a high dollar—rare tools even more so. Common tools sell in cycles, way up one year and leveling off or dropping the next. Braces are way down from a few years ago—as much as a third the value—and Bedrocks and Norrises are way up due to a strong user market. It's a quirk of the auction scene that British tools can sell for considerably less here than in England, and

To look over the crowd, though, you have little idea who has deep pockets and who, like myself, is there to watch and learn. And what an education it is. The auction is a good excuse for tool guys (and gals) to get together and swap stories about their particular tool expertise. There's no better source to learn

about the subtleties and history of tools than from these long-time dealers and collectors who have handled, owned, or in some cases spent a lifetime working with them.

Just being among all those tools is an education. Some museums have tools, but even the best have just a handful compared to the incredible

DAVID STANLEY and his son Ian run an international tool auction twice a year in Leicestershire, England. The tools are similar to those offered at American auctions: many Stanleys and tools by their English competitors, Record and Preston; molding planes; plows; rules and levels; axes and adzes; unique tools from bygone trades; and dozens of those planes dreams are made of—Norrises, Spiers, and Mathiesons.

The crowd is relatively small, and there are no tables for dealers; the auction is the action. Yet there's plenty of competition. One man

I meet owns 161 Norrises and is still going strong. Another has a shop filled with what must have been many years' worth of production of the planemakers he collects and uses. To promote the auction worldwide, the Stanleys produce a lavish catalog, with color pictures and descriptions of almost 2,000 lots—more than twice as many as at the Harrisburg auction. More than three-quarters of the lots are sold to absentee postal bidders or their agents.

Emphasis on postal bids is just part of what sets English auctions apart. Unlike American auctions,

each item has a reserve, a minimum selling price set by the seller. As an agent of the seller, the auctioneer can bid against you if he chooses (and quite surreptitiously) to raise the price to the reserve. No tools are held up at the opening of each lot, and a digital display tracks lot numbers. Add to this a rapid-fire pace—287 lots an hour, or less than 15 seconds for each—so you better stay focused.

On the block were whole shops of tools belonging to clogmakers, coachmakers, coopers, basketmakers, patternmakers, sailmakers, furniture makers, carvers, and carpenters. The variety in this one sale was far greater than at Harrisburg. Handwork survived longer in Britain and on the continent than it did in the United States, and so did the spectrum of woodworking trades and the tools they used.

Where we had mass-produced Stanleys and a great many tools, a British tradesman typically used far fewer tools (and still does). Yet each was beautifully made with striking details and the personalized touches that speak of small makers or the owner himself. Only by seeing the rich variety of these and American tools together at such an auction could I begin to understand the influences they had on one another over the past three centuries. 🪶

The action slows but hardly stops. After hours, hotel rooms turn into instant tool shops as auction-goers gather to hunt for last-minute bargains and to swap stories.

Stanley items for as much or more there. Such isn't the case today; the first Scottish planes come and go, and I never even get off a bid.

Most purchases are headed for collections, so you're competing against this high-end market. And collectors are serious about it. Buying a long-sought-after tool for what might seem like a ridiculous price can bring forth tears. But not all these tools sell for unreal prices. Some do, but there are also plenty of user tools that don't arouse much interest. Since many attendees fly in and out with their loot, heavy or large items can be bargains, such as two nice workbenches that sold for $120 and $125.

Back at the auction, everyone is waiting for the Falconer plow. The auction has to build the proper mood for such a sale through a series of smaller crests: a wooden thread-cutting engine for $8,000, a Tidey double-beveling plane for $11,000 (below estimate and far below an ebony Tidey sold for $27,500 two years earlier), and a Stanley #164 for $4,700.

Until Don Rich's recent death, the Falconer was the premier piece in his collection of coachmaker's plows, a tool he had desired for years but sadly owned only a short time. One of only three known and the only complete version of this unusual plane, it started at $18,000 and a minute later was gone, headed to another collection and never to be used again.

The room all a-titter with speculation about the mystery postal bidder, the grimy Spiers panel plane came up. Not everyone was distracted and it was only by my classic "Statue of Liberty"—bid card firmly planted in the air—that I was the successful bidder. For myself and others it was downhill from here, as more and more seats emptied and only the hardy remained to pick up some bargains.

The end of one auction is the beginning of the next, as high prices bring out more tools from collections, the sellers hoping to get the best prices. Yes, there is a bit of greediness in all this accumulation and chasing after the highest price. But then such sales also attract friends like Craig and Larry who come every year. They spread blue cloths on their hotel beds and cover them with tools—a temporary tool shop with parts of their collections for sale. But the tools are really only a come-on to swapping stories with other tool lovers and enjoying themselves.

> **TWO USEFUL TOOLS** to bring along on tool-hunting forays are a combination square with a 12-in. blade, and a flat-bladed screwdriver. Take things apart. Check the squareness of parts such as the sole and sides of a rabbet plane, the flatness of a bench plane's sole, the backs of cutters and chisels, or the straightness of a backsaw's spine.

What to Look For

You don't have to go to a big auction to get caught up in the euphoria of finding and buying old tools. The problem is getting too carried away in the beginning and bringing home boxes of useless junk. The difference between a worn-out or unusable tool and another with generations of life left in it is not as great as you might think. For a tool bought to be admired in some collection it doesn't make much difference. But if you are looking for tools to tune and put to work, missing parts, cracked bodies, or rust-pitted irons are discouraging and disappointing. They are also part of the learning process. Educating yourself about quality tools and gaining experience finding them takes hard work and time.

Buy the tools you need. Most will be common tools, manufactured in large numbers, and these are affordable. Condition and rarity establish their selling price. Take planes for instance: Two #4 bench planes in the same condition can sell for very different prices. A collector would value the rarer earlier type, a user the less expensive later plane with a lateral adjuster. Chipped japanning, dings, surface rust, or other minor defects can turn off a collector while making a perfectly usable tool more affordable. Bear in mind, if you buy a tool in top condition you will pay more, but you can also get a better price if you decide to sell it again.

The surface pitting on the sole of this Spiers miter plane would turn off a collector and make the tool all that much more affordable for a user. But beware of deeply pitted cutters and rusted-together parts that can ruin a tool.

Repairs usually devalue tools and can even ruin them, such as the #10 rabbet plane in the foreground with a repaired body and a sole that's now warped. Adding a side handle to the #9 (middle) makes the tool easier to use as a shoot plane but unappealing to a collector. Despite the good repair to the side of the #604 (top), holes in the sole diminish its value.

A complete tool is not much more expensive than an incomplete one, but without a good tool guide or lots of experience, you wouldn't know whether the #45 (top) or the #78 (bottom) is complete.

Broken tools aren't a bargain unless you can fix them, and this just adds to the cost. Repairing the wooden parts of tools is not that difficult, nor are basic metalworking repairs (see Chapter 11). If you are willing to take the time, you can learn a lot in the process and end up with a tool that might not have much collector value but is wonderfully pleasing to you. There is one major exception—cracked cast-iron bodies and parts are not easily repaired. Look these sorts of tools over carefully; good repairs are expensive. Look for hidden cracks and tap on the body and hope for a nice high ring.

Is the tool complete? Empty tapped holes might mean a missing part, but unless you are familiar with the tool you might not know. The downside of multipurpose tools—of which Stanley made many—is that parts like fences, cutters, and side handles used infrequently are easily lost. Many common tools have such parts, and because Stanley used unique thread pitches, any missing parts are hard to replace except from a similar tool. Mismatched parts are common and harder to spot, although they don't necessarily affect how the tool functions. To use up its inventory of parts, Stanley was even known to send out new tools with parts of different vintages.

Rust kills tools. You can sand off surface rust, but deep rust welds parts tight and pits cutters so badly they become useless. Some cleaning is inevitable with used tools, but any rust alerts me to look further. Do

Tools marked by the maker are no more usable, but they are worth more when you sell them. The otherwise identical square on the right marked "Stanley" is worth 10 times the unmarked square next to it; the common bevel gauge is worth a fraction of the Southington below it.

the adjusters work smoothly over a complete range? Are the screws that secure parts frozen with rust? Look over chisels and cutters carefully, especially the back that will need to be polished flat for a truly sharp cutting edge. Given the will and lots of time, most rust can be lapped out. It's hard work. Do it once and the next time you might look a little further and find an equal tool with little or no rust for nearly the same price.

Embark on the next level of buying tools, seeking the less common or unusual for many hundreds of dollars per item, and you are verging on collecting. You will need even more education about what you're buying, you will have to look harder, and because of the sums involved, be more wary. You'll be in competition with other collectors and dealers, although they might turn up their noses at a totally usable tool if it's less than perfect. Be patient, as even the rarest tools continue to show up. Investment also becomes a factor, as you wonder how the value of your tools will change over time.

If you buy tools that appeal to you and they are in great condition, they will hold their value or, more likely, grow in value. The overall tool market is fickle enough that prices rise and fall, but the best of the best still increase steadily year after year. But don't think of tools as a retirement hedge. Selling takes patience and luck to find the buyer who appreciates the same beauty you saw in that well-worn cooper's croze. The more unusual the tool,

More planes by late-18th-century cabinetmaker John Green than you are likely to see anywhere else, this collection took a lifetime to assemble, one piece at a time.

chances are the more difficult it will be to sell. But I still believe that in 10 or 20 years we will look back and say how reasonable tools are today—and maybe even wish we'd bought a few more.

I prefer to think about the tools that I have collected over the years as a different kind of investment. Having the best tools has inspired the best in me, to hone my skills and work in ways I couldn't with ma-

chines alone. To earn a living with such beautiful and ingenious objects is a further dividend. Having good tools also encourages my sons' love of woodworking, for while they are too young to use machines, they can quite confidently plane, saw, and carve. Have fun looking for tools, buy the best, and learn to use them well. The rewards will last a lifetime.

Bibliography

Bridgewater, Alan and Gill. *Mastering Hand Tool Techniques.* Cincinnati, Ohio: Betterway Books, 1997.

Dunbar, Michael. *Restoring, Tuning, and Using Classic Woodworking Tools.* New York: Sterling, 1989.

Goodman, W. L. *The History of Woodworking Tools.* London: G. Bell and Sons, 1962.

Graham, Frank D., and Thomas J. Emery. *Audels Carpenters and Builders Guide #1.* New York: Audel, 1946.

Holtzapffel, Charles. *Turning and Mechanical Manipulation, Volume 2: Construction, Action, and Application of Cutting Tools.* London: 1875. Reprint, Mendham, N.J.: Astragal Press, 1993.

Hummel, Charles. *With Hammer in Hand.* Henry Francis duPont Wintertur Museum, Charlottesville, Va.: University Press of Virginia, 1968.

Jackson, Albert, David Day, and Simon Jennings. *The Complete Manual of Woodworking.* New York: Knopf, 1989.

Kean, Herbert P., and Emil S. Pollak. *Collecting Antique Tools.* Morristown, N.J.: Astragal Press, 1990.

Kebabian, Paul B., and Dudley Witney. *American Woodworking Tools.* Boston: New York Graphic Society, 1978.

Kingshott, Jim. *Making and Modifying Woodworking Tools.* East Sussex, England: Guild of Master Craftsmen Publications, 1992.

Korn, Peter. *The Woodworker's Guide to Hand Tools.* Newtown, Conn.: The Taunton Press, 1998.

Lampert, Nigel. *Through Much Tribulation: Stewart Spiers and the Planemakers of Ayr.* Pascoe Vale, Victoria, Australia: Oliver Pub., 1998.

Lee, Leonard. *The Complete Guide to Sharpening.* Newtown, Conn.: The Taunton Press, 1995.

Odate, Toshio. *Japanese Woodworking Tools: Their Tradition, Spirit, and Use.* Newtown, Conn.: The Taunton Press, 1984.

Rees, Jane and Mark. *Tools, A Guide for Collectors.* Suffolk, England: Roy Arnold, Ipswich Book Co., 1996.

Salaman, R. A. *Dictionary of Woodworking Tools.* Newtown, Conn.: The Taunton Press, 1990.

Sellens, Alvin. *The Stanley Plane: A History and Descriptive Inventory.* Albany, N.Y.: Early American Industries Association, 1975.

Underhill, Roy. *The Woodwright's Companion, Exploring Traditional Woodcraft.* Chapel Hill, N.C.: University of North Carolina Press, 1983.

Watson, Aldren A. *Hand Tools, Their Ways and Workings.* New York: Lyons Press, 1982.

Wearing, Robert. *Hand Tools for Woodworkers, Principles and Techniques.* New York: Sterling, 1997.

TOOL CATALOGS

The Cutting Edge: An Exhibition of Sheffield Tools. Sheffield, England: Ruskin Gallery, 1992.

David Stanley Auctions. Osgathorpe, Leicestershire, England. Various catalogs, 1995-1998.

Sheffield Standard List, Illustrated, Containing Prices & Patterns of Machinery, Files, Rasps, Saws, Joiner's Tools, Light and Heavy Edge Tools, Lancashire Tools, Machinists', Plumbers', Tinmens' Tools, Spades, Shears, Anvils, Bellows, Wire, and Other Sheffield Goods. Sheffield, England, 1864.

Stanley Rule and Level Co. *Catalog #34, 1915 Edition.* Reprint Westborough, Mass.: Stanley Publishing Co., 1985.

Thomas Turner and Co. Suffolk Works, Sheffield, England, 1890 catalog.

Tool Shop Auctions. Needham Market, Suffolk, England. Various catalogs, 1996-1998.

W. Tyzack and Sons and Turner, Ltd. Sheffield, England, 1921 catalog.

Index

D

Disston, Henry:
    as sawmaker, 167-68
    saws by, 166, 169
Dividers:
    angle, 49
    proportional, 53
    uses for, 53
Dovetail gauges, making, 59
Dovetail saws. *See* Saws, dovetail.
Doweling, tools for, 155, 156, 157
Drawknives:
    sharpening, 27, 96-97
    types of, 96
    using, 96-97
    See also Scorps.
Drilling, dynamics of, 142
Drills:
    bow, 143, 144-45
    breast, 148
    chucks for, 145-46
    egg-beater, 148
    hand, 148-49
        using, 155-57
    passer, 145
    push, 144, 149
    Yankee, 148

E

End grain, planing of, 118-21

F

Falconer, Thomas, plow plane by, 207, 208, 210
Ferrules, on chisel handles, 81, 200, 201
Filemaking, process of, 136
Files:
    handles for, 137
    mill, 135
    single-cut vs. double-cut, 136
    storing, 137
    teeth of, 135-36
        cleaning, 137
    types of, 135
    uses for, 10, 134-35
    using, 137-38
Firmer chisels. *See* Chisels.
Flea markets, buying from, 204-205
Floats, described, 135
Flush-cutting saws, 171

Footprint Tools, as tool manufacturer, 14, 196
Froes:
    as splitting tools, 68
    using, 69

G

Gimlets, as boring tools, 144
Gauges. *See individual tools.*
Glazing, tools for, 75
Gouges:
    sharpening, 27, 94-95
    types of, 93-94
    using, 95
Grinders:
    choosing, 23
    types of, 23
Grinding. *See* Sharpening.

H

Hammers:
    claw, 71-72
    evolution of, 71, 72
    framing, 74
    sledge, 74
    tuning, 74-75
    veneer, 73
    Warrington, 74
Hand drills. *See* Drills, hand.
Handles, tool:
    catalog of, 82, 199
    making, 200-201
    replacing, 64, 87-89
    wood for, 200
    See also individual tools.
Handsaws. *See* Saws.
Handscrews, as clamping tools, 39
Hand tools, advantages of, 6
Harrisburg International Tool Auction, profiled, 206-208, 210
Hatchets:
    handles of, replacing, 64
    sharpening, 65
    shingling, 63
    using, 64
    See also Axes.
Heat-treating, process of, 193-95
Holdfasts, on workbench, 35-36
Hollow augers, as type of plane, 107
Hollow grinding, process of, 23-24
Honing, process of, 25-27

I

Inshaves. *See* Scorps.

J

Japanese tools:
    chisels, 81, 85-86
    grinding, 24
    saws, 11, 171-72, 173, 175-76
Jennings, Russell, bit design of, 10, 151-52
Jointing:
    technique of (planing), 115-18
    of saw teeth, 177
    of scrapers, 129-30

K

Krenov, James, chisels of, 81

L

Lapping, process of, 24-25
Lapping tables, as sharpening tools, 25, 111
Lee, Leonard, as tool designer, 188
Levels:
    spirit, 52
    styles of, 51

M

Mallets:
    carver's, 70
    types of, 69-70
    using, 70
Marking, tools for, 7
Marking gauges:
    butt, 57
    mortise, 56-57
    types of, 56-57
    using, 58
Marples, William, braces by, 146-47
Maydole, David, hammer design of, 72
Measuring, tools for, 7
Metallurgy, evolution of, 12-13
Miller's Falls, tools by, 149, 186
Miter boxes, described, 182-83
Miter jacks, as clamping tools, 39
Miter trimmers, uses for, 183
Mortise chisels. *See* Chisels.
Mortise gauges, described, 56-57
Mortising axes. *See* Twybills.